LEARNING TO OPTIMIZE MOVEMENT

HARNESSING THE POWER OF THE

ATHLETE- ENVIRONMENT RELATIONSHIP

ROB GRAY, PH.D.

To Sara, for always working with me to "keep it coupled" in our relationship.

To Angus, Molly, and Jonah for creating the optimal level of challenge for us in parenting 😊

CONTENTS

PREFACE: BEYOND HOW WE LEARN TO MOVE

Think about who you consider being the most *skillful* athletes. What is it that separates them from others in their sport? Is it just that they have scored more, won more, and accumulated more stats? Is it all just about performance outcomes? As I am writing this, two of the most skillful athletes of all time have just recently called it a career: Serena Williams and Roger Federer. Are these two tennis greats held in such high regard just because they won a lot of matches or is there more to it than that? I think for most people there is. It's not just about what they did – it's also how they did it.

The most skillful athletes typically are *elite movers*. They seem to be more powerful and smooth and have better rhythm and timing. They seem to be one step ahead of their opponents and behave like somehow time moves slower for them. They take opportunities that others miss, and we talk about them having better "vision". Like a captain steering a ship, they make subtle adjustments to their skill to deal with a raging storm of changes going on around them – new rules, new technology, new equipment, and a seemingly never-ending supply of younger athletes that are going to un-seed them. They continually rise to the challenge of the big moments, moving as if they are alone rather than playing in front of thousands of fans. They seem to be ageless and unbreakable – maintaining their skill despite the ravages of time and the accumulation of injuries to the body they are moving. Come to think of it – they don't seem to get injured as much in the first place! Also, as illustrated nicely by

Williams and Federer, they don't use the same "ideal" movement technique as others – they have their own, unique approach and style to their game that takes advantage of their individual strengths.

In this book, I want to move beyond "How We *Learn* to Move". I want to go beyond just trying to understand how we achieve some basic level of control and coordination over our body so that we can achieve our goals. Go from proficiency to mastery. From adequate to optimal. From having a "lot of moving parts" to being economical and efficient. From solving the *problem* of having too many different options for how to move to exploit the *abundance* of possible movement solutions available to us. From deciding to take the best option available to moving to shape and change the options afforded to us. From perceiving to act to also acting to perceive – moving to gather more information. From feeling rushed and pressured to slowing time down and acting like you knew what was going to happen all along. Finally, I want to consider how we can go from building skills that are easily disrupted and broken to ones that are adaptable and even anti-fragile – getting stronger through being challenged. I want to explore how we can develop optimal movement. That is use movement patterns that yield the maximum performance under a given set of constraining conditions for a given individual athlete[1].

Harnessing the Power of the Athlete-Environment Relationship

"Understanding in practice is a process of *enskilment*, in which learning is inseparable from doing, and in which both are embedded in the context of a practical engagement in the world."

While there is obviously not one simple training method, "hack" or drill that can turn an average tennis player into Serena Williams or Roger Federer, there is <u>one</u> overarching principle that should guide them on this path. Becoming an elite mover is all about establishing, maintaining, and growing the relationship between the athlete and their environment. As Ingold so wonderfully captures in the quote above, the path to becoming elite is not about "*acquiring* skill" or "*becoming* skilled". It is not about pulling something out of the environment that gets stored inside you so you "control the controllables". It is about enskillment – actively doing in a place.

Skill is all about context, symmetry, and using verbs, not nouns. I don't have good marriage skills. I have a good marriage with my wife. Context is everything. I don't think I would like the reaction if I tried to test whether I have good general, out-of-context marriage skills! And, come to think of it, <u>I </u>don't have a good marriage – <u>we</u> do. A "good marriage" is not something one person can possess for themselves. By very definition it is something that is between us – it has mutuality and symmetry. Finally, I don't know about you, but I have learned over the years that you need to *relate* to your partner not just have a relationship. Relate – verb – dynamic and changing, demonstrated through doing. Not relationship - noun – a static state.

In this book, I hope to convince you that moving optimally is all about a relationship. The one illustrated in Figure 1. The athletic environment is your partner. And like a good partner, it has much to offer! It is a rich and abundant source of information that can guide you to success. It invites you to act. You don't need to figure out everything by yourself. By connecting to it you can shape and change it through your movement, increasing the invitations it sends. In Chapter 1, we will revisit this athlete-environment relationship in detail. Showing what it can offer. And making the key point that there is intelligence throughout the system – in all parts of this relationship. In our body. In the environment - through the way, it structures sensory information. Not just in the head of the athlete.

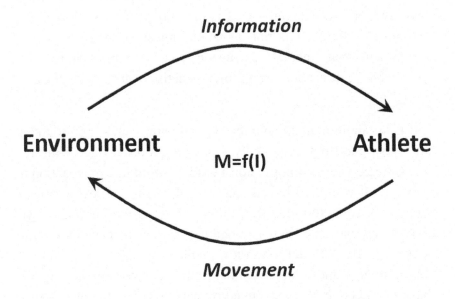

Figure 1 – The Athlete-Environment Relationship

In Chapters 2-4, we will look at the information available from our environment and how we can most effectively pick it up. It seems to me that for a lot of the skills we perform across a lot of different sports we have created a "Matrix". That is, like in the popular Keanu

Reeves movie, we have constructed this complex world around us that requires processing, interpretation, and disambiguation. For example, take the main sport I work in, baseball. We have convinced batters that they need to figure out what type of pitch is coming (a 2 or a 4-seam fastball, or a curveball), whether the pitcher can throw it with something extra (e.g., a higher rate or different axis of spin than usual), whether they are using some type of sequencing of pitches, whether they are using some sort of deception, etc. Blah, blah, blah. Pass me the popcorn. We have created this overly complicated plot when the story is very simple. The only information the batter needs to hit the ball successfully is *where* it will cross the plate and *when* it will be there. Period. In this book, I want to jump to the end of the movie and "see through the Matrix". We are going to shatter the illusion and find the information we need to control our actions, which was just waiting there all along for us to directly pick it up.

In Chapters 5-8, we will turn to the movement side of things. Here, I hope to take some of the massive burdens off our almighty brain. In the popular conceptions of motor control, it has been too controlling in the athlete-environment relationship! Time to back off! We will achieve this in two different ways. First, I want to illustrate that when we create the right types of relationships with our environment, between information and movement, we get a lot of things for *free*. That is, they become simple consequences of our relationship, icing on the cake of movement control if you will, rather than things we must put a lot of mental effort into creating ourselves. Take, for example, anticipation. It has long been assumed that to be "one step ahead" of their opponent an athlete needs to do a lot of complex predictions in their head before they move. Considering the situation, weighting the probabilities of different actions, etc. But again, we have overly complicated this.

"Anticipation" is all about acting. Specifically, it occurs when one part of the system (the athlete) does right now what another part of the system (e.g., a ball or an opponent) will do a few seconds from now. And I know it sounds impossible, but this can be a simple consequence of establishing and maintaining the right kind of information-movement relationship, $M=f(I)$.

The second thing I hope to achieve in this section of the book is to change the way an athlete views their body. For the most part, we assume that it is *hard* assembled. That is, it has a pre-set configuration with pre-set parts that perform specific, pre-set functions. All of these are unchangeable. We own a bicycle with axles, wheels, pedals, etc. that steer, brake, accelerate, etc. For this reason, all the intelligence, all control, comes from the rider. We need to turn the handlebars at the appropriate rate, put force on the pedals in the right amount, and squeeze the brake handle at the right time. The bike doesn't do any of this for us. It is the tool we use to express our skills. It is not skillful in and of itself.

This is not how our body works! Your brain is not sitting on top of a bicycle. While it may seem like it, in reality, the bicycle is made out of Legos! When we consider our body as part of the athlete-environment relationship, it is a *soft* assembly. It can reconfigure and reorganize itself to achieve different tasks. It uses the same parts for different functions and different parts for the same function. It masterfully controls tension to maintain structure and stability. Your body is intelligent and skillful if you just let it be!

In Chapters 9-12, I want to consider Adaptability – how we can adjust and alter our relationship with the environment to keep it strong. Back to my marriage analogy, there is not one way to relate to your partner that is going to be successful forever and ever. Throw kids, mortgage payments, new jobs, getting older, etc. into the mix and you need to continually come up with new ways to interact and communicate. As illustrated in Figure 2, this is also true in sports. Being skillful is not a process of repeating a solution, it is repeating the process of finding a solution[3]. The constraints we face (such as the type of surface we play on in tennis) are always changing creating new movement problems for us to solve. As we will see in this section, two of the keys to being an adaptable problem solver are; (i) giving yourself lots of different options for solving problems and (ii) moving to keep these options available to you for as long as possible. In understanding how this can be achieved we are going to turn decision-making on its head – showing that good decision-making is not typically synonymous with quick decision making rather often we want to delay the decision for as long as we can.

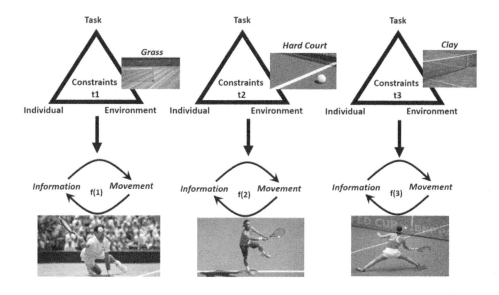

Figure 2 – Adaptability. Changes in the pattern of movement in response to changes in constraints (e.g., playing surface).

In Chapters 13-15, I want to talk about how we can avoid the issues illustrated in Figure 3. That is, letting "adverse constraints" like injury, pain, a high level of task difficulty, and pressure break up the athlete-environment relationship. Sometimes leading to a complete divorce and the end of an athlete's career. I will consider how we can stabilize and strengthen our skills. But not in the way most people expect. We are not going to treat our skill like a glass vase that we handle carefully and place on a shelf out of harm's way. That is just an invitation for it to get smashed to pieces in a competition! We are going to strengthen our skills by deliberately trying to break them during practice. We are going to continue to push and challenge athletes with new movement problems to solve, put pressure on them by doing things like telling them that they might have to give a speech to their teammates after practice, and put their bodies in a lot of variable and unstable positions. We are shooting for "anti-fragility" – not just avoiding performance declines like choking under pressure but improvement and strengthening through adversity.

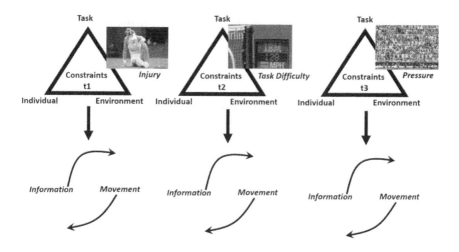

Figure 3 – Disruption of the Information-Movement Relationship by Injury, Task Difficulty, or Pressure from Crowds.

Finally in Chapter 16, I will look at some of the tools I have found to be most useful for supporting the development of the athlete-environment relationship. How can we best achieve data-informed practice design? How can we create a toolbox of cues, constraints, and practice activities for coaches so that everyone is working on the same set of core principles?

Let's Keep Exploring, Shall We?

I wanted to say thank you to everyone who bought, read, and gave me feedback about my first book – *How We Learn to Move: A Revolution in the Way We Coach & Practice Sports Skills*[4]. The response was overwhelming and honestly very humbling. But, most importantly, it gave me a ton of inspiration and motivation to write another one!

One of the most gratifying things coming from my book has been the reactions from most of the coaches, trainers, and athletes I have interacted with. The phrase I use to describe it is: "it just resonates". The logic of this "revolutionary" approach to skill just makes sense to a lot of people. Using it makes practice more alive, dynamic, and fun and keeps things closer to the game itself – which is what we all signed up for in the first place! And in many cases the ideas I present are highly similar to practice activities coaches have developed themselves through years of experimenting and a wealth of experiential knowledge. We are not reinventing the wheel here. We are trying to grow, adapt, and expand our coaching methods through an understanding of the underlying theory of skill acquisition.

This book builds on several of the key principles discussed in *How We Learn to Move*. We are going to be revisiting several of our old friends including variability, self-organization, coupling, and constraints. We will have another look at the Constraints Led Approach (CLA) and Differential Learning. While I have tried to write this to be a stand-alone book as much as possible, I think you will get more out of it if you do read my first one first 😊

So, I hope you enjoy it. Cheers for now. And keep 'em coupled. (Hopefully, if I achieved my goals in my first book, you know what that means now!).

1

HARNESSING THE POWER OF THE
ATHLETE-ENVIRONMENT RELATIONSHIP

"Ask not what's inside your head, but what your head
is inside of."

- William Mace[1]

O ur almighty brain holds all the answers. Or at least that's
what we have believed about skillful behavior for a long
time. The environment around us is chaotic and mysterious.
The things our perceptual systems pick up from it are
impoverished – they are indirect cues to what might be out there.
They require processing and interpretation to be useable for us to
control our actions. Our body, in the meantime, is just the servant
of our brain. Our muscles, tendons, and joints faithfully execute
the programs and plan they are handed from above without any
real intelligence of their own. Becoming elite at a skill, therefore,
involves filling our brains with knowledge, mental models, and
motor programs. Skill lives inside the head.

But what if there is a different route to becoming an elite mover? What if the environment around us is less mysterious than we think and holds many of the answers we are looking for if we just know where to look? As William Mace so colorfully put it in the quote above – what if we spent as much time considering what our head is inside of (our ecology, our environment) as we did what's inside it? What if our body is more intelligent than we once thought, and can solve complex movement problems on its own? To extend Mace's quote – ask not just what's in your head, but what your head is attached to! Let's take a more symmetrical look at skill in which we consider the whole relationship between the brain, body, and environment.

The Information is Out There!

Imagine you have been cast in the lead of a new action movie called "Killer Meteor". A huge meteor is approaching earth and you, as the hero of the movie, are tasked with figuring out how long humanity has before extinction. Since it is an unknown object, you don't know its size…it could be a rock the size of a house that is far away or one that's the size of a beachball that is close to the earth. You also don't know how fast it is going. Oh, no the earth is doomed!

Luckily, scientist and novelist Fred Hoyle figured out an elegant solution to this problem which he presented in his science fiction book The Black Cloud in 1957[2, 3]. Hoyle realized that you don't need to know an approaching object's distance or speed to figure out the time to contact (TTC). You can simply look at the size of the object's image in your eye. As illustrated in Figure 1.1 with a sporting example, for an object approaching at a constant speed, the time until contact is equal to the current image size of the

12

object divided by the rate at which the image size is increasing. Yay, humanity is saved!

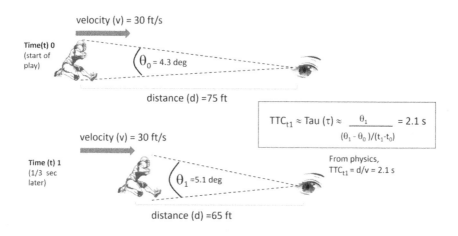

velocity (v) = 30 ft/s

Time(t) 0
(start of
play)

θ_0 = 4.3 deg

distance (d) =75 ft

$$TTC_{t1} \approx Tau\ (\tau) \approx \frac{\theta_1}{(\theta_1 - \theta_0)/(t_1 - t_0)} = 2.1\ s$$

velocity (v) = 30 ft/s

Time (t) 1
(1/3 sec
later)

θ_1 = 5.1 deg

From physics,
$TTC_{t1} = d/v = 2.1\ s$

distance (d) =65 ft

Figure 1.1 – Information about Time to Contact from the Change in Object Size. AKA "Tau".

I use this example to illustrate the incredible power or James Gibson's idea of direct perception. Seemingly complex problems, which surely must require us to do some calculations and computations in our head, simply don't! We don't need to figure out the object's speed and distance to get to the relevant variable (TTC) that we want[4]. It is specified directly by information from the environment. We don't need to make some crude prediction or an educated, best guess. The environment tells us what we need to know to control our actions if we just pick up the right things from it. The information source, in this case, the rate of change of the object's size which was later dubbed tau (τ) by David Lee, is used to control braking when driving a car[5], a long jumper's runup to the board[6], and even how birds close their wings when diving into the water to catch a fish[7].

To understand this a bit more let's look at the information a football player might use when tackling an opponent in different situations. In scenario #1, a defensive player is running toward a punt returner on the other team who is waiting to receive a kick. The defensive player's goal is to close the distance between themselves and the returner as quickly as possible (to be in a position to tackle them) but stop before they hit them to avoid being penalized for interference. In scenario #2, our same defensive player is running toward an opponent that has already caught the ball. So, their goal now is to contact the ball carrier with a large amount of force to potentially cause a fumble but at the same time not run to fast to overrun the play.

How does the defensive player know that they are running at a speed that will achieve their goal in each of these scenarios? Again, this sounds like an incredibly complex problem that requires some computation and prediction. But what if I told you that in both situations the defensive player could achieve their goal by picking up one simple information source from their environment and using it to control their running speed…

As we have already seen, the information source *tau* tells an athlete the amount of time remaining before an approaching object will contact their body. Because it is based on the change in the image size of an object, it works when the object is moving and the performer is still (e.g., hitting a baseball), the object is still and the performer is moving (e.g., long jumping), and for all combinations of performer and object movement (e.g., heading a cross into the net in soccer). So, imagine in scenario #2 above, our defensive player is standing still, and the ball carrier is coming towards them. The rate of change of the image size of the ball carrier (tau) tells the defensive back that the player will contact them in 2 seconds. But, of course, the defensive player doesn't want to just wait for the contact to occur and let the ball carrier gain all that yardage. So, they start running towards them. This, in turn, will cause the image size of the running back to increase at an even faster rate causing the value of tau to change – telling us that the time to contact is now, for example, 1 second.

The rate at which the value of tau changes as athletes and objects move through the environment (a variable dubbed *tau-dot*) is another direct source of information that can be used to control actions without any need for processing or interpretation. As David Lee worked out in his seminal 1976 paper, tau-dot directly specifies how hard the contact between you and an approaching object will be. As illustrated in Figure 1.2, from his analysis we can derive three simple laws that can be used to control contact.

1) If the value of tau-dot is between -1 and -0.5 (Figure 1.2A), you will hit the object while you are still moving and impact it with force. The closer to -1, the harder the force.

2) If the value of tau-dot is between -0.5 and 0 (Figure 1.2B) you will stop moving very close to the object without hitting it. If it is exactly -0.5 you will stop so close to the object you could kiss it!

3) If tau-dot is greater than 0 (Figure 1.2C) you will stop moving a long distance away from the object.

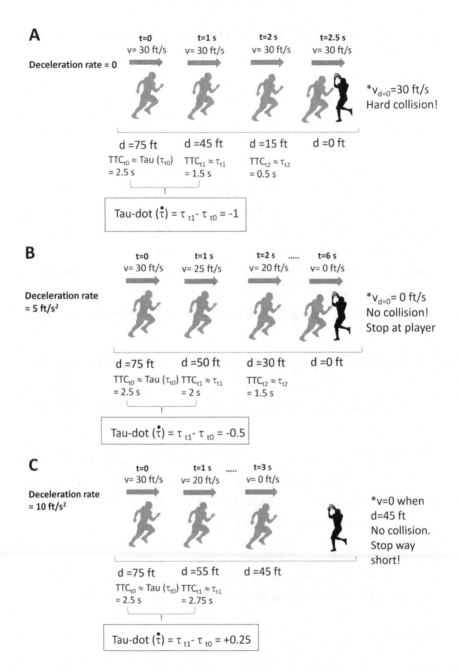

Figure 1.2 – Tau-dot Control Laws

Therefore, in scenario #1, all our defensive back needs to do is adjust their running speed to keep the value of tau-dot between -0.5 and 0 (if it starts getting too negative slow down, it starts getting to close to zero speed up). If they do this, they will achieve their goal of stopping close to the punt returner without hitting them. In scenario #2, our defensive back now wants to run to keep the value of tau-dot less than -0.5. If they do this, they will contact the ball carrier while they are still moving and will impart some force on them. The athlete has achieved their goals just by picking up the right information source and using it to control action appropriately. No need to predict what will happen, try to compute speed and distance, etc.

As an even more extreme example of the information that is out there in our environment, just waiting to be picked up, consider the incredible story of Brian Bushway[8]. Brian, who I was fortunate enough to interview on my podcast[9], started to go blind at the age of 14 and now has no response to light at all. But amazingly he can still "see". Brian has learned to echolocate. That is, he uses the auditory information that naturally occurs in our environment, the sounds bouncing around off things, to localize and identify objects and events. He uses this to mountain bike, ice skate, and perform a host of other activities. Importantly, Brian is also an "active echolocater". He purposely makes sounds (like clicking noises with his mouth) to create auditory reflections he can pick up. This fits perfectly with JJ Gibson's idea of perception-action coupling – we don't only perceive to act, we also act to perceive.

The assumption that the information we get from our environment is impoverished and incomplete, that it needs to be enhanced, processed, and interpreted by our brain, is fundamentally flawed. As we will see in upcoming chapters, researchers have identified information sources like tau and tau-dot (which directly give us the information we need to control our actions) for a wide range of sporting skills – from hitting or catching a ball in baseball or cricket, to picking holes in the defense to run through in soccer, basketball, and rugby. The path to becoming an elite mover is not through building up the brain's information processing power because such processing is unnecessary. The path to becoming elite comes from tuning into these powerful, direct information sources.

Our Highly Intelligent Body

Is your body just a puppet? Is it just a mechanical device that your brain manipulates to achieve its ends? Is it directly involved in the process of being a skillful mover or is it just the route through which skill is expressed? Imagine for a second trying to drive the car illustrated in Figure 1.3A. A car in which each of the four wheels moves completely independently such that they must be controlled by the driver with a separate steering wheel for each. I think most people would agree this is a pretty "dumb" car. It is poorly designed because it is placing way too much burden on the driver. Having to independently control what each wheel is doing would be an incredibly difficult task! The simple solution of course is not to come with a better central controller for this machine – spending hours training drivers to be able to handle using four steering wheels. The solution is to change the design of the car. As illustrated in Figure 1.3B, adding axles that connect the wheels makes it such that they can be controlled by one steering wheel. The parts of the machine are working together to achieve control.

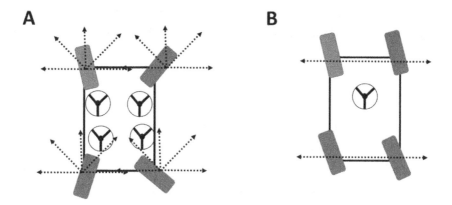

Figure 1.3 – Simplifying the Problem of Control with a Better-Designed Car

Next, think about two different kinds of tents. First, the old-fashioned type of tent that uses ropes and pegs hammered into the ground. I don't know about you, but I have some very frustrating memories of trying to put up one of these! What angles do the ropes need to go to? Darn, there is a tree root in the way so I can't put a peg there! Maybe I need to take a course in tent erection? Or is there a better way?

Now think about the modern one that most people use when camping these days – the pop-up tent. You know the ones that immediately "pop" into shape as soon as you take them out of the bag. What we have here is an example of *tensegrity*. The structure is created by a balance of internal forces – the tension created by the internal tent poles sown into the material – not some external force applied by the user. Once we pull the tent out of the bag, we can pick it up and move it to another location, or we could launch it into space, and it wouldn't lose its shape. As the name implies, tensegrity means integrity through tension. The structure of the tent is maintained by the internal balance of tension between the poles. Not external compression. External forces (applied when you shove it back into the bag) are needed to prevent it from keeping its shape.

I use these examples to illustrate two key principles of controlling movement. First, placing all the burden of control on a central controller (the puppeteer in our brain) and having to specify what each part of the system is doing is difficult. Driving cars with four steering wheels and putting up tents by applying all external forces yourself isn't very efficient. What's more, the number of components that need to be controlled in my four-steering wheel car or a traditional tent is WAY smaller than the number in our body. Consider just what your upper body is doing when executing a sports skill like throwing, hitting, or swinging a golf club:

"In the case of the shoulder, 10 muscles are working at the joint (excluding the many stabilizers and the biceps and triceps). At the elbow, there are six muscles. Four muscles move the radio-ulnar joint, and six move the wrist. That makes a total of 26 degrees of freedom that must be regulated" [10]

So, in other words, driving the human body with the central controller in our brain doing all the work wouldn't require four steering wheels – it would require 26! And we haven't started talking about what our lower body is doing yet.

The second key point here is that solving this control problem is not best achieved by working to improve the central controller – by asymmetrically trying to build up its knowledge, programs, and mental models so that it can learn to specify the values for the components of this system (e.g., what the six muscles around the wrist are doing) for each type of movement in each different situation. By being instructed in how to use multiple steering wheels or how to put up a tent. It is solved by improving the design of the apparatus. As we will see in future chapters, this is exactly what your body does if you train in the appropriate way to allow it. Your body can add the equivalent of axles and internal tent poles!

An example of this can be seen in the development of motor synergies in the body. Consider the recent study by Matsuo and colleagues[11] on baseball pitching. In this study, joint angles (including the elbow, shoulder, pelvis, knee, and ankle) were measured for 12 semi-professional pitchers asked to throw 10 maximum velocity fastballs. These angles were then used to reconstruct the movements and calculate the orientation and direction of the hand at the point the ball was released. When pitching we want these release parameters to have low variability because it makes it more likely the pitch will hit the target each time. But do we get a consistent release point by centrally controlling what each joint is doing? To address this question, the authors compared two types of reconstructed movements illustrated in Figure 1.4. In the first (shown in the top panel), movements were reconstructed using joint angles taken from the SAME delivery. In the second (shown in the bottom panel), the reconstruction used joint angles taken from DIFFERENT deliveries. So, for example, they might have used the elbow angle from pitch #1, the knee angle from pitch #4, and the hip angle from pitch #5. Think about what the difference between these two should be. If skilled pitching involves our brain setting the angles for the different joints, then there should be no difference. If you are using the same elbow angle on each pitch it shouldn't matter whether I take it from delivery #1 or #5. But this was not what was found! The variability in the angle of the hand at the point of release was nine times higher for the DIFFERENT reconstruction than for the SAME.

This suggests two things. First, the angles are not the same on each delivery – they vary from execution to execution. Second, this variation is not just random. The fact that we get better pitching performance when looking at the shoulder and elbow angle from the same delivery indicates that they are varying (and working) together, in synergy. Over rotation of the shoulder which would drop the hand too low at release is compensated for by less rotation around the elbow joint. In other words, the pitcher's body is self-organizing to create an "axle" connecting the joints so that they can compensate for each other. <u>Intelligent body, not just an intelligent controller of the body</u>.

Figure 1.4 – Reconstructed Movements using Joint Angles from the Same or Different Executions

Connecting the Athlete & the Environment

If we take a more symmetrical view of skill, one in which the brain is just part of the athlete-environment system, we will see that we get a lot of the answers we are looking for, for free. By that I mean we can learn to achieve our goals and optimize our movement without the need for complex predictions, mental models, trying to program and control what each joint in our body is doing, etc. Simply by learning to tune into the right information out there in the environment (setting your perceptual radio on the right station) and connecting it with a part of your movement we can achieve amazingly skillful behavior. In the case of Brian Bushway, we can even learn to "see" without sight! Simply by allowing your intelligent body to self-organize, to temporarily redesign itself with axles and internal tent poles that connect the different parts of the system, we can achieve incredible feats of coordination. So, let's begin on the journey of exploring how we can harness this connection between the athlete and their environment.

2

"SEEING THROUGH THE MATRIX": PICKING UP INFORMATION FROM THE ENVIRONMENT

The traditional indirect view of perception and the associated methods for coaching create a Matrix that athletes must navigate. That is like in the popular Keanu Reeves movie, we have fostered the idea that the world around the athlete is this mysterious, complex place that requires a lot of mental effort to interpret and understand. We knowingly accept this idea with statements like "perception is an illusion" or "reality is constructed by our brain". A skillful mover needs to learn to process information, compute things in the brain, and predict what will happen to act. Well, how about we all just fast forward to the end of the movie, and like Neo, discover that this is all just a fabrication?!

In this chapter, we will look at examples of sources of information available from our environment that can be used to *directly* control our movements in sports. From catching to hitting, from running to stopping, from tackling to avoiding being tackled. Using the theory of Direct Perception proposed by James Gibson, we will see that there is information out there that can give us all we need to know to achieve our goals. No need to overly complicate things by involving processors or predictive machines. Finally, we will consider how coaches can go about identifying this information for their specific sports skills and look at ways of manipulating it in practice.

Invariants & Specification

When Gibson started researching perception[1], the conception of how we perceive the world was very much like the Matrix – what we perceive is a fabrication, a construction done by our brain based on the limited cues we get about what is out there in the world. This seemed to be a necessity because, as illustrated in Figure 2.1, the information we received through our senses was ever-changing, variable, and ambiguous. Think about visual perception for a moment. When we view a physically unchanging object it can create multiple different images in our eyes. Its image size changes depending on how far away it is, the shape of its projection on our retina changes based on the viewing angle, and even the contrast and color of it can change based on the background illumination. Think about the now infamous blue/gold dress in which the same photograph was perceived completely differently by people[2]. Using psychology terminology, the same distal stimulus can produce a wide variation in the proximal stimulation we get on the retina. How could we see the pattern of light as coming from the same object when the visual information from it is constantly changing unless we can do some internal processing and computations to correct for these variations in the image? For those that have read my first book, you might notice a parallel with the work of Nikolai Bernstein here. Gibson was facing essentially a perceptual equivalent of the degrees of freedom problem in motor control: too many options, or in this case too much potential information.

A

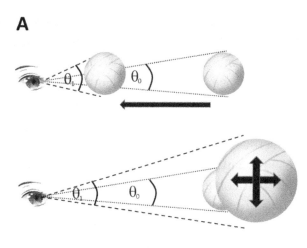

Image expansion = approach or
increase in size?

B

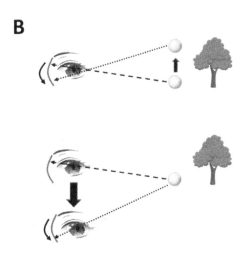

Image movement = object or
self motion?

*Figure 2.1 – Examples of Variance and Ambiguity in the Retinal
Image.*

For Gibson, these "problems" of ambiguity and variance in the retinal image could be solved easily by taking a different starting point for understanding vision. Instead of looking at the physiology of the eye and the retinal image and asking: "what could it detect?", he looked at the physical world and asked: "what information is there that could be informative for achieving our goals?". Specifically, Gibson introduced the idea of the *ambient optic array*. For any point of observation (for example, an eye) there is light that comes from two sources: directly from a light source such as the sun or a lamp, and light that has reflected off surfaces in our environment. Critically, the reflected light is not just random, *it has been structured by the surface it interacted with*. This structure is informative. Let's see how it helps us solve the examples shown in Figure 2.1.

Figure 2.2 illustrates the problem of distinguishing between object approach and increasing object size (Fig 2.1A), from a different perspective. When we first see the object, it has an angular size of θ_0 and forms an angle between itself and the horizon of β_0. A short time later these angles are now θ_1 and β_1. Is the increase in angular size $(\theta_1 - \theta_0)$ telling us that the ball is coming at us, and we need to duck or that someone is inflating it? As Gibson noted, this can be determined easily by looking at the ratio between the angular size and the angular formed with the horizon (θ/β). If the angular size is increasing while this ratio is constant (as shown in Fig 2.2A) the object is approaching. While if the angular size is increasing and the ratio is changing (as shown in Fig 2.2B), the object is changing in size.

A

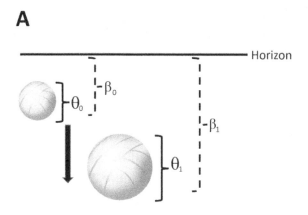

Object approach $\quad \dfrac{\theta_0}{\beta_0} = \dfrac{\theta_1}{\beta_1}$

B

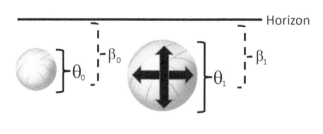

Increasing size $\quad \dfrac{\theta_0}{\beta_0} \neq \dfrac{\theta_1}{\beta_1}$

Figure 2.2 – An Invariant Specifying Object Approach

Figure 2.3A shows the problem of distinguishing between object motion and self-motion illustrated in Figure 2.1 with one simple thing added: the movement of the tree's image. If, as illustrated in the top panel of Figure 2.3A, only the ball was moving then only it's image would move across the eye. The image of the top of the tree (shown with the solid arrow) would be unchanged. Conversely, if as shown in the bottom panel, the viewer's eye moved down then both the image of the ball and the image of the tree would move. As illustrated in Figure 2.3B, during self-motion the images of all the objects in our environment move across the eye. Gibson called this *optic flow* and, as we will see shortly, it provides powerful information that can be used to control our actions. For example, the direction of optic flow tells us what direction we are moving while its speed tells us how fast. But we will get to that.

A

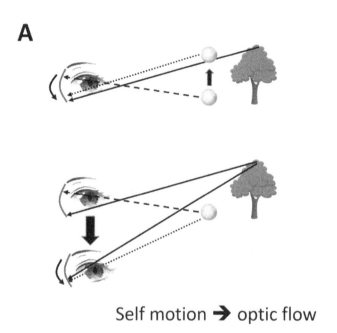

Self motion ➔ optic flow

B

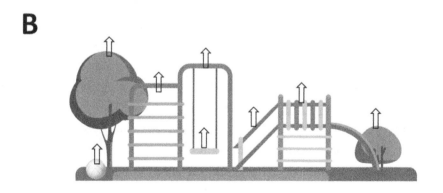

Figure 2.3 – An Invariant Specifying Self-Motion

These simple examples illustrate some of the key points that Gibson was making. First, we can solve "the problems" of perception simply by picking up different sources of information from our environment. No computations, processing, or prior knowledge is required. In Figure 2.1A, we created the problem of ambiguity of image expansion that could easily be remedied through the detection of the θ/β ratio. In Figure 2.1B, we created the problem of ambiguity of image movement that could easily be solved by detecting the relative motion of all the objects in our environment (optic flow) not just the movement of the ball itself. It's not reality that is a construction, it is these ambiguities! The assumption that the information we get from our environment is inadequate and impoverished is an illusion, not our perception. If we consider just what's in our head (the retinal image) we create problems that must be solved. If we look at how light is structured by objects and events in our environment, we solve these easily by just picking up different sources of information. We see through the Matrix!

The second important thing we can see in these examples is Gibson's concept of *invariants*. As discussed at the start of this chapter, one of the reasons that most people believe perception must be indirect is because the information we receive is highly variable and changing. While that is true, these examples illustrate that not everything changes. Some of the information is unchanging. If a ball's physical size does not change then the ratio θ/β will remain constant no matter if moves towards or away, rotates, or bounces. If we are moving downwards while the objects in our environment are stationary then there will be a constant, unchanging pattern of optic flow like that illustrated in Figure 2.3B. As Gibson showed, for any event there are these *invariant* (unchanging) sources of information that can be used to control our actions. We don't need to try and make sense of all the

32

changes through some interpretation process. We just need to pick up the appropriate invariants.

But Rob, I am confused. You just said that the key to perception was picking up these unchanging, "invariants" from the environment. But in your example of the approaching ball, and with the tau and tau-dot examples we saw in the chapter, the size of the object's image (θ) is changing! How is that invariant? Let me clarify. When we use this term, we do not mean that things are all staying the same within one event. We mean that across different events of the same type certain critical features will not change. For example, when an object is coming at you, the tau variable will always *specify* the TTC. This is true whether the object is a golf ball or a car. Whether it was thrown or kicked. Whether it comes from your right or left. Whether it is traveling 100 mph or 1 mph.. etc, and so on. While other features change across these different situations, tau equals time to contact does not. It is invariant in all events in which an object is coming at you.

The final concept illustrated in these examples is that acting in our world often involves the detection of *higher-order information* sources. Instead of detecting simple (lower order) features of our world like sizes, distances, speeds, etc, and then constructing a complex representation in our head, we pick up more complex ratios (like the angular size/horizon angle ratio) directly. As we will consider more in detail, this requires that the learner become *attuned* to this higher-order information through perceptual experience.

Specification – Getting What We Need Directly from the Environment

The last concept I want to consider in this chapter, before getting to more examples and applications, ties everything together: *specification*. One of the main pieces of evidence that is put forth to explain why perception must be indirect is variation in the retinal image. Put another way, on the surface, it seems as though there is a many-to-one mapping between the proximal stimulation on the retina and the distal environment. That is, a given pattern of stimulation on the retinal could be produced by a very large number of different things going on in the outside world. Therefore, the retinal image is ambiguous and must be processed so that we can infer what is happening.

Gibson's identification of invariants in the retinal image turns this notion on his head. If the pick-up of high-level invariants is what our perceptual system is doing (rather than just starting with the low-level retinal information) then there is a one-to-one mapping between the information and the environment. A given pattern of invariance in the optic array comes from one and only one state in the environment. Going back to the simple retinal image size example, if the ratio between an object's angular size and the horizon angle remains constant as the object's angular size increases then this corresponds to one and only one event in the outside world: the object is getting closer. Put in Gibson's words: these higher order invariants are *specifying*. That is, they are specific to one event. We have already seen a couple of examples of this in the last chapter when looking at tau and tau-dot. Let's look at some other sports-relevant specifying information.

Optic flow and Heading

If you are around the same age as me, you are no doubt highly familiar with the starfield screen saver that used to be on every computer with Windows 95 installed. As shown in Figure 2.4, this consisted of a pattern of small white dots on the screen that moved continuously and somehow made you feel like you were moving forward. How is it possible that we could create this complex percept of movement through the world with just a few dots? The answer is information, my friends!

Figure 2.4 – The Starfield Screen Saver. AKA Optic Flow

As we saw in Figure 2.3, when we move through our world (self-motion), the images of objects in the environment will move across our eyes. As first observed by Gibson, this movement (or flow) of the visual (optic) images is directly related to the direction we are moving. All the objects flowing from a single point (as in the starfield screensaver) occur when we move forward. Images flowing inwards towards a point occurs when we move backward. Images flowing right means we are moving sideways to the left. Images flowing left means rightwards movement. You get the idea! No matter what else is going on in the world (e.g., whether we are driving, flying, or running), this optic flow is invariant. It will always be the same for a particular event and, thus, specifying our direction of travel.

Let's look at the case of forward motion in a bit more detail. This was something Gibson was particularly interested in when trying to understand the task of landing a plane. Along with providing information to the pilot telling them, they are moving forwards (duh!), he noted that were other important specifying features in the optic flow. First, the speed of optic flow specifies the rate of travel. If the objects are flowing faster, it means we have sped up. Second, the location of the center of the flow (what Gibson termed the *focus of expansion*) specifies the direction we are headed. Let's look at a sporting example to understand this in more detail.

How does a football player "hit the gap"? That is, how do they know where to run to get through a line of defenders? Do they need to figure out the distance, angle, and speed of movement of each of the defenders? Do they need to know whether they are playing a 3-4 or a 4-3 defense? Must they know what plays their team is running? Nah – that is overly complicated Matrix movie stuff. As the ball carrier moves forward towards the defenders there will be optic flow – outwards movement of the images of other players on the field. As illustrated in Figure 2.5, to get through an opening all they need to do is adjust the direction they are running so that the focus of expansion is aligned with the gap between the defenders. The focus of expansion specifies the direction of heading no matter what play is being run, what team you are playing against, etc. By creating a simple information (the focus of expansion) – movement (direction of running) relationship the player can achieve their goal.

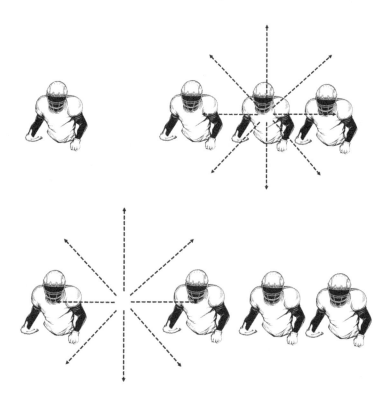

Figure 2.5 – Hitting the Gap Using Optic Flow

Before we get to other examples, let's consider the starfield screensaver for a little bit more. It illustrates another important point. If there is invariant information (like tau and optic flow) that uniquely specifies an event in the world than if I can use some technology to artificially recreate this information, it should cause people to perceive that event. Case in point – our screensaver. Another example of this is virtual reality (VR). When all the objects you are looking at are moving, this uniquely specifies self-motion. That is why when we make everything you are looking at in a VR system move (using a head-mounted display or large screen) it makes you feel like you are moving. If we recreate the information, we recreate the event it specifies.

Information from Gaps and Coupling Taus

So, our player in Figure 2.5 can ensure they will hit the gap if they adjust their running direction to keep the focus of expansion on that location. How do they know the gap will still be there when they arrive? Another key point here. Although there is information in our environment that uniquely specifies different events, the world around us is dynamic. Events in our world (balls to catch, gaps to run through, players to tackle) are not going to be there forever! In most sports, they are not going to be there even a few seconds from now. So, we need information about the timing of events. Fortunately, we can get this easily too through the use of a variant of tau.

As illustrated in Figure 2.6, the world around us is filled with visual angles. Critically, these angles are not just created by objects in our environment like balls, teammates, and opponents but also by the *gaps* between these objects. In Figure 2.6A, the gap between the two defenders creates an image with a visual angle ϕ_1, the gap between the ball carrier and the line of defenders creates a visual angle ϕ_2 (Fig 2.6B), and the gap between the ball carrier and the sideline creates a visual angle ϕ_3 (Fig 2.6C). Just to name a few.

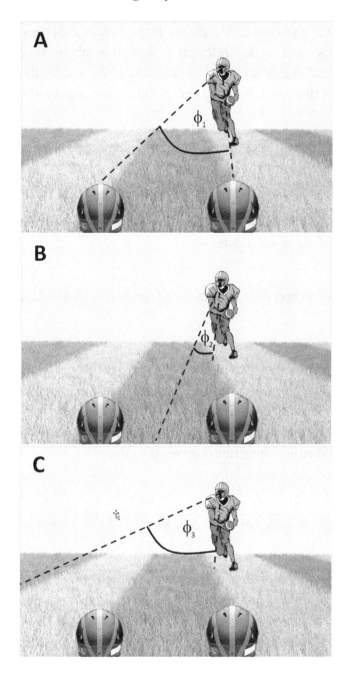

Figure 2.6 – The Tau of Gaps

Just as was the case with tau, the rate of change of these visual angles specifies action-relevant information about time. More generally, if we define "tau" as any angle divided by the rate of change of that angle then we get the following information:

-the tau of the angle ϕ_1 specifies the time until the gap between the defenders will close

-the tau of the angle ϕ_2 specifies the time until the ball carrier will reach the line of defenders.

-the tau of ϕ_3 specifies the time until the ball carrier will reach the sideline.

As first proposed by David Lee[3], one way this gap information can be used to control action is by coupling (or linking) taus. For example, if our ball carrier wanted to ensure that they "hit the gap" they can couple the tau of ϕ_1 to the tau of ϕ_2. More specifically, they could adjust their running speed so that:

$$\frac{\phi_2}{d\phi_2/dt} = k\,\frac{\phi_1}{d\phi_1/dt}, \text{ where k<1}$$

That is, the tau of the gap <u>to</u> the defenders is kept less than the tau of the gap <u>between</u> the defenders. If this relationship is maintained the ball carrier will be ensured to get to the gap between the defenders before it closes. No need to know about formations, calculate distances or predict movements. They have achieved their goal by coupling taus. Let's look at another example.

So far, the information we have been talking about is all visual but, of course, we do have other senses. Imagine we now have a baseball batter hitting a pitch as illustrated in Figure 2.7. How do they get their bat to the right place at the right time? Assume that the batter wants to hit the ball when it's at the front of the plate and with arms fully extended to generate the maximum force. We can again describe this in terms of two closing gaps. First, we have the tau of the distance gap between the ball and the front of the plate, which is specified visually by the tau of the angle ϕ_{ball}. Second, we have the tau of the gap between the bat and the front of the plate (ϕ_{bat}) which is specified proprioceptively to the batter. In this case, the rate at which the gap between the current muscle length and the length at full extension is changing. This can be thought of as a type of force gap. The tau coupling strategy here would be for the batter to control their swing so that:

$$\frac{\phi_{bat}}{d\phi_{bat}/dt} = \frac{\phi_{ball}}{d\phi_{ball}/dt}$$

If the batter maintains this tau coupling relationship, the gap between the ball and the front of the plate will close at the same time as the gap between the bat and the front of the plate. Their swing will be "on time" no matter the pitch type. In coming chapters, we will consider more information from senses other than vision but let's next look at a couple more sport-relevant sources of specifying visual information.

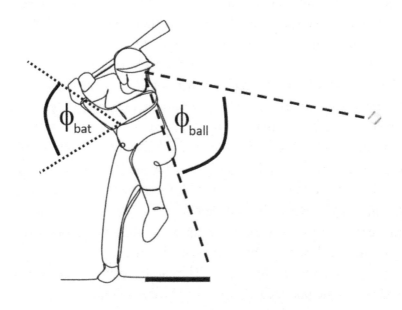

Figure 2.7 – Coupling Taus in Baseball Batting

Information for Running to Intercept a Moving Object

Imagine now that you are an outfielder trying to catch a flyball. How do you know that you are running in the right direction and at the right speed to intercept the ball before it hits the ground? Surely, this must involve some sort of prediction. Nope, again there is simple information out there just waiting to be used. Chapman (1968)[4] demonstrated that a flyball can be caught successfully if the fielder adjusts their running trajectory based on the optical acceleration of the ball's image on the eye. Figure 2.8 illustrates how a flyball traveling in a parabolic path (solid circles) creates a projection on the fielder's eye (open circles). In panels A & D, when the fielder is running too fast such that the ball will go over their head, the ball's image will be accelerating – as it gets closer the position of the image will change by greater amounts. Conversely, in panels C&F, when the fielder is not running fast enough such that the ball will hit the ground before they get to it, there is a deceleration in the optic image. If the fielder speeds up when the optic image decelerates and slows down when the image accelerates, it will create a constant velocity of the ball's image (Figure 2.8 B&E) and will be in the right place to catch it when it comes down.

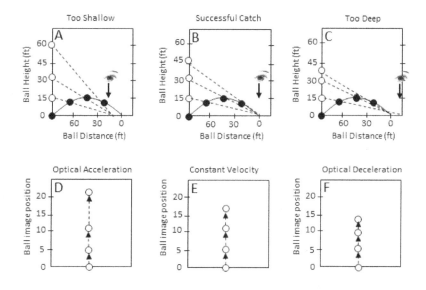

Figure 2.8 – Control by Optical Acceleration Cancellation

How about a football defender running to tackle a ball carrier? How do they get to the right place at the right time? Well, hopefully by now you might have guessed there is a simple answer! To achieve this goal the defender can use the *constant bearing angle strategy* illustrated in Figure 2.9. When the play starts, the visual angle between the defender and the ball carrier is β_0. If the defender runs to keep this angle the same (speeding up when it gets smaller and slowing down when it gets bigger), the paths of the two players are guaranteed to come together, as shown in Figure 2.9A. And this will be true no matter what "jukes", "jives" or speed changes the ball carrier makes. Conversely, if this angle decreases or increases, they will not intercept the ball carrier, as shown in Figures 2.9B and C.

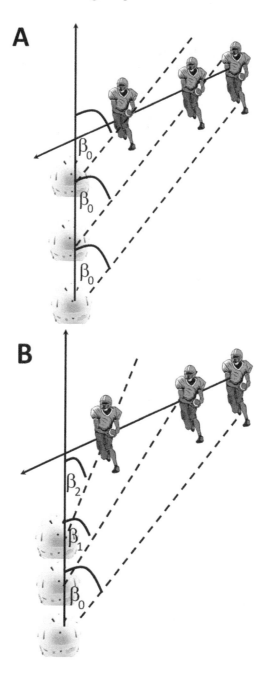

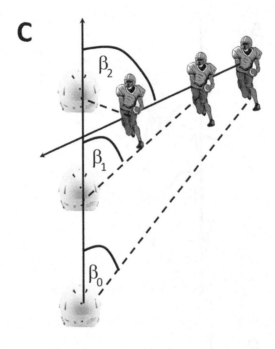

Figure 2.9 – Control by Maintaining a Constant Bearing Angle. A: Constant bearing angle leading to tackle. B: Decreasing bearing angle resulting in the tackler not getting there in time. C: Increasing bearing angle leading to overrunning the play.

I could go on and on with examples of different information sources but hopefully, I have convinced you of the point I made at the start of this chapter. If we take the time to look at the world around us and drop the false assumption that it is this mysterious, ambiguous, and overcomplicated place we can see through the Matrix. Our environment, in reality, is a plentiful garden of information sources (of taus, angles, and optic flows) that can be used to achieve our goals. It is a cooperative partner in the control of action if we just accept its invitation to meet for a drink 😊

How to Identify the Relevant Information for your Movement Skill

How can a coach go about identifying the specifying information that is or could be used by athletes in your sport? To foreshadow a more detailed discussion of practice design coming in future chapters, the information that the athlete will use to control their movements in competition is what they also use in practice. So how do we know what information they are using and what is available? I think this could be done on two different levels.

If you are mathematically inclined, you could go through the effort of identifying the specific variables. Calculating the appropriate angles, rates of change, etc. If you want to go this route, fortunately, a lot of the work has already been done for you. For understanding variables related to time and movement, I would recommend looking at the seminal work by David Lee[5], James Todd[5], and James Cutting[7]. For consideration of spatial information, for example about the slant and slope of surfaces like a golf green, check out the amazing work by Koenderink and van Doorn[8]. But I think for most coaching purposes, identifying the exact mathematical formulae and equations is not necessary.

More important for me is that a coach have a conceptual understanding of the information sources involved. What are the important gaps, angles, and movements for the different skills you are trying to develop? What action-relevant variables does your athlete need: how much time is left, how close am I to something, which way am I headed? When players on the opposing team move, what remains invariant depending on the defense they are playing? When a pitcher throws a different type of pitch what remains invariant about the ball flight? If you do this, I think you will see the fatal flaw with a lot of the practice drills we typically use. An athlete is not going to learn to couple their movement to the tau of the gap between two defenders when those defenders are stationary cones! The relevant information is not there. This leads to the last topic I want to briefly consider in this chapter.

How Can We Design Practice to Help an Athlete Become Attuned to Specifying Information?

Our environment is asking us out on a date. It wants to be in a relationship with us. But we need to accept the invitation. By that, I mean we need to learn to pick up these invariants and specifying information sources we have been discussing. In the following two chapters, we will consider two important ways this can be achieved – getting the athlete to look in the right place and focusing their attention on the right things. But let's consider some basic things we can do with practice design.

First off, you cannot give explicit instructions to an athlete on how to find and use information. "On the next pitch look at the ball's visual angle, now divide that by the rate of change of its angle". "If the tau-dot value from the punt returner is less than -0.5 you are running too fast and are going to get called for interference". Nope, doesn't work that way! These types of statements are for coaches and analysts to understand and describe the skill, not coaching cues. When an athlete uses these information sources, they are not doing mental calculations in their head like when solving a calculus problem. They are just detecting the information and coupling it with some aspect of their movement. This can only be learned through direct experience with the environment- you must go out on that date not just talk about it!

Second, we need to create practice environments that have sufficient variation in conditions so as not to avoid our athletes from accepting the wrong invitations. Consider, for example, hitting a baseball launched by a pitching machine that is always at the same distance and has the same pitch speed. In this case, the distance of the ball is information I can use for timing my swing. If the ball is traveling at 60 mph, when it is 44 feet away it will arrive in 0.5 seconds. So distance is informative about time under these conditions. 44 feet means I have .5 sec. But, of course, this is non-specifying information because as soon as I turn up the speed dial or move the pitching machine further way, 44 feet equals 0.5 sec will no longer be true. Unlike with tau, there is not a 1:1 relationship between an object's distance and its time of arrival. 44 feet is not specific to only one time of arrival of the ball like a tau value of 0.5 is. If we use practice conditions with too low of variability like this we can create situations in which an athlete will develop information movement control laws that will not transfer to the game.

Finally, we need to "amplify" the information wherever possible. By this, I mean, creating situations in practice that exaggerate or emphasis it. A great example of this can be seen in small-sided games used in sports like soccer and basketball. By reducing the size of the field and/or playing area we are reducing the size of the gaps (and making them change more often) than what occurs in a full game. This gives the athlete more opportunities to experience how their movement influences the value of the tau of the gap between defenders, for example.

We will look more at how a coach can help an athlete pick up information in future chapters but let's next consider an important factor in determining what information the athlete is getting – where they look.

ROB GRAY, PH.D.

3

———

OPTIMIZING THE CONTROL OF GAZE

Where should you look when you are acting? The answer seems obvious – we should be looking at whatever we are interacting with! The ball, our opponent, the net, a teammate, etc. But it's not that simple. If we look at our opponent, where on their body should we look – their head, their feet, their face? Also, if we are going to move our eyes and look at different things when should we be switching from one to the other? For example, when making a golf putt we need to look at both the ball and the hole, but when do we look at each of these things? If you are a football quarterback, you need to look at both the defensive players and your receivers, but when?

As a further example of the challenge of controlling gaze (that is, where your eyes are pointing) consider the task of baseball batting illustrated in Figure 3.1. Obviously, to hit a ball thrown by a pitcher you need to look at the ball. But, in the early part of the pitcher's delivery, it is not visible – it is hidden from view by the pitcher's body. Well, you might say: I will just move my eyes to the location the ball will be when it comes out of the pitcher's hand (the "release point") and wait there for it. But, as can be seen in Figure 3.1, the release point is typically at a location in space that can be a large distance from the pitcher's body, and during the early part of the delivery, there is nothing there to lock your eyes on.

Figure 3.1 – Where to Look When Batting?

The answer to the question of "where to look" also seems to be a lot more important than we might think. Figure 3.2 shows some eye movement data I recently collected from two different baseball infielders looking in at the back catcher before the ball is hit. Each grey dot represents a fixation – a time when the player stopped and rested their eyes to look at something. On the left is gaze data from a college shortstop while on the right is a shortstop that has played in major league baseball (MLB) for over 5 years. See the difference?

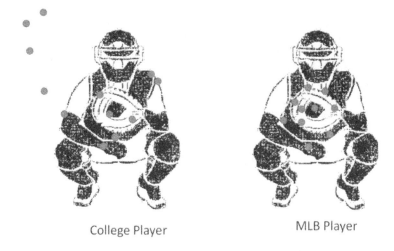

College Player   MLB Player

Figure 3.2 - Gaze Control in Baseball Infielders of Different Skill Levels

Figure 3.3 shows data from a flight simulator study my graduate student Jon Allsop and I conducted[1]. Here we have fixations (+'s) and saccades (movements of the eyes to get fixation from one place to another, lines) while the pilot is landing the aircraft. The top panels are from a low-pressure condition. In the study, we next put the pilots under performance pressure by putting a video camera in front of them and telling them that the recording might be used in one of my lectures on "choking under pressure" and by offering them a monetary prize for a soft landing. The net results were a decrease in performance from low to high pressure (harder landings), an increase in heart rate (by about 10 BPM), and the gaze behavior shown in the bottom two panels of Figure 5.3. See the difference? I call it the "bird's nest effect".

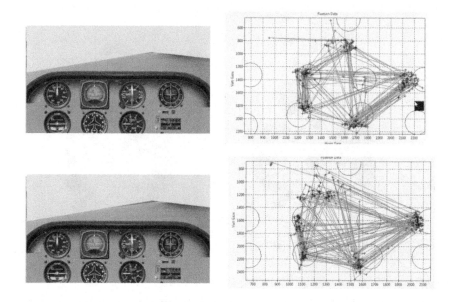

Figure 3.3 – Gaze Data in Low- and High-Pressure Flight Simulator Landing Conditions

The results from a large body of research have shown that when we compare good vs bad or even great vs less great performance, we very often see a difference in how gaze is controlled. Elite athletes look at different things at different times than lesser-skilled athletes. In situations where a skilled performer is doing well (e.g., low pressure) we tend to see different patterns of gaze as compared to situations that are associated with poorer performance (e.g., high pressure). Even when we look at a series of executions of the same action under the same conditions (e.g., a golfer making a series of putts from the same distance or a basketball player making a bunch of free throws) we can often see differences in their gaze behavior between successful and unsuccessful attempts. Answering the question I posed at the start of this chapter seems to be very important for an athlete!

Why is the control of gaze so important for the control of action? The first reason relates to the pickup of information. In Chapter 2, I hopefully convinced you that the world is full of a ton of useful information that can be used to guide our actions. Taus, flows and bearing angles are everywhere! But unfortunately, as illustrated in Figure 3.4, we don't see it everywhere. Our high-resolution, detailed vision is supported by the *cone* photoreceptors in our eye which only account for a small area of our visual field. It is about the size of two thumb nails at arm's length. All the other parts of the visual scene are being handled by the *rod* photoreceptors which have worse resolution than the computer monitor you had 20 years ago! Although the importance of seeing, visual acuity, in sports is typically WAY oversold (a point I will get back to shortly), we will indeed pick up more information in parts of the visual scene close to where we are fixating. We need to have our eyes pointing at the location where the information is!

Figure 3.4 – World Vs Visual Resolution

The other reason gaze control seems to be so important is a bit of an odd one. Often when we move our eyes to the right place, we get control of the movement of the rest of our body for free. That is, our body just seems to come along for the ride. Take, for example, the task of steering around a curve in the road when riding a bicycle or driving a car. As discussed in Chapter 2, control in this situation can be achieved by creating an information-movement relationship where the angle of the steering wheel (or handle bars) is coupled to information related to our heading direction provided by the focus of expansion of the optic flow. Simply put, we can get around the curve safely by adjusting our movement so that focus expansion stays in the center of the road. How do eye movements effect this? As first documented by my Ph.D. advisor, Martin Regan[2], they can complicate things a lot. When we move through the world and keep our heads and eyes still, we get the nice patterns of optic flow we saw in Chapter 2, like the starfield screen saver. But if we also move our gaze (with a head and/or eye movement) we alter the flow pattern as illustrated in Figure 3.5. Moving our gaze causes movement of objects across our eye that is combined with the movement of objects created by our whole body moving through the world. This produces a complex pattern of total optic flow for which the location of the focus of expansion no longer specifies the direction we are heading in the same way.

Figure 3.5 – Shifting Gaze Distorts Optic Flow. Left panel: looking at and moving towards the person. Right panel: Moving towards a person while shifting gaze. Arrow indicates the focus of expansion.

How do we solve this problem? By controlling our gaze appropriately. Specifically, it has been shown that when driving around a curve, we tend to keep our eyes fixated on the tangent point of the curve. This simplifies the optic flow pattern and allows us to use the focus of expansion for steering more easily. Weirdly it also seems to pull us around the bend. Research has shown that when we keep our eyes on the tangent point, the control of steering can be modeled like a metal spring. That is, we steer as if we are being pulled towards a particular informational relationship: one in which the location of the focus of expansion is aligned with the center of the road. We can stray a little bit from this, but like a spring, if we go too far we get pulled back.

Another example of this can be seen with gaze training. What should we do when a golfer is not very good at putting? The typical answer is we need to somehow change their pattern of movement with some technical cues and instructions. "Swing the club like it's a pendulum". "Keep your arms in the shape of a triangle". Stuff like that. But what if we ignored their movement for a second and just tried to improve their gaze control. This is exactly what Sam Vine and colleagues did[3]. A group of golfers was given video feedback showing them where they look when putting with the simple instruction: "keep your eyes fixated on the back of the ball for 2-3 seconds before you start your putting stroke". What was found? This group of golfers reduced their number of putts per round by roughly 2 while no change was found for the control group. Somehow changing their gaze (we will explore why shortly) changed their movement without any instructions about how to change their movement. Improved putting "technique" was an added benefit, icing on the cake, of improved gaze control.

So hopefully you are convinced that looking in the right place at the right time is critical for effective sports performance. But how do we know what is "right" and what is "wrong"? Is there only one correct place to put your eyes when controlling a movement? Or, like with the movement itself, are their individual differences? Is there room for functional variability in gaze control? How can we design practices to improve gaze control? Let's have a look ☺

Gaze control strategies

Visual Search: Looking Where the Information Is

One way that we could effectively control our gaze is to try to move our small area of high-definition vision around our environment to the locations where the information is. Take for example the task of saving a penalty kick in soccer. Research has shown that when saving a shot, skilled goalkeepers use the information provided by the kicker's body movements and the ball[4]. Specifically, early in the kicker's run-up, the goalkeeper looks at the shooter's head to get information related to the direction of the kick – we tend to look in the direction where we are going to shoot. They then quickly move their fixation to the ball itself. This allows them to pick up two useful sources of information. First, the tau of the gap between the kicker and the ball provides information that can be used to time the early part of the dive (e.g., beginning to put more force into the left foot for a dive to the right). Once the ball is struck information related to its time to contact (tau) and direction of travel (the change in bearing angle) becomes available.

What do lesser-skilled goalkeepers do? Simply put, they look everywhere! Research has shown that lesser-skilled athletes tend to look in more locations, fixating for shorter amounts of time, and often stopping in places where there is no useful information for controlling the action. This has been found in soccer and other sports including baseball (see Figure 3.2 above), tennis, volleyball, and boxing. They do not seem to be picking up the specifying information sources we talked about in the last chapter and are easily distracted by other things.

A similar effect can be seen in research on the so-called "quiet eye". As first documented by Joan Vickers[5], if you examine the final fixation athletes make before they begin their movement (e.g., the last look at the ball in golf putting or at the rim in shooting a basketball free-throw) it tends to be of longer duration for more skilled athletes than lesser skilled ones. In other words, just like we saw in the soccer example, their eyes are "quieter".

Visual Pivot Points & Gaze Anchoring

What do we do if we don't know where the information is going to come from (e.g., the release point problem illustrated in Figure 3.1) or if there are just too many important things in our environment to try and fixate on all of them? As an example of the latter, consider the task of a basketball point guard. To make an accurate pass the player needs to gather information about their teammates and the defense spread over a large area of space. It's not as simple as just fixating on a small number of areas. We could try to jump our eyes around a lot and guess where things like release points are going to be. But is this what skilled athletes do? No.

In such situations, the preferred strategy seems to be to park your eyes for a while in a location where there is no useful information. For example, over the past couple of years, I have been doing a lot of unpublished measurements of eye movements in professional baseball batters. One of the things that I have found is that during the pitcher's windup a lot of highly skilled batters fixate their eyes on the logo on the pitcher's hat. This is an example of using what is called a *visual pivot point*. The batter is looking at the logo for two reasons. First, it allows them to pick up information from the pitcher's body movements in their peripheral vision. Second, this is a convenient place to move the eyes from once the ball is released. So, instead of trying to fixate on the area in space where the pitcher is going to release the ball (where there is nothing currently that can change for different types of pitches), the batter just lets their eyes wait on a nice big and bright target in a place somewhat close to where the release point is going to be.

What about out basketball point guard? Here, research has shown that skilled players typically use *gaze anchoring*. That is, they keep their eyes fixated on the center of the play so that they can gather information about the positions and movements of other players using their peripheral vision. The most striking example of this can be seen in the studies by Ryu and colleagues[6]. In this research, the eye movements of expert and lesser-skilled basketball players were measured while they were watching videos of unfolding basketball plays. The authors also did something clever. Using the output from the eye tracker, they placed a big black circle on the screen and moved it around so that it always appeared in the location the player was fixating. So, in other words, you couldn't "see" what you were looking at! What did they find? Adding the circle did not affect the decision-making ability (e.g., who to pass the ball to) of expert players while it resulted in a decline in performance for the lesser skilled ones. Presumably, this is because the skilled players weren't gathering information from where they were looking – they were just anchoring their eyes there so they could get information from the periphery.

Gaze anchoring can also be seen in martial arts. Think about it, in an MMA fight should you fixate on your opponent's left or right hand? Should you try and jump your eyes back and forth? What if you are looking at their right hand and they throw a punch with their left? Ouch! A much better strategy is to park your eyes in the middle and pick up information about the punch in your peripheral vision. This is indeed what skilled martial arts athletes seem to do.

Hausegger and colleagues[7] recently compared the gaze behavior for two different martial arts disciplines: Kung Fu (in which attacks are made equally using both the arms and legs) and Tae Kwon Do (where attacks are made mainly with the legs).

Consistent with the use of gaze anchoring, the Tae Kwon Do athletes fixated on a sport 35% lower on their opponent's body than the Kung Fu athletes. Both are putting their eyes in the center of where all the information is going to be.

At this point, I think we need to have a frank discussion about something that gets under my skin a lot – the role of visual acuity in sports. As we have been discussing, visual acuity refers to your ability to see the details in an image – the resolution of your visual system, if you will. It is typically measured using the famous Snellen eye chart. For this, we calculate a ratio that expresses the distance at which the person being evaluated can read a letter as the top number and the distance at which a "normal" person can read the letter as the bottom number. So, 20/20 means the person being evaluated has normal vision – what they can read from 20 feet, an average person can read from 20 feet. If the denominator is less than 20 it means the person has better than normal vision. For example, 20/10 vision means that a normal person needs to be 10 feet away to read, you can read from 20 feet. You will often hear that being an elite athlete requires this type of higher-than-normal visual acuity. And if you don't have supranormal acuity as an athlete, you should use one of the training programs and devices out there that can be used to improve it. Let me try to explain the flaws in this logic.

First off, if visual acuity is so critical why do athletes seem to be using their peripheral vision so much? As we have just seen, when using the visual pivot point and gaze anchoring strategies, athletes are picking up information in areas of the visual field being processed by rod photoreceptors. This results in a dramatic decrease in acuity. Hold out your thumb at arm's length. If you keep looking at your thumb and I moved an object, the equivalent of 10 thumb nails to the left or right your acuity would drop by

50%. That is, it would go from 20/20 to 20/40. What you could read from 40 feet way if you are fixating, you now need to be 20 feet away. If I moved the equivalent of 20 thumbnails your acuity would drop by 90%. Visual acuity in peripheral vision is terrible!

How can athletes in many sports, like baseball, basketball, and martial arts, be so successful in using peripheral vision to pick up information? The answer is quite simple. Most of the information sources we use to control our actions in sports do not require high resolution – the details are irrelevant! Think about our soccer goalkeeper again. Do they need to be able to read the logo on the ball to save it? No, of course not. They need information like tau which is based on coarse details (the expansion of the entire ball's image) not fine details.

This can be seen in research examining the use of information sources like tau in peripheral vision. Recall, that if you move an object 10 degrees (thumbnails) away from the fovea your acuity drops by 50%. If you moved it 30 degrees your acuity would decrease by about 95%. What happens if instead of asking about details, you ask the person to make a judgment about the object's rate of expansion (i.e., whether it was expanding faster or slower than the last object you saw)? For this source of information, there is no significant change in performance when you move an object from the center of a person's vision to 32 degrees into the periphery[8]. At the distance of the penalty kick spot, that is the equivalent of the width of roughly 28 soccer balls!

The first reason the importance of visual acuity in sports has been massively overstated is that for most of the information sources we used to control our actions, seeing details (high resolution) is not required. Further evidence of this can be seen in the cricket study by David Mann and colleagues[9]. Here cricket batters were required to wear lenses that blurred their vision. It was found that visual acuity needed to be reduced to 20/200 before any significant changes in batting performance could be observed. That's pretty much legally blind!

The second reason why I think the role of visual acuity needs to be downplayed in sports is that there is no evidence to show that improving acuity through training has any effect on performance. In sports training, we often fall into a simple logical error: a professional athlete has x while a lesser skilled one does not, therefore if we train the lesser athlete to get better at x it will make them as good as the pro. If x is visual acuity these seem to make sense to many. But what if I make X equal to a "ton of money"? That means training a lesser skilled athlete in good financial investing would make them a pro?! Or how about we make x equal to "attractive spouse"? Would improving dating skills help sports performance?! Just because an elite performer has something does not always mean that it should be a focus of training. We need to do a task analysis to determine whether it is relevant to the skill in question. And, as we have just seen, visual acuity does not seem to meet that criterion.

Finally, if you don't believe me, let's put our money where our mouth is. In 2016, the developers of the app Ultimeyes (which primarily focuses on improving visual acuity) were required to pay a fine of $150,000 to the FTC[10]. Why? Because their claims like "users would benefit from comprehensive vision improvement for activities such as sports..." were determined to be "deceptive" because there was no "competent and reliable scientific evidence" to support them. We need to stop our obsession with visual acuity. As we will see, there are way more effective and relevant ways we can train vision in sports. But before getting to that I want to look at a couple more ways gaze can be controlled.

Tracking Moving Objects: Keep Your Eye on the Ball and Your Head Still?

"Keep your head still and your eyes on the ball". Two common mantras you will hear in sports coaching. But is that good advice? Or even possible to achieve? So, far we have mostly focused on fixating – keeping our eyes in one spot or moving them between spots. What do we do when the object starts moving? How do we track the movement of the ball with our eyes? While we can do a lot with peripheral vision, there is not much visual information available if the object moves completely out of our view. To understand this problem, let's again look at the task of hitting a moving ball like in baseball, cricket, or tennis.

Early research on this topic produced a very unexpected result. Keeping your eyes on the ball when hitting was impossible! In 1954, Hubbard and Seng[11] visually inspected 35mm films of MLB batters to determine when they were moving their eyes and head. Surprisingly, all movements seemed to stop at about 200 msec before the point of contact or when the ball was roughly 15 feet away from the plate. This result was later confirmed in a seminal study by Bahill and LaRtiz[12] conducted some 30 years later. Eye movements were recorded while batters viewed a ball moving along a rope at about 40 mph. It was found that novice hitters lost sight of the ball when it was about 10 feet from the plate. Even when they brought in a major league player, Brian Harper, the result was the same. He could only visually track the ball until it was about 5.5 feet from the plate. It appears "keeping your eye on the ball" was impossible to achieve! For vision researchers, this result was not too surprising given the speeds involved. A major league fastball travels at speeds up to 1000 degrees (thumbnails) per second while the fastest human eye movements ever recorded are only about 90 degrees per second. Your coach has been speaking nonsense!

But hold on a second, the story is not over. In a 2013 study, Mann and colleagues[13] investigate eye movements in cricket batting. For this, they addressed a few limitations of previous research. First, they had the batter hit the ball (off a ProBatter pitching machine) not just watch it. Second, they used pitch speeds much closer to what is faced in the game (75 mph whereas in cricket top speeds are in the 80s). And, finally, they looked at a truly elite professional: Justin Langer[14], a multiple record-holding international-level cricket player from Australia. For a lesser skill club level batter, the story was like what was reported in previous research: when the ball got close (at about 450 msec after ball release), the batter's eyes could not keep up with the ball so they could not keep it in sight to the point of contact. For Langer, a very different pattern emerged. Not only did he not lose sight of the ball before the point of contact, but his gaze began to get ahead of the ball at about 320 msec after the ball release and waited for the ball to arrive. It's like the eyes are the hare and the ball is the tortoise in the race!

Why did they find such a different result for the elite batter? Two words: head movements. Instead of trying to follow the ball by only using rotations of the eyes, which as we have seen are slow, Langer coupled the rotation of his head to the rotation of the ball. This resulted in a change in the direction of *gaze* (which is produced by a combination of eye and head movements) which could easily keep up with the ball. So, the other coaching mantra is wrong too! You don't want to keep your head still while performing sports skills like hitting. Head movements are a critical component of the effective control of gaze.

This is a very important point. It's not stabilizing your head that is the key to skillful performance – it is stabilizing your gaze. Just ask the birds. I think most people have seen examples of the incredible ability of hunter birds like the kingfisher or hawk to keep their head still and locked on their prey[15]. In these videos we typically see the bird sitting on a perch that is moving around with them making small adjustments to its body position to keep its head still. But sometimes we take the wrong message from these. These birds are not successful hunters because they keep their heads still. They are successful because they keep their gaze (the direction their eyes are pointing) still. In these examples, the bird is not doing any other action other than watching so it can stabilize its gaze using body movements. But what if they are using their body for something else?

Let's ask the pigeon. Have you ever wondered why pigeons bob their head up and down while they walk? Do they secretly have headphones playing heavy metal? No, they are stabilizing their gaze. When we walk or run or jump or do any other kind of action it is going to cause changes in our gaze direction if we don't do anything to compensate. Try running with a video camera that doesn't have any built-in stabilization or gimbal system. It's like that! If a pigeon just walked and did nothing else, it would lose sight of that French fry you dropped on the ground because with each step their gaze would be moved from the impact. To compensate for this, the pigeon holds its head still for a moment as it steps forward to maintain focus on the fry. It then jerks its head forward in a sudden motion so that it catches up with the rest of its body. Just like we saw with Justin Langer, they are purposely using head movements to help keep an object of interest in sight[16].

So, the bottom line is that not all head movements are bad. We need to consider if they have a purposeful function in tracking objects as they or we move before we try to coach them out of our athletes. If they seem to be just by-products of the forces of the athlete's body movement (e.g., due to a batter having an exaggerated stepping action) then we might want to address them. But, we don't want to try to teach pigeons to stop bobbing their heads.

Visual Scanning

So far, we have only considered how gaze control can support action control. That is how controlling where we look (like following a moving ball or establishing a visual pivot point) can aid us in executing a movement like hitting a ball or making a pass. We are talking about perceiving to act. But notice that in our information-movement relationship the arrows go in both directions. We not only perceive to act we also act to perceive. That is, sometimes our movements are not to achieve some goal like making a shot or stopping a penalty kick. They are to gather more information. A great example of this is the visual scanning behavior we see in many sports.

Visual scanning in soccer has been studied in an excellent series of studies and in-game analyses by Geir Jordet and colleagues[17]. When a soccer player receives a pass there could be many different possible actions to choose from: pass (with a few different options), dribble into space or shoot. How does the player know which of these opportunities for action is available at each moment and select between them? The first thing we do know about this behavior is that to do it effectively at a high level of competition it must be done prospectively. That is, the player must have already begun the process of action selection before they receive the ball. This is reflected in the common instructions from coaches: "Don't turn blind" or "check your shoulder". Skilled soccer players engage in visual exploratory actions in which they move their bodies, head, and eyes to visually perceive the game around them. In doing so, the player can perceive the availability of space and other players, which provides information about the opportunities to act (or affordances). We will consider the topics of action selection and decision-making in more detail in Chapter 10.

Research on visual scanning behavior in soccer has shown that it has lots of benefits for sports performance. Take for example the 2018 study McGuckian et al[18] which examined the extent and frequency of in-game head movements in the Australian National Premier League. On the one hand, players that turned their heads less frequently and by smaller amounts before receiving the ball tended to make highly predictable, simple passes to a teammate close by. On the other hand, players that made larger, more frequent head movements were likely to choose other options including turning to carry the ball and passing to an area that was opposite to the direction the ball was received from. Effectively controlling their gaze to gather information resulted in the players perceiving more opportunities for action and being more creative in their play. And look Ma -we have beneficial head movements again!

OK, now to the million-dollar question: how can we train our athletes to have more effective gaze control?

Practice Design to Improve Gaze Control

To understand how we can improve gaze behavior in sports let's first consider how NOT to do it. Existing research on gaze training and a lot of anecdotal evidence suggests that you can't just explicitly tell an athlete where to look. Instructions like "fixate on the pitcher's hat" to a baseball batter, "look at the shooter's head then the ball" to a soccer goalkeeper, or "turn your head more to keep your eyes in front of the ball" to a cricket batter simply do not work on their own. Even giving an athlete a target to follow that goes to the key information sources during a video highlight of a play doesn't help. There are two problems here. First, like with any movement of our body, we are not very good at taking on explicit instructions about moving our eyes or head. Everything we know about gaze control in sports is that it is an emergent, self-organized behavior. That is, it arises from the athlete interacting with their environment and constraints there within. It's not controlled by a boss in your head – look here then there, stop and view the ball for a while, etc.

The second problem is one of attunement. Although we could use feedback from the muscles in our eyes and neck to know where we are looking at any given moment, we don't seem to pick up that information very well. Our gaze is pushed and pulled around by eye-catching objects in our environment and reflexive adjustments without us detecting this. If you don't believe me, try wearing an eye tracker for a while. This can be particularly revealing, and embarrassing when you are interacting with other people!

So, if we can't just tell our athletes where to look, what can we do? Let's look at four basic principles we can use to guide our training. Note, for these, I am going to consider both big and small budget options.

Using Augmented Information

One of the ways the control of gaze in sports can be improved is by using augmented information to improve attunement. In plain English – we are going to give you some extra feedback about your gaze direction so you can become more sensitive to it and use it as information when controlling your action. The most obvious (and most expensive) way to do this is, of course, to have the athlete wear an eye tracker while performing their skill and use its output to provide information. This can be seen in the "quiet eye" training I discussed earlier in the chapter. An instructional constraint (e.g., "keep looking at the ball longer before you putt") combined with augmented information (watching a video that shows you where you look when acting) has been shown to improve performance in golf[3], soccer[19], and basketball[20].

Another interesting example of this is eye movement sonification. For this, the output of the eye tracker is used to change some parameters of a sound played while the performer is executing a movement. For example, it could get louder when they move their eyes up, lower in pitch when they move their eyes right, etc. A research study using this methodology in badminton found that the sonification information resulted in faster and more accurate decisions when making judgments about shot direction while watching videos[21].

But what can I do if I don't have an eye tracker, Rob?! Well, there are a couple of things. First off, it is sometimes possible to tell where an athlete is looking from their gross head position captured from in-game video. If available, this can be used in question/review sessions. But the key here is we don't want to use it to "correct" the athlete i.e., you should have been looking over there on this play. We want to use it to guide them: "See, in this play, there is a lot of space over there that you could have used". We want to use it to point out affordances – possible opportunities that they might take next time on the field.

The other cheap and cheerful method for improving gaze control is the use of secondary tasks. That is, we are going to add constraints in practice so that the athlete has to make a judgment about something in an area we want them to be looking. For example, in baseball batting practice I like to put pieces of tape on things. "Was the tape on the pitcher's hat oriented vertically or horizontally?" "When you hit the ball did it go to the right or left of the piece of tape on the ground?". As another example, it has been well documented that Barry Bonds used to practice hitting tennis balls with numbers written on them, reading out the numbers while the ball was in flight. Other examples include asking the batter to make a judgment about the fielders (is the shortstop or second baseman closer to the bag?) or placing a piece of wood across the plate with numbered balls cut in half and asking the batter to say which number the ball crossed the plate. In all of these cases, the batter will not be able to do the secondary task we have added unless they are looking in the location we want: the pitcher's hat, the ball in flight, or the point of bat-ball contact. I am not telling them where they must look – I am adding a constraint (more task-relevant information in certain locations) that encourages them to look in those places.

Constraining to Afford

One of the reasons having effective gaze control in sports is so important is that typically we don't have a lot of time to waste looking all around. Things happen in seconds or even fractions of seconds. If we don't gather information quickly and efficiently, we are not going to pick it up. Therefore, another way we can improve gaze control is by amplifying this effect in practice by adding constraints. We are going to try to encourage the athlete to change where they look by increasing the time pressure.

An example of this is using visual occlusion activities in practice[22]. By blocking the athlete's vision during different parts of the unfolding action we encourage them to find ways to gather information more quickly and efficiently. This can be done using glasses that can be opened and closed via a remote trigger or similar results can be achieved by just telling the athlete to open and close their eyes at certain times. In a late occlusion drill, the athlete starts with their vision un-occluded until shortly after the event begins (at which point, the lenses are closed, or they are told to shut their eyes). Successfully achieving an action like hitting or catching a ball under this task constraint requires them to have their gaze in an effective location (e.g., a pivot point on the pitcher's hat) to pick up the ball quickly and it necessitates using information early in the event (e.g., from the pitcher's delivery and the early part of the ball flight). We are taking away the option of looking all over the place that we see in many novice performers. In an early occlusion drill, the athlete starts with the lenses/eyes closed, and then they are opened after the event begins. This can be used to encourage the athlete to explore more effective solutions for tracking moving objects (e.g., incorporating head movements). There is a lot of evidence from a wide range of sports, which I reviewed in this podcast episode[43], that this type of systematic occlusion can lead to improved performance. By increasing the temporal constraints on the action, we encourage the athlete to better self-organize their gaze control.

Scaling

Another practice approach that can be used is to do the exact opposite of what we just described. One of the challenges with controlling gaze is that we often have small objects move quickly which can make it difficult, especially for younger and lesser skilled athletes, to look in the "right" places. By slowing things down a bit and/or making the movement of targets cover a smaller area we allow the athlete to develop more effective gaze control.

A good example of this can be seen in the study by Oppicci and colleagues[23]. Novice soccer players were split into two groups: a control group that practiced with a regulation soccer ball and a group that practiced using a futsal ball - a smaller, heavier ball that does not bounce around as much. The futsal-trained group showed a greater improvement in a passing test using a regulation soccer ball, especially in a time-constrained scenario where they had less time available for the action. Underlying these performance improvements were significant changes in gaze behavior. Players in the futsal group spent less time fixating on the ball and more time shifting their gaze between the ball and the players on the field. Presumably, the lower demands of tracking the ball's movement allowed them to shift their gaze to other locations on the field.

Practicing with Variable Directionality

The final principle for designing "gaze practice" is particularly important for improving visual scanning behavior. If we want to encourage our athletes to search for information we need to vary the locations where the information might be! A good (or bad) example of this can be seen in the well-known soccer Rondo drill shown in Figure 3.6. For those unfamiliar, in this activity players standing in a circle must pass the ball through an area with 1 or more defenders. This popular activity removes all need for visual scanning because the players always know where their teammates and defenders are[24]. A much better way to develop soccer skills is the use of small-sided games in which players are moving the ball (or defending) goals located in different locations.

Figure 3.6 – The Soccer Rondo Drill

As a final method for getting the eyes to the right place to pick up information, we can make sure to get the athlete's attention there first! Let's focus on that next.

4

FOCUSING ATTENTION IN THE RIGHT PLACE

T think about a time when you have been bored or distracted. Heh, maybe it happened in the first few chapters of this book, but I hope not! But if it did, you likely experienced something that we all have at one time or another – reading without really reading. That is when your eyes move over all the words in a paragraph, but you don't absorb any of them. If you were given a test right after you would score a zero. Another common example of this occurs in driving. You are traveling along a street thinking about something you are going to do when you get home and suddenly realize you don't remember anything that happened on the road in the last 10 minutes. These cases illustrate the point that looking at something and paying *attention* to something are not the same thing!

Although there is information all around us in the outside world and coming from within our bodies, we do not perceive it all equally. We have been provided a powerful tool to use (or occasionally misuse!): attention. Our attention works like the combination of an amplifier and a filter. For some of the information, we boost the signal while for the rest we turn the signal down so that it is not as strong or often missed completely.

Think about what our life would be like if we couldn't do this. Imagine being at a party where every voice was perceived with equal strength. It would be maddening. And the inability to selectively attend to things can be a symptom of some mental disorders like schizophrenia.

But attending is more than just blocking out distractions. Over the past 20 years or so I have taken (an admittedly slightly sadistic) pleasure in seeing how I can mess up an elite athlete's performance by shifting their attention around. In one of my first studies on this topic[1], I gave baseball batters secondary tasks (done while they were batting) that drew their attention to different areas. So, for example, to get them focused on the crowd I would play a sound coming from the stands and ask them to say whether it was high or low-pitched. Or to get them to focus on their body, I would play a sound and ask them to say what direction their hands were moving (down or up) when they heard it. The results (in terms of errors in the timing of the swing) are shown in Figure 4.1. The most striking effect can be seen when you compare the two conditions on the left side of the figure. Simply by drawing attention to their hands, I turned highly skilled college players into worse hitters than you see at your local park on the weekend. Oh, where have you gone Joe DiMaggio?!

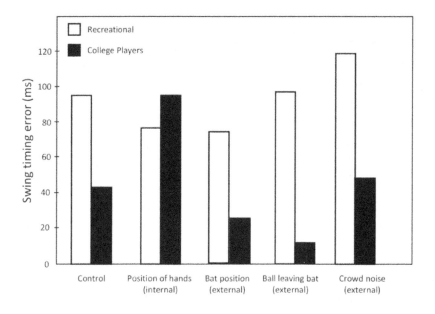

Figure 4.1 – Attentional Focus and Baseball Batting

But attention has both a dark and a bright side. Looking at the rest of the results, we can see that when I got the college players to focus on the ball leaving the bat (in this case, by having them judge whether the ball went to the left or right of a cone on the field) improved their performance relative to when they were just hitting as they normally would (control). For lesser-skilled recreational players we could also make their batting performance better (attending to the bat position) or worse (attending to the crowd). I quickly began to realize that this shifting attention around was very powerful. Insert evil laugh here!

In follow-up studies, I began to dig deeper into what was happening when we focus our attention on different sources of information. I found several interesting effects. First, I made batters focus on different areas of the plate by giving them different task goals[2]. For example, I would tell a left-handed batter that they had to hit the ball to the left side of the field. This task is much easier to achieve when the ball is further away from the body. When the pitch location was further from the body they perceived the ball to be larger than when it was closer. Batters who had a bigger increase in perceived size hit more balls to the instructed location. Stated another way, when the ball was where the batter was focusing their attention, it looked like a beachball to them – it looked more "hittable" causing them to swing more at these pitches and achieve better performance outcomes. Attention amplifies information that can be used to achieve our intended action.

The next thing I looked at was the effect of attention on remembering events[3]. For this, I asked college baseball batters to hit in two of the conditions described above: one in which they were attending to the ball leaving the bat and one in which they were attending to their hands. Unbeknownst to them, the pitcher had a distinct pattern. All of the fastballs were thrown inside (close to the batter) and all the curveballs were thrown outside. After hitting for a while in these attention conditions, I then asked them to hit in a condition with no attention task and where the pitcher's pattern was reversed. What was found? When batters focused on the ball they again performed better (relative to a control condition) but also showed clear evidence that they had learned the pitcher's pattern. Specifically, their performance dropped sharply when I reversed the tendency. Conversely, when the batters were focusing on their hands, they performed worse overall and showed no evidence that they picked up on the pitcher's pattern. Paying attention allows us to better learn from experience. That is, adjust our information-movement control based on the sequence of events, an effect we will look at in detail in Chapter 12.

Finally, I have most recently looked at how attention influences the pattern of movement[4]. Using force plates in the ground we can measure when the batter shifts their weight to their back foot to load force and when they shift their weight forward to transfer it to the ball. I have found that for highly skilled batters there is a synergy or functional coupling between these two movements. If the backward weight shift takes a bit too long or starts too late, the forwards shift is sped up, and vice versa. This way the batter always gets the bat to the ball on time. But what happens if I shift their attention around? When it is drawn to the ball, this coupling gets stronger. When it is drawn to the hands it starts to break apart. So, having our attention in the right place seems to help our body better self-organize.

Notice again, we are not just talking about where the athlete is looking. This is something different than gaze control. Although in most cases our gaze and attention work together – we look at the thing we want to pay attention to – this is not always the case. If we focus just on vision, sometimes we want to look at a different location. For example, a "no-look" pass in basketball. But critically, attention is also multisensory. When I get batters to focus on the movement of their hands in my studies, they don't start looking at their hands while swinging. They shift their attention from the visual information about the incoming ball to the proprioceptive information about the movement of their hands.

Hopefully, I have convinced you of the importance of attention. You have been given this incredible resource that you need to use wisely. It can make or break performance. When you put it in the "wrong place" it can take you from being elite to average in a heartbeat. A simple shift in attention to the "right place" can produce multiple benefits including improved action selection, better learning from experience, and better self-organization of movement. So, let's dig a bit deeper. What can research tell us about the right and wrong places? What causes our attention to go to different places? And how can we better train it to go where we want?

Dimensions of Attention: The Rights and the Wrongs

In sports science, we tend to be a bit wishy-washy. There are very few laws or absolutes we talk about. We tend not to want to commit to things. You maybe should practice this way but "it depends". For every study that demonstrates one thing, there seem to be contradictory findings. When studies are consistent, they tend to be few and only look at a narrow range of sports performed by not-very-skilled participants in a narrow set of conditions. None of this is the case when we compare an internal vs external focus of attention!

An *internal* focus is when you direct your attention to the positions or movements of your body while executing a skill. This is what I had my baseball batters do when I asked them to make a judgment about the movement of their hands during the swing. If you think about it, we use a lot of internal focus of attention instruction in coaching (e.g., "Push off with your back foot", "Keep your knees bent", "Snap your wrist"). Why? Because they go hand in hand with the traditional way we have coached for many years: attempting to correct technique so our athletes have the ideal movement. Van der Graaff and colleagues[5] recorded the audio from baseball practices run by six coaches from the Netherlands over four weeks. Of the 717 instructions given, 70% were internally focused.

So, what's the problem here? Well, as I was alluding to at the start of this section, compared to the trickle of evidence we see for most effects, there is a relative tidal wave of research showing that the use of internal cues is not the most effective way to coach. In 1998, Gaby Wulf from UNLV compared internal versus external focus of attention instructions when participants were learning to balance on a platform[6]. Instead of focusing on the body, an *external* focus involves attending to the effect the movement of our body has on something in the outside environment. For example, the movement of the bat or the ball leaving the bat in my baseball studies. In the balance experiment, participants were told to either "focus on your feet" (internal) or "focus on the markers on the balance board" (external). Balance performance was significantly better for external instruction, while the internal instruction was no different than saying nothing at all.

When I first read this work, I didn't believe that such a subtle change in wording could have such a large effect on performance. In Gaby's study, the markers on the board were only a few inches from the feet. They were essentially attending the same location in space for both instructions. How could "feet" vs "markers" matter so much? I talked to Gaby at a conference to try and see if there was something else done in this study that I was missing. Her response was: "try it for yourself" ☺

So, to convince myself, I included two different conditions in one of my early studies that I honestly expected to be no different: attending to the hands versus the bat while swinging. How could this matter? The hands are holding the bat and moving with it? But, as you can see in Figure 4.1, it did. The college players in my study hit much better when I changed one word in my task instructions: "hands" to "bat". Since then, I have found the same effect multiple times. While it may sound crazy, you get the same type of performance benefits when you change "turn your stomach towards the pitcher" (internal) to "turn your belt buckle towards the pitcher" (external) and when you change "push off from your back foot" (internal) to "push off from the ground" (external). If these is nothing else you take from this chapter it is this: the words you use as a coach are very powerful so choose them wisely!

Since the first study in 1998, there have been a total of 73 studies with 1,824 participants that have demonstrated superior performance for external focus of attention instructions and 40 studies with 1,274 participants that have shown better motor learning[7]. Furthermore, it has been shown that the benefits of adopting an external focus are both "sticky" (you still see them in retention tests 24 hours after training) and transferable (they result in better performance for tasks in which the participant was not trained). These studies have examined almost every sport, skill, and motor task you can think of. I frequently say on my podcast: "Please stop doing internal vs external studies for some new skill that hasn't been tried yet". You don't need to. We know what the outcome will be! External always beats internal. Before asking whether this is indeed a universal truth in coaching, let's first consider why we get this result.

Why are External Focus of Attention Instructions Better?

There have been three explanations put forth to explain why an external focus is better for performance and learning than an internal focus. The first, proposed by Wulf and colleagues, has been called the "constrained action hypothesis". Based on the most popular theory of skill acquisition (Fitts & Posner's Three Stage Model[8] shown in Figure 4.2), it argues that internal focus instructions hurt performance by disrupting automaticity. It does not allow the execution of the skill to occur unconsciously, using proceduralized knowledge. Instead, when I tell you to "focus on your hands" you start consciously controlling your movement. You start thinking about where your hands should be and execute the movement step by step like you did when you first started learning the skill. Getting your attention away from the body with an external instruction prevents this from occurring. As illustrated in Figure 4.2B, an internal focus causes you to regress to an earlier, novice stage of skill acquisition.

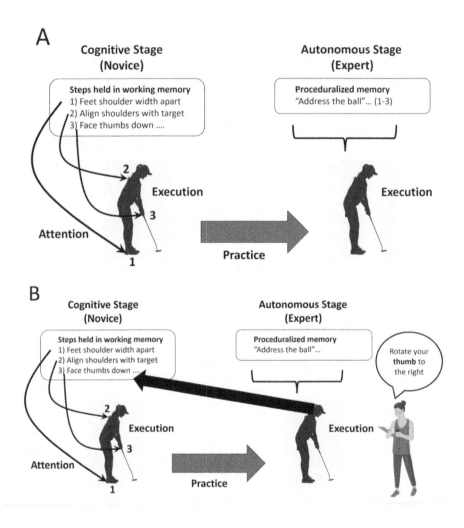

Figure 4.2 – The Constrained Action Hypothesis

The second explanation aligns with the ecological approach to skill acquisition. Recall, that in this view, skillful performance emerges from a process of self-organization. The concept of automaticity (the idea that we reach a stage where top-down control and working memory are no longer involved) is non-sensical because these things were never involved in controlling your movement in the first place! In the ecological view, internal focus of attention instructions results in inferior performance and learning because they are constraints that disrupt self-organization. When a coach tells you to focus on your hands, knees, or feet it causes you to try and control what these body parts are doing rather than letting them coordinate with the rest of your body own their own. This results in suboptimal control of movements. Evidence for this can be seen in studies measuring muscle activity using EMG[9]. When you tell an athlete to focus on their biceps while doing an arm curl you get more activity in that muscle. Remember attention enhances and amplifies things. But, hopefully not surprisingly by now, along with this comes worse lifting performance.

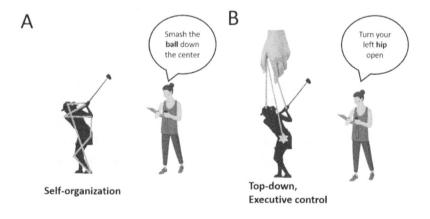

Figure 4.3 – Attentional Focus and Self Organization

The final explanation is an informational one that is consistent with both skill acquisition theories. As nicely discussed in a recent article by Henrik Herrebrøden[10], it is often the case that the external focus of attention conditions used in many of the studies in the past provided more information to the performer (that can be used to control and adjust movement) as compared to the internal conditions. Take my study shown in Figure 4.1. Telling a batter to focus on the "ball leaving the bat" is getting them to pay attention to the details about the outcome of their movement – what is called knowledge of results feedback. If their attention is on this location, they might detect more information about the ball's speed, direction, and spin after contact. All of this could be useful for making adjustments on the next pitch. Contrast this with the internal condition in which they were required to focus on the "movement of their hands". There is not any direct information there that can be used to improve the swing (controlling the bat). In many, but not all cases, the information the athlete needs to pick up (e.g., the taus and flows we discussed in Chapter 2) is in the external environment so directing attention externally is likely to improve this.

This effect can also be seen in research evaluating the CLA. In a study I published in 2018[11], I compared different methods for teaching batters to increase their launch angle and hit the ball in the air more. An internal focus of attention training group was given the instructions: "get your hands under the ball," "move your arms at an upward angle," and "drive up, off your back foot." An external group was told to: "get the bat on the same plane as the incoming pitch," "drive the ball over the infield," and "contact the bottom half of the ball." So, no reference to the body. For the final group, I used a CLA. Specifically, I placed a wall across the field, and batters were only instructed to "hit the ball so that it went over the wall". The CLA group showed the greatest increase in launch angle (and exit velocity and home runs) with the external focus group coming in second. Both groups were significantly better than the internal focus group.

In the paper, I proposed that the superiority of the CLA group may have been an additive effect. Adding the wall across the field is both a constraint that encourages exploration for a new movement solution and it is something that is going to induce an external focus of attention. Indeed, as a manipulation check, on some of the trials, I asked batters to make secondary judgments about the position of their hands. The accuracy in doing this was 72% for the internal group, 52% for the external group, and 49% for the CLA group. A constraint added to the practice environment can not only encourage exploration it can also lead to a beneficial external focus of attention.

Some Caveats and My 2 Cents on the Internal Vs External Debate

Based on this large body of research we have been discussing, should we never use internal focus of attention cues in coaching? Should we accept Gaby Wulf's conclusion that there is "no room for internal foci"? I have had coaches tell me that there are occasions where they have spent several minutes struggling to think of a way to say something about their athlete's arm without using the word "arm". Is this a good thing? Do we need to be <u>that</u> careful with our words?! In my opinion, no. From my experience researching and applying these ideas in practice, I have personally come to conclude these four things.

1) *The last cue or instruction given to athletes before they execute their movement should ideally be external*

If you look at research on focus of attention, you will see that most of the cues and instructions evaluated are ones that were given to the athlete right before attempting to execute the skill. In other words, what we are trying to influence is "what's going in their head" during movement execution. In general, I agree that promoting an external focus in this way is a good thing – it allows for better pickup of information to control the movement and self-organization instead of top-down control. That is why there is this overwhelming body of evidence in support of external cues. In my experience, if the last thought you put in an athlete's head before they step up to the plate, the penalty kick spot, or the free throw line is an external one it will result in better skill execution.

But what about cases for which the information the athlete is using is from an internal sense? What about skills like those in gymnastics, figure skating, dancing, and martial arts for which having a particular form is part of a successful performance outcome? In Chapter 2, I discussed how we could control movements like a baseball swing by coupling a visual tau (from the ball) to a proprioceptive tau (related to the extension of the arm). Would skill execution be better in these situations if we used an internal cue to direct attention to the location of the information (e.g., "focus on the extension of your lead arm while swinging")? Yes and no. Yes, I think it would benefit performance by directing attention to the location of the information used to control the movement. But, no, this does not require the use of internal focus of attention instructions. It is possible to have your cake and eat it too.

Adopting an external focus of attention does not necessarily require the athlete to attend to something physically present in the external environment. It can also refer to a fictitious object. What I am talking about here is the use of analogies - metaphors for the pattern of movement that do not refer to its specifics. "Swing like a rainbow" (tennis), "crack the whip" (volleyball)", squash the bug" (baseball), and "reach into the cookie jar" (basketball) are all cues that I have heard used at various times. Last time I checked, there were no actual rainbows, whips, bugs, or cookies involved! When we use analogies, we are getting the athlete to focus on the movement of their body (i.e., proprioceptive information) without talking directly about the body. We are getting the form or pattern of movement we want without inducing the problems associated with an internal focus. To get your hand in the imaginary cookie jar you need to pick up information about the movement of your hand. We can have information pick-up without a direct, internal focus. For these reasons, I think it's better to use an analogy that an internal cue for the "final" instruction before skill execution.

2) *Internal cues have their place and time when working on activities to develop the skill*

So yes, giving an athlete an external cue (or analogy) to focus on during the execution of the movement is likely to result in the best performance outcome. But, I don't agree with the blanket statement that there is <u>no place</u> for internal focus of attention instructions because practice design is not just about performance outcomes. It is also about developing, learning, and exploring movement solutions. And there is a lot more to coaching than what you say right before skill execution. For these reasons, I think internal cues can be effective. Let me give a few examples.

Perhaps, the most striking example of the effective use of internal focus instructions can be seen in differential learning (DL) [12]. This coaching methodology involves having the athlete execute the skill using a randomly chosen set of variations, in body position, movement, etc. The goal is to never have them perform the same movement twice. This is thought to promote "stochastic resonance", a strengthening of the movement through the introduction of random noise, and greater adaptability through experiencing more of the possible solution space. By my count, there have been a total of 12 different published studies (for sports including shot put, speed skating, soccer, baseball, weightlifting, volleyball, and golf) comparing DL to traditional, prescriptive coaching [13]. It was found that DL was more effective for training in 10 of these studies. So the method works! But what do DL instructions typically involve? Examples used in one of the most recent studies on volleyball include: "Stand on one *leg*, change *leg* while executing the serve", "Circle your *head*", and "Keep your *elbows* extended". Ahhhh..internal cues!! When we get an athlete to explore the movement space and try different movement solutions we don't so much care about the performance outcome so I think internal cues can be effective. In reality, I am not sure how we could get an athlete to try all the different positions and movements involved in DL any other way.

But I should point out that the "thing you say last should be external" rule does still seem to apply here. In a 2021 study, Oftadeh and colleagues [14] examined DL training that combined internal and external cues for practicing shooting in soccer. Participants again practiced using random variations of body position and movement but with slightly different instructions for how this was achieved. In the DL-external condition, an internal instruction ("shoot the ball with the middle of your foot" or "shoot with your left *leg* bent") was immediately followed by an external one ("…focusing on the upper left corner of the *goal*"). In the DL-internal condition, two internal focus of attention instructions were combined (e.g. "shoot the ball with the middle of your *foot* focusing on the impact your *foot* makes with the ball"). What was found? The DL-external group had significantly higher shooting scores after training. To me, this shows that internal cues about how to position and move your body can be effective when used at the right time (not last!) and for the right purpose (to encourage exploration rather than successful performance).

I think this also applies when using the ever-growing number of technologies for tracking movement in sports. For example, when we are reviewing an athlete's biomechanical analysis with them I don't think we need to jump through a bunch of hoops trying to avoid using internal language. When I see a baseball pitcher's "front side flying open" or them throwing with "all arm" this is the language I use to discuss the issue with them. For many athletes, I find that providing an understanding of the details helps to motivate them for some of the weird practice activities that will follow! Speaking of which, I of course don't use this type of language when working on a practice activity to help them find a better movement solution. Here is again where I would again try to use mostly external cues (e.g., "try to get the connection ball to go forward when you throw'). So it is not the case that we can never use internally focused language as a coach.

Finally, I think internal cues can be useful for practice activities designed to work on "feel". As human beings, we are visually dominant creatures. Although there is proprioceptive information available to tell us if our hip is "locked" or not or if our shoulder is "open" or not, most of us do not have a lot of experience using this information. I know I was like this. "Keep your hips more open"-"I have hips?!" Therefore, effective training sometimes involves getting athletes to become attuned to this information by feeling what it means to have a body part "hinged", "locked" or "open". We are purposely trying to create the "negative" side effect of an internal focus of attention instruction – attention to a specific part of the body so we want to refer to the body! For more information on "feel" please check out Toner and Moran's great paper[15] on "somaesthetic awareness".

3) *Trying to develop and use external versions of common internal cues will make you a better coach – but don't give yourself a hernia while doing it!*

One of my favorite activities to do with coaches is an exercise in which we try to expand our coaching vocabulary by creating external focus of attention cues. Take a classic internally-focused cue from your sport. How can we reword it to be external? Can we come up with an analogy for the form of the movement? For example, in baseball batting hitters are commonly instructed to "Get your back elbow up" (internal). To get them to make the same type of movement we could use "make your bat touch the sky" (external) or tell them to "move the bat like a jackhammer" (analogy).

Other dimensions we can play with are the distance and directionality of the cue. Is the external object referred to near the athlete or far away? We can tell a baseball batter to "turn your belt buckle" (close), "throw the head of your bat" (further), or "drive towards to pitcher" (even further). Research has shown that close cues are more effective for lesser-skilled athletes while experienced athletes can benefit more from far cues[16]. Directionality refers to whether we are guiding you towards

94

("throw your bat towards the pitcher") or away ("push off from the ground") from something.

Although I don't agree with the idea that we should only be using external cues, I like going through this process for two reasons. First, it just gives you more tools in your toolbox. If your favorite internal cues aren't working – try one of the new external ones you have just developed. Second, I think trying to convey different movement patterns in different ways can increase our understanding of movement. It makes us think about what the key features are and observe them more closely. But again, I don't think we should push this too far. If it's easier to explain something to an athlete by referring to their body, just do it! In the ecological approach, we are trying to move away from over-constraining athletes by forcing them to use one ideal technique. We want them to explore, solve problems and be creative rather than prescribing a solution for them. The same should be true for coaches.

4) *What makes for an effective cue is highly individualized and, if you let them, your athletes will help you find it*

The final thing that I have learned about cueing is that effective cues are often individual, don't always need to be very specific, and can sometimes be a completely inaccurate description of the movement involved. In terms of individuality, one of my favorite methods for generating cues is to use some constraint to get an athlete to move or position their body in a certain way and then ask them to describe what they felt. I then use their own words to make the cue. It felt like I was really "stretching" = "feel the stretch", etc. Sometimes they come up with their own esoteric analogies – "it felt like the waves when we went to Hawaii when

I was 10" = "feel the Hawaiian waves". Whatever it takes to get the athlete back to that area of the solution space! This can often involve completely inaccurate descriptions of what is going on. For example, one of the hitters I worked with for a long time liked to focus on "driving the bat down to the ball" when his bat moved up to it. It doesn't matter! We want them to be an elite mover, not a biomechanist.

In terms of specificity, research has shown that some of the best cues are more holistic. For example, in a 2016 study[17], Mullen and colleagues compared the effectiveness of holistic cues (ones that direct the athlete to the overall "feel" of the movement rather than some part of their body or object in the environment) with more traditional cues. Specifically, while performing a simulated driving task one group of participants was told to focus on "smooth", "glide" and "easy" while steering (holistic) while a second group was told to use a "9:3 grip" (referring to the position on a clock), "turn using the outside hand", and make "small movements of the wheel". During the competition, the holistic group had significantly faster lap times and fewer instances of going off the course.

A similar effect was found by Becker and colleagues[18] when comparing different types of cues for jumping in gymnastics. The external focus cue was "focus on jumping as close to the orange cone as possible", the internal focus cue was "focus on extending your knees as quickly as possible", and the holistic cue was to "focus on making your movement feel explosive". The holistic cue resulted in the same improvement in jump distance as the external focus cue, both of which were significantly better than the internal one. So, I think holistic cues are something that coaches should also consider adding to their toolbox.

In Chapter 16, we will look at some simple tools that I like to use for developing cues and instructions. But let's next consider a problem: once we get our attention to the right place through effective cueing how do we keep it there?

Why Does our Attention Run Astray and What Can we do About it?

If you listen to athletes describe what happened after a bad performance or an extended period of bad performances you will often hear them say something like: "I lost my focus", "my head wasn't in it", or "I couldn't get my timing down". In many of these cases, what they are referring to is a shift in attention. Try as we might keep it in the right place, our attention often goes exactly where we don't want it to! This is an effect I have been fascinated with for many years, so let me give some examples from my work in this area.

Why do athletes "choke under pressure"? Making your movement "pressure proof" is a topic I am going to discuss in detail in Chapter 13, but let's consider it briefly here first. The most popular and evidence-based explanation for why athletes fail under pressure is that it causes their attention to turn inwards towards their body[19]. Stated another way, it causes a shift from using an external focus (good when we want to perform well!) to an internal focus (bad!). Why? Imagine having a putt to win the Masters or a free throw to win the NBA title. When the stakes are at their highest, our brain wants to take over the operation and make sure we do everything just right. As illustrated in Figure 4.4, this can result in a detrimental change in the way we control our movements.

Figure 4.4 – The Creeping Hand of Internal Focus of Attention

As evidence, consider the study Rouwen Canal Bruland and I did on golf putting[20]. In this study, we played sounds through a pair of speakers placed near the hole while the golfer was putting. After they had made their stroke, they would hear a prompt "Hole" or "Club". If they heard "Hole", they were instructed to say whether the sound was presented from the left or right speaker. If they heard "Club" they were instructed to say whether the sound occurred closer to the beginning or end of their backstroke. What we were trying to do here is not shift their attentional focus around (like I did in my batting study shown in Figure 4.1), but rather just figure out where their attention was. Remember when you focus your attention on something you pick up the information better.

What was found? In a low-pressure pre-test when they were just putting, their accuracy in the "Hole" task (about 80% on average) was much better than their accuracy in the "Club" task (at the guessing level of 50%). This occurred because skilled golfers adopt a far, external focus of attention. They are not paying attention to the movement of their body during the backswing, so they have difficulty making judgments about it. We next added pressure in the form of a monetary prize for best putting performance, losing money for really bad misses, and the threat of emailing their results to all the other golfers in the study. We found that for about half of the golfers this resulted in significantly more missed putts ("Choke") while for the other half there was no change in performance ("Clutch"). But what happened to their attention? The "Choke" players got much better at the "Club" task (70% accuracy on average) and worse at the "Hole" task (<50%). This suggests that the pressure caused their attention to shift inwards, focusing on the movement of their body.

Another situation that can cause attention to go to the wrong place is a performance slump. In many sports, athletes can go through extended periods of bad performance for reasons completely out of their control. In the 2022 MLB season, the league batting average (proportion of times getting a hit) was .243. Based purely on probability, there is roughly a 5% (1 in 20) chance that a league-average hitter could go three complete games (a full series) without getting a single hit. Given they play roughly 50 or so series in a season, we would expect this cold slump to happen at least twice. All this is to say that athletes are going to have ups and downs in performance purely based on probability and luck. But, if they are not careful in the way these are handled it can turn into more than that!

In a 2013 study, Jon Allsop and I investigated the effect of performance streaks on attentional focus[21]. To do this we brought a group of experienced baseball batters into our VR batting lab and adjusted the pitch parameters (e.g., speed, number of different types) for each batter until they all had a .500 batting average (i.e., getting a hit every other pitch). We then just let them hit for a while. As expected, we found that during this period, some batters kept the same level of performance ("Normal"), some increased their performance ("Hot Streak"), and some decreased ("Cold Streak"). To measure their attentional focus we used the same method as was described for my golf study above. After the batter had completed their swing, they were asked to say whether their hands were moving up or down at the time the sound was played. The results can be seen in Figure 4.5. All batters were equally bad (65% accuracy) at doing this in the equalization phase in which they were all performing well. This was expected because good hitters use an external focus. But the story was different when they started to have streaks in performance. The cold streak batters got better (80%) at the "hands" task while the hot streak batters (50%) got worse.

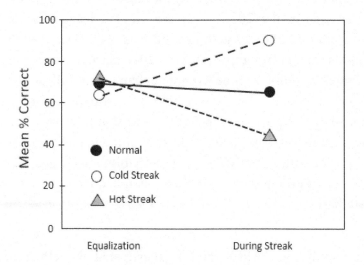

Figure 4.5 – Shifts in Attention During Performance Streaks.

What this study illustrates is that streaks in performance can cause shifts in attention. A bad bounce here or a lucky catch there that makes a batter go three games without a hit can easily cause them to turn their attention inwards in an attempt to "fix" things. And as we have seen – this is the last thing in the world they should be doing! We must help our athletes stay the course and trust in the process during slumps. To achieve this, I like to take players that are struggling and use some practice activities designed to have a far, external focus. For example, I might place a piece of tape on a screen in front of the batter and ask them whether the ball went over or under the tape line. Or I might ask them to say how the fielders are positioned while they are waiting for the ball to be pitched.

While we are on the topic of streaks, do athletes get "hot"? If you are interested, please read through my simple explanation of the controversy surrounding the so-called "hot hand" in Box 4.1.

Box 4.1 – A Simple Resolution of the "Hot Hand" Controversy

For a long time, there has been an argument as to whether athletes can get "hot" or not. That is, can they raise their performance above its normal level at different points in a game? Every fan in the world will tell you: "yes"! We use phrases like "he's on fire" or "she can't miss". While almost every statistician will tell you: "no"! Who's right? The fans are. Let's see why.

To answer this question, researchers came up with what seemed to be a very simple test. Look at your success rate after a series of successes and compare it to your baseline performance. For example, we could look at a basketball player's shooting % after three makes and compare it to their % for the full season. The simple prediction is, that

---

if the "hot hand" exists, the shooting % should be significantly higher after the three makes as compared to their normal performance. They have raised their level of play. While there are some slight differences depending on what stats method you use, there is no evidence at all that this occurs. The success rate on the next shot is the same when you are on a "hot streak" as your normal level of performance. Athletes are like coins. You can't change the probability of getting a head no matter how many heads you got in a row. There is no "hot hand". Case closed.

But, as it turns out, the test we have been using is flawed. As Ben Cohen[22] so nicely put it, "the hot hand has been hiding the hot hand for years". Think about what happens when a basketball player makes three 3 pointers in a row. Two things are likely to occur. First, they are going to get more confident and start taking shots even further away from the hoop. Instead of toeing up the 3-point line, they might launch one from 5 feet behind it. Second, the way they are being defended is likely going to change. If you make three in a row, the defense is not going to just let you keep firing away. They are going to play you tighter. From modern data which tracks the position of all the players on the court, we can confirm that these two things do happen. Therefore, all else being the same, both effects should cause your chance of making the next 3-point shot to go **down**. So, the fact that the shooting % doesn't change is evidence for the "hot hand" not against it. To keep making the same shots under more difficult conditions (deeper shots, tougher defense) a player needs to raise their level of play. Which they do seem to be able to do. Case closed – but with a different verdict.

The final "attentional shifting" factors I want to look at here are pain and injury. When athletes are recovering from an injury, it is very common for them to shift their attention inwards toward their bodies. This effect can occur for two reasons. First, pain is powerful information that our attention gets automatically drawn towards. Second, it is very common for recovering athletes to want to monitor their injured body parts to make sure they don't hurt them again. This latter effect can be seen in a study I published in 2015[23]. For this, I recruited baseball batters recovering from ACL knee surgery. All were completely pain-free and were given full clearance to play. I again used a similar method to attempt to assess where their attention was focused. When they heard the word "knee" after their swing they were asked to say whether their leg was bent more or less (around the knee) than a reference angle during the swing. When they heard "elbow", they did the same except for their arm. Finally, when they heard "Ball" they were asked to say whether the ball went to the left or right of a cone on the ground. The results can be seen in Figure 4.6. When asked to make a judgment about their uninjured arm, the ACL-recovering athletes were just as *bad* as the uninjured, expert comparison group (65% accuracy) and worse than a group of uninjured novices (80%). Skilled batters do not normally focus internally on what their elbow is doing so they are not good at telling you about it! But the story was different for the leg. Here, the performance of the recovering players was just as *good* as the novices (80%) accuracy and far better than the uninjured, expert controls (63%). Their attention had shifted inwards towards their recovering knee. Finally, notice the results for the "Ball" task. The injured, experts were exceptionally good at this (>85% correct) while both the recovering players and novices were far worse (<70%). The ACL batters' attention had been pulled away from the bat-ball contact. As we would expect based on these attentional effects, the recovering batters hit significantly worse (by roughly 100 points of batting average) in the study than the expert controls.

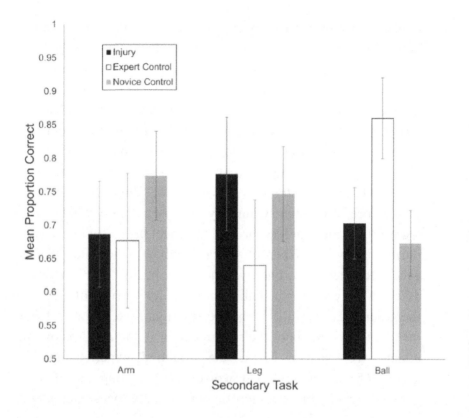

Figure 4.6 – Injury Recovery and Attentional Focus

So, to sum up, this chapter, research has clearly shown that there are right and wrong places to focus your attention as an athlete. The specifics of what is right and wrong depend on what you are trying to achieve. Is the focus just on performing well now or is it on further developing the skill (through exploration of the solution space and improving "feel") so you can perform better in the future? At the same time, we are trying to get our athletes to put their attention in the right places with appropriate cues, instructions, and constraints there are forces out there trying to pull it somewhere else. In coming chapters, we will look more at how we can improve attentional focus and make athletes more resistant to it being pulled, but next, I want to put more focus on the other side of this relationship we have been admiring – how do we use all this wonderful information from our environment that we are directing our gaze at and focusing our attention on to *move* our body.

5

MOVING TO CONTROL THE "CURRENT FUTURE"

magine you are playing Ultimate Frisbee. Someone has thrown
you a long pass, high in the air that you are trying to catch
(Figure 5.1). As we have been discussing, there is visual
information in the environment that specifies the frisbee's
direction of travel, speed, and time to contact. You have visual and
proprioceptive information related to the speed and direction you
are running and kinesthetic information about the position of your
hands. The central question we want to tackle in this chapter is:
how do we use this information to move our bodies?

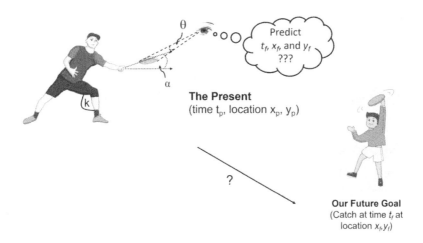

Figure 5.1 – How Do We use Information in the Present to Control the Future?

Let's think in detail about exactly what we are trying to achieve here. We are trying to control the future. That is, we are trying to move to make some event (our hand clasping around the frisbee) happen a few seconds from now. Considered this way, two key questions arise. First, to make an event happen in the future do I need to know the future? That is, do I need to know exactly when the frisbee will come down to a catchable height (e.g., in 2.5 sec) and where exactly on the field (e.g., 10 feet from the sideline) that will occur? Second, if I do need to know the future, is the information I am getting from the environment in the present sufficient for this purpose? Or do I need to process or supplement it in some way?

For most people, the answer to the first question is of course you do! How could I make an event happen in the future without knowing the details of that future event? How could I get to the right spot on the field at the right time to catch the frisbee if I don't know where and when that is? What a silly question! While it might seem silly, its answer turns out to create a major fork in the road in our understanding of the control of action. If you believe that we need to know the future to control it, you have pre-defined the job of our brain. It is a predictive machine. Its job is to try and make predictions about the events that will happen in the future. And its method for achieving our goals is predictive control.

It also determines the answer to our second question. If we assume that we need to predict the future to control it, then the information from the environment is <u>not</u> going to be sufficient for several reasons. Although I have been incessantly touting the idea that there is all this rich and useful information in our environment, it is not all that useful for making predictions. To foreshadow, we don't use it for that purpose, but let's humor the idea. Start with the most optimal conditions: an object directly approaching our head at a constant speed. As discussed in Chapter 1 (Figure 1.1), the optical variable tau tells us the future. Its value is equal to the time to contact so it tells us exactly when the object will hit us. So, when people predict the time to contact using tau they should be pretty accurate, right? Wrong! Figure 5.2 shows what you get when you ask people to predict TTC based on tau[1]. As you can see, they make HUGE errors. For an actual time to contact of 6 sec, people predict that it will arrive in less than 4 sec.

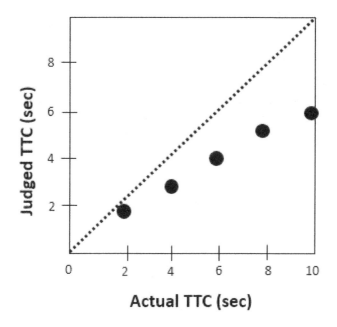

Figure 5.2 – Accuracy of "Predicting" TTC Using Tau

The situation gets even worse when we move away from these "optimal" prediction conditions. This is what I did for my Ph.D. dissertation. I tried to break tau. I started with the "we have to predict the future" assumption. From there, I showed that there are a lot of conditions for which it is not a reliable source of information. These included very small objects (the rate of expansion can be too small to detect)[2], rotating or spinning objects (the rotation can cause the image to increase in size which changes the value of tau)[3], and objects passing off to our side. Tau alone is not good for predicting the future, so we are going to need to add something else.

Now I fully admit that, at that time, I didn't understand how tau is used in the control of action. The title of my dissertation is: "Estimating time to collision..". That first word makes me cringe now. I had chosen the wrong path by assuming that we need to predict, judge, and estimate what will happen in the future to control our actions. I was able to "break" tau because I had assigned our perceptual system a job that it is not qualified for, prediction. While I am proud of that work and it, of course, helped to get me where I am today, I don't think those studies have much value anymore. I was asking completely the wrong questions. But before I get to that, let's consider a couple more reasons why the information in our environment is insufficient for prediction.

Let's return to our Ultimate Frisbee example. Imagine that when we first see the frisbee leaving the thrower's hand we predict that it will be at a catchable height in 2.7 seconds at a position that is 10 feet from the sideline. Cool, let's just go there and wait. But what if there is a gust of wind? Or imagine instead we are trying to tackle a ball carrier in football or rugby, and they decide to accelerate? We are out of luck. Our prediction about the future is no longer accurate because, in the time between making the prediction and the future event, the conditions have changed.

The next issue we have is the potential for interruptions. If I just use the information for the environment how can I deal with periods when there is no information available at all? For example, imagine that while our frisbee player is running to catch the frisbee they see a tree branch that has fallen on the field. They look down for a couple of seconds to avoid it. Is it game over now? They stopped getting information about the frisbee's trajectory. Did their control of action just stop? Other more common examples of this that can happen in sports are a fielder looking away briefly to "find the wall" in baseball, a football receiver "checking for the sideline" while the ball is in the air, and a soccer player looking at one teammate and then passing to another.

The final problem is one of time. If I am going to just use the information from the environment and nothing else to control my actions, then what do I do when that information is only available for a very short amount of time? Consider baseball batting. In the game I was watching last night a pitcher threw the ball at speed of 103 mph! The time between when tau (and other sources of information from the ball's movement) become available and when the ball crosses the plate is 370 msec for this pitch. The time it takes the bat to get from the hitter's shoulder to the plate is about 200 msec. So, we have 170 left. But it also takes time for the light reflected off the ball to get to our eyes, and travel to the visual areas in our brains. and a command to get sent back out to our muscles. Even for a very simple movement of the hand, it takes about 150 msec for this to occur[4]. We have a whopping 20 msec left to gather information from the environment before we act. This simply can't be enough.

So, the bottom line is that if we need to predict the future to control it then just picking up information from the environment is not enough. We need to supplement or process it in some way. Let's look at how that might be done.

Internal Model-Based, Predictive Control

To solve these problems (that we have created for ourselves!) we are going to use an internal model in our brain. That is, we are going to take some information from the environment and use it in a representation of the outside world we have created. Within this representation, we are going to add other sources of information (not directly available from the environment) and process things to get our prediction. This idea can be followed from some of the earliest research on motor control:

"the brain 'imitates a physical process by creating an internal model of reality with a similar relation-structure, thereby enabling prediction of external events in the physical world" (1948)[5]

.. to the most cutting-edge research in the area today:

" internal models are 'putative neural systems that mimic physical systems outside the brain, whose 'primary role is to predict the behavior of the body and the world''. (2022)[6]

An example of this type of internal model and how it could be used for predictive control in frisbee catching is shown in Figure 5.3. There are three key components here. First, we assume that these is not enough information available while the frisbee is in the air (typically called "online" information). Therefore, instead of using just specifying information that is directly related to some action variable, we also use non-specifying information or "cues". Take for example the launch angle, α in Figure 5.3. If the thrower launches the frisbee at a steeper angle it will typically travel higher and further. But not always because it depends on the speed at which it is thrown. Launch angle is indirectly related to the landing location of the frisbee – it suggests what the future might be. It is a cue or a hint. But, that's OK because we are going to add more cues.

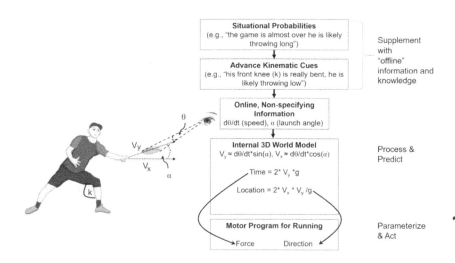

Figure 5.3 – Predictive Control Model of Frisbee Catching

The second key feature of our model is that we are going to supplement the online information we get from the environment with other things. First, we can use our knowledge of the situation and thrower as cues. He/she might have clear action tendencies we can exploit – they always tend to pass low and hard. Or there could be situational patterns. It is late in the Ultimate Frisbee game, and we need to score so the thrower is likely to throw me a long pass toward the end zone. We call these *situational probabilities* referring to the fact that the probability of different events (e.g., a pitcher throwing a fastball) varies as a function of the game situation (e.g., the number of balls and strikes). Almost all sports have these and most teams are now spending a lot of money on "analytics" trying to figure them out. Second, we can use *advance cues*. These are any aspect of the behavior (in particular, the movement kinematics) of the thrower that can be used to anticipate trajectory. For example, as shown in the figure, a greater knee angle (k) is a cue that the throw is likely to be low. Again, these are only hints to what might occur – I can make a short throw at the end of the game or throw high with a bent knee.

The final piece in our predictive control story is the internal model itself. It takes in all the information, processes it, and comes up with a prediction. The frisbee will be at x_f, y_f, and time t_f. This information is then used to parameterize a stored motor program for the action. Run with force f in direction d. A common feature in the processing stage is to weight the different information sources based on their reliability. For example, if the thrower doesn't have any clear tendencies, we would use that less in our prediction.

This internal model solves the problems we have been discussing. Tau is not good for prediction when the frisbee will arrive in some situations. That's OK, we are going to add other sources of information and our previous knowledge, so it doesn't have to be perfectly accurate. The conditions might change while the frisbee is in the air. We can handle that by *updating* our model frequently. That is, we can give our internal model new values for the angles used in the calculation as the event unfolds. We can handle interruptions because we have made a prediction and can just keep controlling our actions using that when there is no information coming in. This frisbee will only be in the air for a short time. No worries, we are going to supplement this with information that becomes available before the throw has been made.

We might have solved our problems, but we have also broken the performer-environment symmetry I discussed in Chapter 1. Our relationship has become very asymmetric and unbalanced. Whether we can execute the action of frisbee catching successfully or not depends almost entirely on the quality of the prediction machine in their head. How well does their internal representation of the world correspond to the real world? How much knowledge have they acquired and stored in their memory about things like player tendencies, advance cues, and situational probabilities? The performer has all the power in the relationship now. The environment is just this confusing Matrix again ☹

We have also created some complications that most people don't talk about very much. First off, how long do our predictions last and how often do they need to update? If my model needs to be updated all the time, then what value is it? What if I told you I have this great new model that can predict who will win the Super Bowl but for it to work, you must give it the score in the game every minute? Would you pay for using such a model? No! It's not predicting anything. It's not giving you any more information than what you can get from your own two eyes.

Second, who or what looks at the prediction the model spits out? Other than for very simple movements like reaching with your arm to pick up something, I am unaware of any model of this type that explains how the prediction is used. There are no complete models for any sporting skill to my knowledge. What do we do with our prediction that the frisbee is going to be at x_f, y_f at time t_f? How do we use this to control the movement of our body? Do we just put a force into our legs that is inversely proportional to the time remaining? All we have done here is shifted the problem of the control of action around. We started with an event in the outside world: X. Now we have an event inside our head: I predict X.

115

Because our brain has done a lot of processing and computation, we feel like we have accomplished something. But have we?

Next, if being able to perceive and act on the world around us depends on an internal model and previous knowledge then where did all this come from? As Gibson so wonderfully put it: "Knowledge of the world cannot be explained by supposing that knowledge of the world already exists"[7]. How could we ever acquire knowledge about a player's tendencies and game situations if we need that information to perceive in the first place? How could we develop an internal representation that processes the ambiguous cues from the environment if we need the internal model to disambiguate the information? The logic of predictive models of action is completely circular.

But, most importantly, all of this is just not necessary. We have started with the wrong answers to the questions I posed at the start of this chapter. NO, we do not need to know the future to be able to control it. And, YES, the information in the environment is sufficient for achieving our goal in the future because we are not going to try to predict it. Let's look at the alternative…

Returning to the Intended Definition Of "Perception"

To understand the alternative approach to action control we need to first change our view completely of what perception is for. The word "perception" comes pre-loaded with a lot of assumptions that most people stopped questioning a long time ago. Take the Wikipedia definition:

"**Perception** (from the Latin *perceptio* meaning 'gathering, receiving') is the organization, identification, and interpretation of sensory information in order to represent and understand the presented information or environment"

We have the built-in assumption that the job of our perceptual system is to "represent" and "understand" and this requires processing ("organization", "identification", and "interpretation"). Our perceptual system is a computer. But did you catch the inconsistency in this definition? Look at the terms used for the Latin word "perceptio" from which "perception" is derived – "gather", "receive". No computation or processing. No representing or understanding. Just taking it in. It suggests something like a radio receiver or satellite dish, not a computer.

Where we go wrong is by assuming that we need to "know" about the world before we can act on it. That is, we need to judge, estimate, gain knowledge, interpret, or understand things about our environment before we can move. If we are going to catch a moving frisbee we need to identify what it is. We need to judge its time contact. We need to know the distance it was thrown from. We need to estimate its speed. Notice, we have done something sneaky here: we have separated sensation (the gathering and receiving of information) and perception (the interpretation of that information). This is something you will see at almost every university around the world. When learning about this, we take a class called "Sensation AND Perception". But I am here to tell you we have been thinking about this all wrong.

When we want to act on our environment, we just need to *use* information *from it* we don't need to *gain knowledge* about it. This is a tricky point that was difficult to understand for me as evidenced by my Ph.D. dissertation title. For example, take tau. As shown back in Figure 1.1, the value of the perceptual variable ($\theta/d\theta/dt$) gives us the value of the physical variable time (e.g., 2.1 sec). In Gibson's words it *specifies* a particular event in our environment: contact in 2.1 seconds. But when acting we don't ever know this value. We don't perceive tau so that we can "know", "judge" or "estimate" TTC ("it's going to hit me in 2.1 sec") when acting. We perceive tau because it can be *used* to guide the movements of our body. The knowledge step in between is unnecessary.

We need to take back the definition of perception and return it to its Latin form. We perceive (pick up, gather, and receive) information from our environment so that it can be used to control our movements. There is no sensation and perception, only perception. The intelligence comes in how the information is gathered (which information source we pick up, where we look, where we attend) not in how it is processed or interpreted. Let's see how this can be achieved by looking at our frisbee example.

Prospective Control and the "Current Future"

Before we dive into all the details, let me make one point first. Do you believe that catching a frisbee requires all the computation, prediction, use of previous knowledge, and probabilities illustrated in Figure 5.3? Do you believe that it requires the incredible supercomputer that is the human brain? If so, I would like to point out the fact that most dogs are way better at catching a frisbee than you are! We like to think that the incredible feats we see in sports are uniquely human. But they are not! Intercepting or avoiding moving objects. Moving through gaps. Coordinating movements with others. These are all seen throughout the animal kingdom. Why? Because they can be achieved using very simple, universal methods of action control.

Figure 5.4 illustrates an example of such a method (called the "Linear Optical Trajectory" strategy[8]) that can be used to catch a frisbee. Here is how it works. At time t_0, when the frisbee is released by the thrower, it creates an optical projection on your eye. A short time later (t_1), after the frisbee moves through the air, it will create another optical projection (shown with the white circle) in a different location on our eye. A short time after that (t_2) it will create another, then another (t_3), and so on. The movement of the frisbee creates an optical trajectory or optical path. This optical trajectory is *specifying information*. That is, it corresponds to some event. If, as shown in Figure 5.4A, the optical trajectory is straight or linear (that is, it moves equal amounts vertically and laterally during each time interval) this can only happen if it comes down to the ground in the location where the eye is (i.e., a successful catch). If instead, as shown in Figure 5.4B, the optical trajectory is curved it corresponds to other events. Curving in one direction specifies the event that it goes over the receiver's head. Curving in the other direction means it will hit the ground in front of them. In other words, not catching. The amount of curvature will be related to how far they miss it. The optical trajectory is useful for the control of action due to its 1:1 correspondence with these different events. It is *specification*.

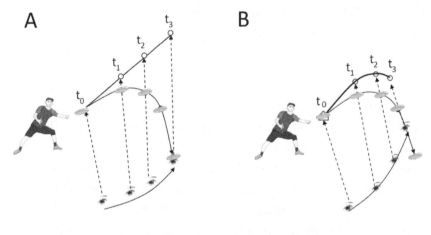

Running Direction = a*(Curvature of OT)

Figure 5.4 – Prospective Control in Frisbee Catching

But how do we use this information? Easy. We start running towards the frisbee. If the optical trajectory is linear, we just keep running in the same direction. If the optical trajectory curves down, we turn a bit to the right. If it curves up, we turn to the left. What we are doing here is creating a simple information-movement relationship. A perception-action coupling. If we run to keep the optical trajectory linear, we are absolutely, positively guaranteed to create the event that we will intercept it.

Notice how we are using the information. Emphasis on *use*. We are just linking it to some aspect of our movement (the direction we are running). We are gathering it and coupling it. At no time do we use it to acquire knowledge. While executing the strategy we have no idea where and when it will come down to the ground. We don't know the future. We are not trying to predict it. We don't need to. We don't need to consider any player tendencies or situational probabilities. If we control our movement to keep this simple information-movement relationship satisfied, we will achieve our goal. End of story.

It's a control method so simple a dog could use it. And in fact, they do! In a 2004 study, Dennis Shaffer and colleagues[9] equipped dogs with video cameras mounted on their heads. They then threw a bunch of frisbees for them to catch. Hey, sometimes research is just playing in the park with your dog! What did they find? The running paths used by the dogs were consistent with them trying to maintain a linear optical trajectory. The dogs didn't just run to a spot on the field and wait for the frisbee to come down. They caught it on the run, with changes in their running direction occurring when the optical trajectory started to curve.

The method of catching illustrated in Figure 5.4 is an example of *prospective* control. Here we are still trying to make some event (our hand clasping around the frisbee) happen in the future (a few seconds now). But we are not achieving it by trying to predict and directly control what happens in the future. Instead, we are trying to control the "current future". When we find a specifying information source for a particular event and link it to our movement it informs us about the relationship between what we are doing in the present and what will happen in the future. If I am running such that the frisbee has a linear optical trajectory (present) then I will catch it (future). My current future is a successful catch. So, I just need to keep on keeping on. If the optical trajectory is not linear (present) than I am going to miss it (future). My current future is not aligned with my goal, so I need to change the way I am moving. Referring to some of the information sources we discussed in early chapters, here are a few other examples:

-If a football special teams player is running such that the value of tau dot is -0.8, their current future is a hard tackle of the punt returner.

-If a rugby player is running such that the focus of expansion is centered on the gap between defenders, their current future is getting through the gap.

-If the tau of the gap between the front of the plate and the ball is equal to the tau of the gap between the current arm position and full extension, then a baseball batter's current future is hitting the ball

We don't need to know the future to be able to make an event happen in it. We don't need to know the present! Again, it is all about the athlete-environment relationship. If we establish a relationship between an appropriate movement parameter and an information source from the environment that is specifying for the event we are trying to achieve, we will be successful. There are also several distinct advantages of this method as compared to predictive control.

The first is just parsimony. Compare and contrast Figures 5.3 and 5.4. Prospective control is simpler. Whereas we need several boxes, arrows, values, and equations to describe what is going on in predictive control, prospective control can be described in one line of text: the information-movement control law, direction of running = f(optical trajectory). But, Rob, you are exaggerating how much goes into a predictive control model! Nope. See Figure 5.5 for an example of one of the most cutting-edge models of that type. But, Rob, I can't control action based on one simple control law. Yep, you can. A couple of my colleagues here at ASU, Mike

Mcbeath and Tom Sugar have taken just the simple control law shown in Figure 5.4 and used it to successfully program a catching robot![10] With predictive control, we are back to the Matrix again. Overcomplicating the story when it is completely unnecessary.

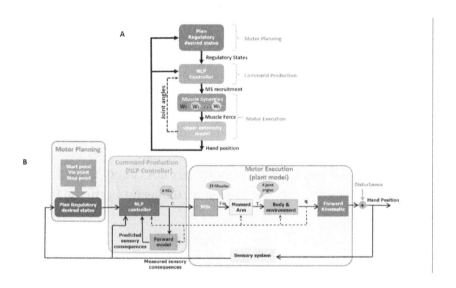

Figure 5.5 – Example of a Predictive Control Model[11].

The second issue is that despite all this text, boxes, and arrows in predictive models, they don't tell us what to do in the end. So, I have predicted that the frisbee will be at a catchable height in 2.7 seconds at a position that is 10 to the right of where I am now. What do I do? Do I program my body to make a beeline to the landing location? That would make sense, but people don't do that – we almost always catch things while we are still moving. Do I program my body to turn 1 deg per second so that it becomes aligned with the landing location in 2.7 seconds? Processing information to get a prediction is not enough – we need to know what to do with that prediction! We have been spending so much time on perception (as described in the new distorted definition, not the Latin root), we haven't bothered to address action.

Prospective control solves the perception and action problems at the same time. What do I do with the perceptual information? Simple!

-If the optical trajectory of the frisbee is curved I rotate my body around my midline while running with the amount of rotation being proportional to the magnitude of the curvature.

-If tau-dot is -0.8 and the punt returner has not caught the ball yet, I reduce my running speed by an amount that is proportional to the value of tau dot.

-If the tau of the gap between the front of the plate and the ball is greater than the tau of the gap between my current arm position and full extension, I increase the rate at which my arm is extending (by increasing muscle contraction) by an amount proportional to the differences between the two taus.

Because prospective control is expressed as an information-movement relationship, we can't avoid talking about the movement like is done for most predictive control models.

Third, prospective control is more robust in the face of changing constraints. A gust of wind changes the frisbee's flight path. No need to recalculate, re-predict, or reprogram the movement. Since the gust is going to change the optical trajectory, we just need to maintain our information-movement control relationship, just like we were already doing. Your shoe comes off so you can't run as quickly anymore. No need to recalculate, re-predict, or reprogram the movement. Slowing down is going to change the optical trajectory so we just need to maintain our information-movement control, just like we were already doing. Since we are using information from the environment in the first place, we don't need to do anything different or special when the information changes due to some unforeseen circumstance.

Finally, despite what many people think, prospective control can easily handle the problems of interruption and time we discussed earlier in this chapter. Let's start with interruption. In Figure 5.6, the only information I have available to catch the frisbee is the optical trajectory. What happens if I looked away from the frisbee for a second to avoid running into a park bench? I don't have the optical trajectory information anymore. Surely, I must then need to predict where the frisbee is going to land to keep running in the right direction. No, that's unnecessary because remember we are not controlling what is happening in the present, we are controlling the "current future". Or more accurately we are controlling the current future if nothing else changes. Imagine at time t_1 in Figure 5.6 we have established the information-movement relationship. Our running speed and direction are such that the optical trajectory is linear. If we keep running in the same way and the frisbee continues to travel on the same parabolic flight path, we don't need any more information to catch it. Our current future, given the conditions in the present, is a catch. We can easily handle the removal of optical trajectory information at times t_2 and t_3 if we have established our control relationship before that point.

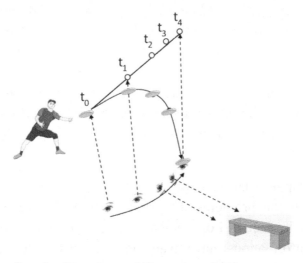

Running Direction = a*(Curvature of OT)

Figure 5.6 – Prospective Control with Interruption of Information

This is also part of the reason why time is also not a problem for prospective control. Let's return to our baseball batting example where we have only a very short time to pick up information from the ball in the flight. Research has shown that batters can handle this quite easily. For example, it has been shown that the variability of point of contact between the bat and ball was not significantly different between a full view condition and one in which only the first 150 ms of the ball's flight was visible[12]. How is this possible without predicting where and when the ball will cross the plate? Again think "current future". If in the first 150 ms the batter picks up information about the tau of the gap between the ball and the front of the plate and couples with the tau of the gap between their current arm angle and full extension, they created a current future of the bat and ball getting to the front of

126

the plate at the same time. If this relationship is maintained this current future will be true even if the information is removed. Or if the time until plate crossing gets so short that information from the ball flight can no longer be used to alter movement. Establishing a prospective information-movement control law does not require that we are always receiving information for the full duration of our movement.

The other way that we can prospectively control our actions for very fast-moving objects that can only be viewed for a short time is by using information before the ball is released to anticipate the trajectory. We can use the situational probabilities and advance cues illustrated in Figure 5.3. But, hold on, isn't anticipation synonymous with prediction? Not necessarily…

Strong Anticipation

Anticipation is another word whose definition has been distorted by theoretical assumptions. In common usage, it has become synonymous with cognitive processing, prediction, and expectation. In sports, we use it to refer to a process whereby an athlete predicts what their opponent is going to do. I anticipate a fastball, a run to left, and a serve down the line. And as illustrated in Figure 5.3, this is typically though to involve a lot of mental processing. To anticipate I need to consider the game situation, my opponent's tendencies, etc. But again, this is not where it started. The original Latin root, *anticipatus*, refers to movement coordination rather than mental processes. Specifically, it means "to follow a path before".

If we want to get all mathematical about it, anticipation can be defined as one aspect of a system maintaining a negative phase relationship with another aspect of the same system. A negative phase relationship is like a shift in time – that is, what one part of a system is doing right now is the same as what another part of the system will do a few seconds from now. To understand this further, let's revisit an example from Chapter 2 – a defensive player in football running to tackle a ball carrier. Our system is the combined behavior of the two players.

Figure 5.7 illustrates three different strategies a defensive player might use to tackle the ball carrier in a situation where the ball carrier is accelerating. The first (Fig 5.7A), is by far the dumbest: run right at the ball carrier. In other words, run to make the bearing angle (β) equal to zero. With this strategy, there is a *positive phase relationship* in our system. That is, the defensive player is doing now what the ball carrier was doing a short time ago. As most people know, the problem with this strategy is the delay in our perceptual-motor system. It takes time for the defensive player to pick up the bearing angle with their vision, send that to the motor control areas in their brain, and then execute a motor command to turn their body. By the time all that is done, they are executing a movement based on something that happened in the past so are always behind the ball carrier.

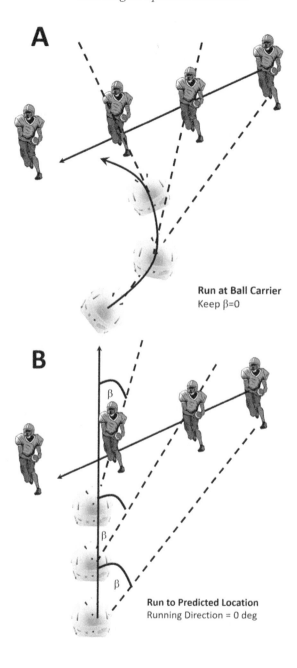

A

Run at Ball Carrier
Keep β=0

B

Run to Predicted Location
Running Direction = 0 deg

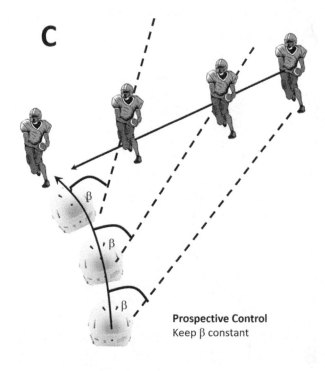

Figure 5.7 – Control Strategies For Tackling In Football

The obvious solution to this problem for most is, of course, to make a prediction. Figure 5.7B illustrates this strategy. The defensive player has predicted where the ball carrier is going to be and is executing a motor program to run straight to the location. This is not going to work either because the ball carrier is accelerating. By the time the defensive player gets to their predicted location, the ball carrier will have blown past. For this strategy, there is no real phase relationship between what the two players are doing because the system has been broken apart. As the play unfolds, the movements of the defensive player are completely uncoupled from the runner – they were preprogrammed beforehand. But, Rob, couldn't this strategy work if we just updated our prediction? We will get to that but let's look at the last strategy.

Figure 5.7C illustrates prospective control. The defensive player is running to keep the bearing angle constant. When the ball carrier accelerates it causes β to get smaller. In our coupled system, this causes the defensive player to turn away from the ball carrier which increases β. What we have here is a *negative phase relationship* between the two players. What the defensive player is doing now (adjusting their running direction to keep β constant) is based on what the ball carrier will do a few seconds in the future. They are turning away from the ball carrier so that they head to where they *will be* not where they are now or where they were in the past. In this situation, the defensive player is anticipating. They are following the path of the ball carrier before they get there!

In prospective control, you get anticipation for free! It is a natural consequence of maintaining the information-movement relationship. Stepp and Turvey call this strong anticipation[13]. A property is "strong" when it arises from the system itself based on its lawful properties and when it holds across a wide range of situations. As we have seen, this is true for prospective control. The bearing angle control law illustrated in Figure 5.7C works no matter how the ball carrier jukes or jives, accelerates, decelerates, etc. Because we are using information online as the event unfolds, we are going to be responsive to any changes in the conditions or constraints that might occur.

But you might ask: what about the visual-motor delay? Wouldn't it be a problem for prospective control too? By the time I change my running direction based on the bearing angle, the bearing angle is going to change. I will leave it up to you to explore yourself if you are interested[14], but in a coupled system delays actually help to stabilize control.

Of course, we could get these same effects with the predictive control strategy illustrated in Figure 5.7B. If at each time interval, the defensive player updated their prediction based on current visual information, they would alter their running direction resulting in a curved path like that shown in Figure 5.7C. This is "weak" anticipation because it arises from a model of the system via internal computations or representations. It is weak because it is adding a lot of unnecessary complexity. Why would I go through all the trouble of processing, weighting, and predicting if I don't have to?

Notice that, in my acceleration example, predictive control is only going to work if we continue to pull in current information from the environment. If we are going to do that, why not just continually use the current information by coupling it to our movement i.e., prospective control? A prediction is a best guess about what will happen in the future. We use it in situations where we don't have all the information e.g., we try to predict the winner of an election because we don't know how everyone is going to vote. But would you try to "predict" the outcome of an election after the votes are all counted? No, you would say what the outcome was because you have all the information. If you establish an appropriate prospective control relationship with your environment, you have all the votes!

Two more points. First, if we believe that athletes use prospective control does that mean that they completely ignore all situational probabilities, opponent tendencies, and advance cues? Are they just purely reactive and in the moment? That seems dumb. Well, the answer is No, they don't. We will revisit all of this in Chapter 12. As we will see a system that uses prospective control can learn through experience (i.e., change based on tendencies and probabilities) without an internal model based on previous knowledge. And it can use advance cues (e.g., the body language of an opponent) to control movement rather than make predictions.

Second, prospective control has a very important implication for something we tend to obsess over a lot in sports: reaction time. That is the speed of our first movement. How quickly we react to some stimulus. As I will discuss more in Chapter 9, if we use prospective control, it renders reaction time almost irrelevant. It is not going to be a rate limiter on performance. It is much more important to react to the right information than just reacting quickly. Sometimes reacting slower will be better! But we will get to that.

134

6

PINK ENVELOPES NOT PUSH SIGNS: AFFORDANCE-BASED COACHING

Think back to when you were a kid on a playground. Did you just do the things you were *supposed* to be doing there? Sliding on the slides. Swinging on the swings. Climbing on the climbing frame. Or were you a naughty little girl or boy that also did things that the equipment wasn't built for? You know things like standing on the swings to launch yourself in the air, climbing up the slides, hanging off safety railings, or seeing if you could leap between two different structures. Well, I am here to relieve you of any residual guilt you might be feeling. It wasn't your fault if you did those things. You were just accepting the invitations from your environment.

All around us our world is inviting us to act. Sit. Climb. Lay down. Walk. Hit. Catch. These invitations are what JJ Gibson called *affordances* – opportunities for action provided or offered to us by our environment. A flat surface affords sitting. An opening affords walking through. Notice my choice of words here. I didn't say a chair affords sitting or a sidewalk affords walking. The affordances we pick up from the objects in our environment are not limited to just the functions that the objects might have been "designed for". Take the two examples illustrated in Figure 6.1. On the top, we have the designer of this space trying to tell us "Use the nice, paved sidewalk to get to your car" while our environment is shouting "you can get to your car faster by just walking across the grass". On the bottom, we have a surface with a handle sticking

135

out that screams "pull me" so we must add a "push" sign that overrides this. We are all just naughty little children on playgrounds – picking up invitations to do things we are not "supposed to".

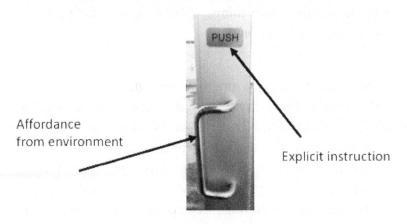

Figure 6.1 – Affordances vs Explicit Instructions

Why is this relevant to coaching? Well, I think it's time for a big shift in the mindset of how we coach. For a long time, coaching has been about trying to directly manipulate and change the athlete. We have been doing this in two main ways. First, like in the examples in Figure 6.1, coaching has involved sticking up "push" and "walk here" signs all over the place. Explicit instructions telling the athlete how WE want them to act in their environment. Keep your knees bent, and your elbow up, and make sure to snap your wrist. We have been trying to tell them how to play while, for the most part, ignoring what the playground might be inviting them to do.

Second, we spend a lot of time trying to directly change the "abilities" of our athletes. We have them hit baseballs off tees or repeat the same golf swing over and over so they can develop better "technique". We have them run around cones or through ladders so that they can develop better "agility". We have them do a bunch of squats to make them stronger. We have them following objects on a computer screen to give them better attentional focus and reaction time. The assumption is that they will just be able to pull these abilities out and use them in the right way and at the right time when they get back in the game.

In this chapter, I want to try and convince you that there is a better way. That is, instead of trying to directly change and manipulate the athlete, we need to think about changing and manipulating the affordances available to the athlete instead. We need to think about invitations, not instructions. Far fewer "push" and "walk here" signs and more opportunities for action picked up directly from the practice environments we design. We need to move away from the asymmetric focus on building up and storing abilities and techniques within the athlete like they are a bank account. We need to think about increasing the number of invitations the athlete gets on the field and making some of them more inviting than others. We want to become affordance-based coaches. Let's see how.

Affordances in Action: Selection & Control

How do athletes use these affordances to control their actions? To understand, let's start at the very beginning. Imagine you are going to start playing baseball. You walk up to a rack of baseball bats. How do you know which one you should use to achieve the best performance? What weight should it be, how thick, and what length? Or imagine you are starting to play tennis. You are in the pro shop surrounded by racquets strung with different string tensions. How do you know which one is going to allow you to best control your shots? What we are talking about here is, of course, the perception of affordances. What opportunities for action do different pieces of equipment afford us? Does a heavy bat afford swinging fast? Does a tightly strung racquet afford hitting the ball accurately? Can we perceive not just the physical dimensions of an object but what it affords us? What information do we use?

Not surprisingly, JJ Gibson was all over this problem! In 1966, he introduced the concept of dynamic touch[1]. When an object like a bat or racquet is grasped and wielded – that is lifted and moved around in space – it creates deformations in our body tissue. There will be changes in the length and tension in the muscles and tendons. Critically these deformations are not random. They will depend on the physical characteristics of the object being wielded. Heavier objects will create more tension in the muscles than lighter objects, longer different than shorter ones, etc. So, just like we saw in the last chapter for vision, objects in our environment structure the information we receive from our senses – that is, they

138

alter it in a way that is directly related to its properties. Therefore, it is possible that we can perceive the affordances of objects directly through information provided by our sense of touch. Let's look at a few research studies that have investigated this.

In racquet sports, there is a general belief that playing performance is enhanced if the "right" string tension is chosen for match play. Often, we hear that elite players prefer a particular string tension that must be frequently checked during a match. Broadly, higher string tensions allow for more transfer of force (and thus higher velocities) but are sometimes more difficult to control (i.e., lower accuracy). In 2013, Zhu investigated this issue using an affordance approach[2]. Twelve adult badminton players (4 experts, 4 recreational, and 4 novices who never played) were first asked to determine the difference between string tensions on racquets and select the tension that would allow for the most powerful stroke. The same racquet strung with 8 different tensions (ranging from 16-30 lb) was used and participants were only allowed to press the strings with their fingers, with their eyes closed and ears plugged.

What was found? All players in the study had a clear preference for a particular string tension with novices tending to prefer racquets with lower string tension than the intermediate, recreational players. What happened when they were tested on the court with all the different racquets handed to them in random order? As shown in Figure 6.2B, the recreational players seemed to be very good at perceiving the affordance. Their shot velocity was highest when playing with their preferred string tension. These players were very good at picking out the racquets that would result in the best playing performance just by pushing the strings with their fingers a little! However, as can be seen in Figure 6.2C, this was not the case for the novices. The did not consistently produce the highest shot velocity for their preferred racquet. So, the first key point here, *accurate affordance perception typically requires experience.* We need to learn to pick up the information from the environment that conveys the relevant opportunities for action by interacting with the environment. Similar effects have been found in other sports. Experience performing the action is required to do things like pick the best ball size and weight for maximal distance throwing and pick the best weight distribution of a hockey stick for stickhandling.

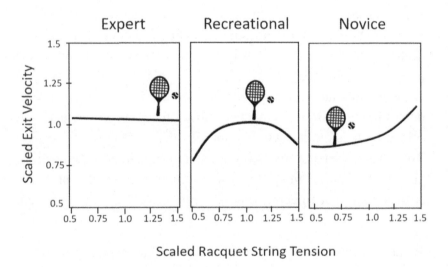

Figure 6.2 – Scaled Exit Velocity of Forehands for Different Racquet String Tensions. Values are divided by the mean. Racquets show the mean preferred string tension.

If the novices in the tennis racquet study were not picking up the affordance, then why did they tend to prefer lighter racquets? Also, note that in Figure 6.2C, the line is not completely flat – the shot velocity tended to be higher when they played using tighter racquets. What's going on here? The answer can be seen when we look at the differences in movement patterns used to produce the stroke. From the motion tracking data, it was found that the recreational (and expert) players used multiple degrees of freedom. Starting with a side stance, they rotate their body towards the ball using the ankle, knee, and pelvis. They then transfer this force to the racquet with shoulder, elbow, wrist, and finger movements. So, lots of body parts are involved! Novices, on the other hand, stood facing the oncoming birdie and generated racquet speed primarily by just flexing and extending the elbow. In other words, novices seemed to be freezing the degrees of freedom – not moving the lower body, wrist, and fingers to simplify the shot. But this, in turn, gives them far less precision in the shot control. They can't make subtle adjustments to the racquet movement. How do they solve this problem? By using a lower string tension which results in less variation in the shot direction after contact. So, the second key point here, the *affordances we perceive depend on the movement patterns we can produce*. If we can't precisely control the racquet head using multiple degrees of freedom in the movement, we won't perceive that a more tightly strung racquet affords good performance.

So, the first key role affordances play is **selection**. Here we have been looking at selecting equipment, but the perception of affordances also allows us to select which actions to perform. As we have seen in previous chapters, the information from the environment tells us things like whether a gap between defenders affords running through, whether a ball affords catching or whether a ball carrier affords tackling. Therefore, we can use this information to select the appropriate actions during game play. As an example, consider a simple selection problem: should I swing at an oncoming pitch in baseball or not?

In a study I published in 2020[3], I investigated this question for a particular batting task. Batters were required to hit the ball to the opposite field. So, if you were standing behind the batter and they were on the left side of the plate, they had to hit it to the right side of the field. Mechanically, this task is much easier to achieve for pitches that are further from the batter's body ("outside" pitches) than for one's close to the body ("inside" pitches). Therefore, a simple affordance-based prediction is that skilled batters might select the action of swinging for outside pitches and select the action of not swinging for inside ones. Do batters do this? Yes, but just as we saw with the badminton racquet example, it depends on their experience and training.

Figure 6.3 shows the results for a CLA training group and a control group (that just did regular repetitive batting practice) in my study. With training, the CLA group showed better action selection – they swung at fewer pitches that did not afford the intended action of hitting the ball to the opposite field. But know what? I never actually told them to do this. At no time in my study did I tell the CLA training group which pitches to swing at – they improved in their action selection on their own. I will get to the details of the "secret sauce" in the training that helped to make this happen shortly, but let's just make the third key point for now. If an athlete can pick up affordances in their environment, they can select the action that is likely to be the most successful (shoot, pass, drive, swing, don't swing, etc) on their own without a coach telling them which play to run or if this happens then do that. The environment is sending them invitations to be successful if they just learn to open them!

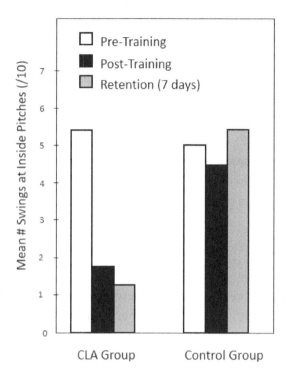

Figure 6.3 – Change in Affordance Perception in the CLA

Once we have selected which equipment to use or which actions to perform, affordances play another key role. They help us more effectively execute the action. As the first example of this let's now consider the results for expert players in the badminton racquet study. Even though the experts in the study have clear preferences for a particular string tension, as can be seen in Figure 6.2A, it didn't matter in the end. The expert players could produce a high-velocity stroke no matter which racquet they were handed. Why? Because they could perceive the affordances of the different racquets and adjust their movement patterns accordingly. For the racquets with less tension, experts used more wrist and finger flexion to compensate for the lower energy transfer from the strings to the ball. They are showing adaptability or what Nikolai Bernstein termed *dexterity* – the ability to find a movement solution that works under different conditions. But, if they can produce high-velocity shots with any racquet, why do experts have a preference for higher-tension ones? Well, as we will see in Chapter 8, being an elite mover is not just about performance – efficiency also matters. Using wrist and finger movements to compensate for lower string tension comes with a cost. These smaller muscles are going to get more easily fatigued. Therefore, high string tensions are preferred because they give high velocity with lower energy costs.

Another important role affordance perception plays in the control of action is by helping an athlete to "play within themselves". That is, to execute actions in a manner that takes into account their individual constraints and action capacities. To understand this let's return to the problem of catching a flyball in baseball. As we saw in Chapter 2, a simple prospective control law a fielder can use to catch the ball is to couple their running speed to the optical acceleration of the ball. As illustrated in Figure 6.4A, if the image of the ball is decelerating, the fielder is too shallow to catch it. So, they need to run back toward the wall at a speed that's directly related to the amount of deceleration. If the image is speeding up, they are too deep and need to run at a rate directly related to the amount of acceleration. If they adjust their running speed so that the optical acceleration is zero, their "current future' will be a successful catch. Put another away, the optical acceleration information source tells the fielder the required running speed to achieve their goal.

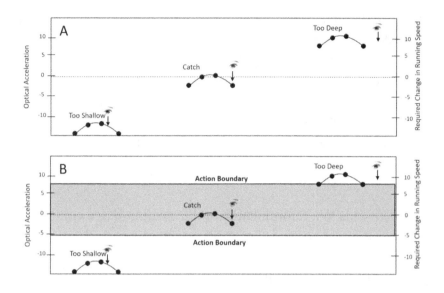

Figure 6.4 – Affordance Based Control in Catching a Flyball

But, as first noted by Brett Fajen[4], something is missing here with this simple information-movement-based control. What if the required change in running speed is greater than the change in speed that can be produced by the fielder? What if the optical image of the ball is accelerating and they are already running at the maximum speed? As illustrated in Figure 6.4, our abilities (what Gibson called "effectivities") create action boundaries in the information-movement space. Within the boundary, the action is afforded. Outside it is not. We need affordance perception. Does the ball afford "catchability"? We can't simply couple our movements to information in the environment. We need to know whether this coupling is going to be in vain or not.

An athlete must be able to detect the location of these action boundaries because typically when we reach one, we will need to change our intention or goal. For example, when the required change in running speed crosses the action boundary for a baseball outfielder, they may change their intention from catching the ball in the air (which is no longer afforded) to playing it off a bounce. Failure to do this can result in the player completely missing the ball because they are running too fast, and it bounces too close to them. This is what we mean when we say an athlete is "playing within themselves". They are acting in a manner that considers their own action boundaries.

This also leads to a reformulation of information-based control to *affordance-based control*. To be successful in our goal, we can't just establish an appropriate information movement control relationship and move to maintain it. We also need to act to keep the required changes in movement within our action boundaries. We can't just pick-up information. We need to also detect affordances. Imagine the ball is hit to you and you initially run in towards it even through the ball is going over your head. This is a very common occurrence in baseball. This will cause the optical image to decelerate because you are now too shallow. No problem, if you are coupling your running to the optical acceleration, it leads you to change direction and run away from the ball. But there is a problem if you run too far in and cross your action boundary. If you want to get an early jump on the ball you need to be sensitive to affordances. You need to move to keep within the action boundary. As it turns out, this is exactly what skilled baseball outfielders do!

Oudejans and colleagues[5] compared the performance of experienced outfielders (including one player from Major League Baseball) to that of novices when moving to catch flyballs. The experts were significantly *slower* in initiating the movement of their feet after the ball was launched (by 85 ms, on average) than the lesser-skilled players. Further analysis revealed that this was

146

particularly the case for balls hit over the head that was misplayed by the novices. In 48% of the trials, novices begin running forward for a ball hit over the head while this occurred in only one trial (0.5%) for experts. In such situations, the novices initiated their movement nearly 100 ms faster than the experts. For the remaining trials in which the novices successfully began running backward, their movement initiation was only about 25 ms faster than the experts suggesting that errors are occurring because they are moving too quickly! Waiting to move both allows more information to be gathered and decreases the likelihood the fielder will cross an action boundary by moving in the wrong direction. As we will consider more in Chapter 9, "good" decision-making is often not synonymous with fast decision-making. In fact, like in this case, the opposite is often true – waiting to decide which direction to run for as long as possible results in better fielding. Being slow is good. But we will get to that!

So, to sum up, to successfully achieve our goal not only do we need to use affordance perception to select the action we are going to attempt to execute, but we also need it to control our actions. Specifically, we need to detect the borders between the possible and impossible. In the catching example, the fielder needs to detect when they are getting close to a situation in which the required running speed is greater than their maximum speed and act to not cross this boundary. If we do cross an action boundary we need to detect this so that we can appropriately change our intention. We will consider how an athlete can improve their ability to do this shortly, but next, I want to explore an exciting opportunity if we use affordance-based coaching: it may be possible to move an athlete's action boundaries.

Action Capacity vs Skill

Imagine again that you are a baseball outfielder, and a ball is hit over your head. The information is telling that your current future is not a successful catch. You need to turn and run away from the ball. But, what if, like many lesser experienced fielders you are not very good at executing this movement solution? As I have tried to illustrate in Figure 6.4B, you will likely have different action boundaries when running in toward the ball as compared to when running back away from it because coordinating your body to turn and run at a high speed is more difficult. As a result, for balls hit over your head, you are likely to perceive the ball is not catchable and instead choose to play the ball after it bounces on the ground or hits the wall. You didn't receive the invitation to catch the ball from the environment because you are limited in your action capacity – in this case, your ability to execute the turn-and-run movement solution. You have allowed the batter to get on base ☹

But let's look at this as a glass half full. So, the invitations an athlete receives from their environment depend on their action capacities. Well, if this is true then we can just do the thing you see in every romantic comedy movie. We can take the awkward and nerdy girl/guy that wasn't getting asked to the prom, give them a makeover, and viola invitations coming from everywhere! If we can increase an athlete's action capacity appropriately, we can increase their field of available affordances. We can give them more options and opportunities to act! But what exactly is an action capacity and how does it relate to skill?

As we have seen in previous chapters, being skillful is about a relationship between the performer and their environment. I would define *skill* as the ability to use information from the environment to find and execute a movement solution to realize an affordance that will achieve one's intention. In other words, the ability to establish and maintain a functional relationship with one's environment. Skills are information-driven, have a clear purpose, and involve deciding between different available affordances. I would define an *action capacity* as a physical or psychological ability that influences the field of affordances for a given task. They influence the number of invitations we receive and determine the location of our action boundaries. Let's look at a couple of studies of this relationship between capacity and skill.

In a 2008 study[6], I examined how baseball batters adapt to an increase in bat weight. After letting them hit for a while with a standard 32 oz bat, I handed experienced college players a bat that was 38 oz. This led to a temporary timing error in the swing – the bat movement was about 40-50 msec too slow to contact the ball. But after about 5-10 swings, the batters adjusted and were consistently hitting the ball again. What was interesting was how they adjusted. Half the batters in my study adapted to the heavier bat weight by increasing the force of their movement. EMG recordings revealed that they were increasing the amount of muscle activity so that they were able to swing the 38oz at the same speed as the 32 oz one. The other half did something very different. They showed no change in muscle activity or force generation. Instead, they adapted by starting their swing slightly earlier.

Why did batters adapt in different ways? Because of their action capacity. In a separate session, I gave the players bats of increasing weights and asked them to swing as fast as possible while hitting a ball off a tee. Yes, batting tees are good for something! When you do this, you find that as bat weight increases so will bat speed

- but only up to a point. The additional weight allows the batter to generate more momentum in their swing but eventually, it becomes too much. For each batter, I determined the heaviest bat at which adding a bit more weight made their swing speed slow down. This was their maximum bat weight capacity. As you can probably guess by now, the batters that had a bat weight capacity at or above 38 oz just swung harder while those that had a capacity below had to adjust the timing of their swing. And this difference turned out to have consequences for performance. The batters that had to adjust the timing of their swing had fewer hits. Specifically, they were less able to hit outside pitches and pitches at high speeds. Reducing their action capacity with the heaver bat reduced their available movement solutions resulting in a reduction in the number of invitations they received from the environment. Some pitches no longer afforded hitting.

In a 2010 study, Matt Dicks and colleagues[7] examined the relationship between action capacity and skill in soccer goalkeeping. The relevant action capacity in the study was the goalkeeper's movement time (MT, how quickly they could get from the middle of the net to one of the corners) which was measured in a baseline test. For the seven experienced goalkeepers in the study, there was a surprisingly large range in this measure. For example, for diving to the top right corner of the net, one goalkeeper's MT was 690 msec while another keeper had an MT of 1038 msec for the same location. They next measured the time when the goalkeeper's started their diving movement for penalty kicks during a game. This again was quite variable. One of the goalkeepers started their dive nearly 300 msec before the kicker struck the ball while another keeper waited until about 50 msec before the point of contact. What is going on here? Are goalkeepers just variable and inconsistent? No, they were using affordance-based control. When the authors combined the two measured quantities (the MT and the start time) into a ratio, they found that all the keepers were doing the same thing. They were starting their dive right about at the point when the time remaining before the ball reached the goal was equal to their movement time. They were moving right at their action boundary. And again, just as was found in my batting study, action capacity had a direct effect on save performance. The three goalkeepers with the fastest movement times (who started their dive later) were the only ones that successfully saved a deceptive penalty kick during the study. Greater action capacity (faster MT) gave some of the keepers an invitation from the environment (wait longer to gather more information) that others did not receive.

Here is our opportunity again. When athletes have greater action capacities (like quicker movement times and the ability to generate more force to swing a heavier bat) they are given more invitations to act from their environment (wait longer or swing harder). This in turn has the potential to make them more skillful. If these invitations are relevant to their goals/intentions, they are accepted at the appropriate times and the athlete can realize them, they are likely to have better performance as shown in the hitting and soccer studies described. So, how as coaches can we best take this opportunity?

Coaching to Increase the Number of Invitations an Athlete Receives

How do we know what the relevant action capacities are for our sport? Once we identify them, what is the best way to train them to increase the likelihood we influence the skill? For me, there are three basic principles we should be following:

1) Conditions not Positions

To be an elite mover there are a few principles or conditions that must be met. For example, to achieve maximal transfer of force in skills like throwing and hitting we need to: (i) take force from the ground and load it into our body, (ii) transfer this force through our body (e.g., from our back foot contact the ground to our hand holding the ball) without losing it all along the way, and (iii) dissipate the force at the end of our movement. These are the conditions we must satisfy. But critically, this can be done using a variety of different body positions. They are no positions that we have to be in. There is not one "correct" technique.

Compare the two baseball pitchers shown in Figure 6.5. Effectively transferring force through the body requires stopping the movement of the lower body at some point and putting all the force into the rotation of the upper body. The pitcher on the left is achieving this by using a movement pattern you see in many sports called "lead leg blocking". By extending their lead leg straight they are essentially braking the motion of the lower part of the body just as they are rotating their torso and shoulder. The thrower on the right is doing something very different. Their lead leg is bent because they are transferring force from the upper body to the lower body by dropping their back knee to the ground and rotating their right hip forwards. Both athletes are meeting the condition (transferring the force moving though the lower body into the torso and shoulder) but using different positions.

*Figure 6.5 – Two Different Movement Solutions for Stopping
Rotation of the Lower Body in Baseball Pitching,*

Why do we see individual differences like this? There can be a variety of reasons including different body dimensions and different training experiences. But it is also likely due to differences in the action capacity. For example, the thrower might be using lead leg blocking because they lack mobility and flexibility in their hip and pelvis. They are not afforded this movement solution because they lack the relevant action capacity to produce it. If we work on improving this capacity in training it could potentially give them more invitations to act. This in turn can make them more adaptable. For example, it might allow them to perform when the surface is a bit more slippery so their lead leg slides then it is locked or if they develop an injury in their front knee. But critically, we are not correcting their technique by instructing them that they must drop their back knee and rotate their hip. We are only going to give them the invitation to use that when they self-organize their movement. We are not prescribing positions – we are giving the athlete more opportunities to satisfy conditions.

Before we get into more details about exactly how we do this, let's look at the third condition I mentioned above: dissipating force.

This is something we often overlook. Why do we care what an athlete does after they let go of the object they are throwing or contact the object they are hitting? Why do we care about their follow-through? It doesn't change the outcome of the action in any way because the athlete can't impart any more force into the object they are interacting with. Well as it turns out it is more important than we might think! There are forward-acting effects in movement – what I do earlier in my movement will influence what happens later. But there are also backward-acting effects. In particular, your body is not going to give you a Ferrari accelerator if you provide it with Volkswagen brakes. Dissipating force ineffectively by sharply stopping a movement or putting it all into one arm or knee is going to cause protective mechanisms to kick in. Your body is going to put a limiter on your acceleration (resulting in your not being able to throw as fast or hit as hard) to protect you from injury.

So, in developing an athlete's action capacities we want to focus on training that gives them more different ways to meet the conditions for effective movement. More invitations. This starts by:

2) Provide an effective stimulus for change

Changing an athlete's action capacities requires giving their body a reason for changing. To understand how we can promote this let's first look at a way NOT to do it. In baseball batting, rotational velocity (the ability to get the bat from the shoulder to the plate) is a critical action capacity. If a batter has a high rotational velocity, it invites them to wait a bit longer to start their swing, allowing them to pick up more information from the ball flight. One of the most common drills used to improve "bat speed" is having an athlete hit a ball off a tee telling them to swing as fast as possible. But ask yourself, why would your action capacity change in this situation? It's just a ball sitting there. There are no timing demands. You are hitting with the bat you always use. There are no increased demands on your movement. Why would you change anything? The answer is you wouldn't. This is why "bat speed" drills like this are typically accompanied by a lot of verbal instructions from the coach: extend your arms, bend your back knee, etc. Positions NOT conditions. Here we are doing things the wrong way. Trying to increase action capacity by telling you how to position and move your body. We are putting up "push" and "walk here" signs again. We must because we haven't created a practice environment that invites us to move in different ways. We haven't designed affordances into our practice activity.

Four different things in our environment promote change. *Variability* – I can't keep using the same movement solution because things around me are changing. *Instability* – I need to change something because I keep getting knocked out of my movement pattern. *Constraints* – I must change because there is something in my environment that is making it such that my movement solution doesn't work. *Overload* – the force and/or timing demands of the movement are increased such that I need to move differently. Figure 6.6 shows a practice activity that I like to use to encourage changes in the action capacity of rotational velocity instead of hitting off a tee. Here, the athlete is moving to rotate a plastic cylinder filled with water (aka an "aqua bag") that weighs as much as 50 lbs (overload). The movement of the water creates unpredictable changes in the load (instability) as I ask them to hit circular targets in different locations (variability). To shake things up I might also add a hurdle by their lead foot that they must step over (constraint).

Figure 6.6 – Aqua bag Rotational Activity. Aqua Bag Rotational Activity. Photo Credit: Randy Sullivan, Florida Baseball ARMory.

But Rob there is no ball! There is no information from the external environment driving the movement. Aren't you violating your catch phrase "keep em' coupled"? Yes, indeed I am. This is because I am trying to help the athlete increase their action capacity of rotational velocity NOT the skill of hitting. I am challenging them to meet the conditions of effective rotation NOT trying to get to develop their "swing technique". I am trying to increase the number of affordances available to them when they attempt the skill of hitting. I am not trying to get them to repeat a particular movement pattern. I am not giving them solutions. I am giving them more available tools to find their own solutions. I am also thinking about this in a very different way than traditional strength and conditioning because I am focusing on.

3) Adaptability not a linear progression

When people hear the term "action capacity" it often suggests strength training using the bench press or squats. That is, our goal is to progressively increase the weight to produce a progressive change in a specific ability – the capacity to generate force and move the bar upwards. Or think training in long-distance running. We want to systematically increase and periodize the training conditions to produce a progressive change in capacity. For me, this is the wrong way to think about increasing action capacity for sports that involve coordinating movements of the entire body. Let me illustrate with a specific example.

One of the most used tools for increasing action capacity in baseball pitchers has been weighted balls. A regulation baseball weighs 5 oz. Training with heavier balls (up to 17oz) has been shown to result in an increase in pitch velocity (by as much as 11 mph) in several studies[8]. But this seems to come at a cost. In 2018, Reinold and colleagues[9] conducted a randomized control trial of weighted ball training. The changes in pitch velocity were like earlier research: 3.3% increase in pitch velocity from pre-post training for the weighted ball training group with no significant change for a control group. But the most striking results came when looking at injuries. Six of the 19 participants in the training group suffered injuries with no injuries reported for the control group. There were four elbow injuries in the training group (24%) that required medical attention, including two olecranon stress fractures, one partial UCL injury, and one UCL injury for which surgical reconstruction was recommended.

What is going on here?! Kinematic analyses revealed that the increases in pitch velocity associated with the weighted ball training were the result of an increase in the maximal shoulder external rotation. For the training group, there was a significant increase in shoulder external rotation from pre-post training of 4.3 degrees on average, while there was no significant change for the control group. Having a larger degree of rotation during the early cocking phase of the delivery effectively allows the pitcher's hand to be in contact with the ball over a larger distance resulting in greater force generation. Previous research has shown that higher values of shoulder external rotation are correlated with both higher pitch velocities and increased torque forces in the shoulder and elbow.

The problem here is that we are again focusing on positions NOT conditions. As has been the case in most weighted ball training, the Reinold et al study used simple linear progressions in the training stimuli. Over the 6 weeks of training, the ball weight was systematically increased (2, 4, 6, 16, and 32 oz) along with the throwing intensity (from 75% to max effort). This seems to encourage a relatively simple change in the movement pattern – a change in the POSITION of the hand and shoulder at the point of cocking (i.e., when the arm begins moving forward).

What should we be doing instead? Focus on adaptability. That is the ability of the pitcher to change their movement solution to meet the CONDITIONS of effective force transfer under different constraints. Progressively increasing ball weight and effort are encouraging a simple (and seemingly dangerous) change in the existing movement solution. Instead, I would propose that we should randomly vary the ball weight. Because the manipulation of task constraints is now challenging the pitcher with the problem of going from light to heavy and heavy to light, they cannot make a simple adjustment (rotate their shoulder more) with each new ball given to them. Instead, they must learn to pick up the properties of the ball and adapt their coordination pattern appropriately.

OK, so we have increased an athlete's action capacity through training that focuses on the conditions for effective movement, provides a stimulus for change, and emphasizes adaptability. We have given them more invitations to act in the sporting environment. But what if they don't accept them? What if a batter's rotational velocity increases but they still start their swing early? Has it all been just a waste of time? The final piece in the puzzle of affordance-based coaching is increasing the chance invitations get accepted by connecting capacity and skill training.

Using Pink Envelopes – Amplifying Invitations in the Practice Environment

As coaches, we must accept that trying to tell an athlete what to do is a waste of time. First off, we don't know what they should be doing. Should a new baseball pitcher I am coaching use lead leg blocking or back knee drop and hip rotation? What body positions are needed to achieve these? I don't know! That is up to them to figure out through a process of self-organization. Even if I did know what to tell them, it's not likely they would listen anyways. Research examining how effectively athletes implement technical instructions has shown that "push" and "walk here" signs don't work. They don't result in the desired changes in behavior. Movements happen way too quickly and involve too many parts for these explicit instructions to be incorporated. So, what is there left for coaches to do? Let the practice environment do the talking for us!

Effective coaching is all about manipulating affordances – changing the invitations an athlete receives from the environment. While we can't tell an athlete what to do, we can change the practice environment such that some invitations never arrive while others come in bright pink envelopes. What I am talking about here is using the CLA. We want to add constraints to the practice environment that are going to take away or de-stabilize an athlete's existing movement solution and invite them to try something else.

As an example, imagine that I worked with a baseball batter to increase their rotational velocity using the activity shown in Figure 6.6. I haven't made them more skillful by doing that. I have given them the potential to be more skillful by increasing their capacity and moving their action boundaries. To increase the chance of realizing this potential, I would follow up the aqua bag by using the CLA during hitting practice. To amplify the affordance of waiting to start the swing I might use early visual occlusion where the batter starts with their eyes closed or occluded when they ball is released and opens them when it's part of the way to the plate. To amplify the affordance of hitting the ball over the defense I might have the outfielders play shallow or move the fence in. I am not putting up "push" or "walk here" signs. I am taking the handle off the door or opening up a new path.

In Chapter 16, we will look at some tools a coach can use to become more proficient at manipulating affordances. But first I want to look at something that we often overlook when talking about movement skills – what we do before we start to move.

7

———

STRONGER TENT POLES: HARNESSING MUSCLE TENSION & BIOTENSEGRITY

Imagine you are in one of those strong man competitions and you are challenged with pulling a car with a rope. When the signal goes off you have 30 seconds to see how far you can move it. Figure 7.1 illustrates two possible starting positions you could use. Which do you think would result in the best performance? I am guessing you said the one illustrated in the bottom panel. Why? Because the rope in the top one is not tight. Therefore, the first part of the puller's movement is not going to move the car. It is going to be used up just by tightening the rope. I use this example to illustrate the topic we are going to consider in this chapter – tension. Your muscles work very much like the rope and the car. Having appropriate tension in them is a good thing and solves a lot of the problems of movement control for us. Let's see how.

Figure 7.1 - Illustration of the Effect of Muscle Slack

Muscle Tonus & Removing Slack

As Frans Bosch nicely describes in his book Anatomy of Agility[1], the muscles in the human body are not just sitting there, tensed, and ready for action, as we might assume. They are not ready to produce power, control movement, and protect your joints, tendons, and ligaments as you move. Instead, they typically hang like slack ropes when we are relaxed. Why is this important? Because for many sporting actions, the time we have available to generate force is quite short. We are only in contact with the primary force generator (e.g., the ground) for a relatively short amount of time. Take a baseball swing for example.

Figure 7.2 shows the ground reaction forces produced during a typical baseball swing. Hitters generate bat speed through a coiling or loading process that begins with a shift in weight onto the back leg (i.e., furthest from the oncoming ball). This is achieved by lifting the front foot off the ground (*Stepping*). As the hitter drives forward out of the coil, the shift in weight to the front foot begins when the lead foot returns contact with the ground (*Landing*). This force is then transferred through the upper body, to the bat, and then (hopefully!) to the ball. So, the *Stepping-Landing* period in the swing, which we can see typically lasts about 300 msec, is critical to hitting the ball hard. The batter needs to load up as much force as they can during this brief window.

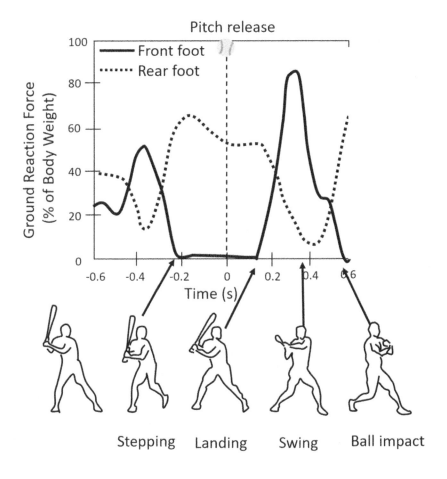

Figure 7.2 - Ground Reaction Forces in a Baseball Swing

Loading force into the back leg involves muscle contractions that create elastic tension. Like an elastic (or rubber) band, our muscles stretch and create a pulling force in the things they are attached to. For example, the force you feel in your fingers as you keep pulling on an elastic band. But if our muscles are not ready, the contractions will initially not create this elastic tension. Instead, like in Figure 7.1, they will just be used to straighten out the muscle. *Muscle slack* can be defined as this delay between the start of a muscle contraction and the production of the elastic tension we want[2]. It is wasted time. It is time we could have been using to generate force if our muscles were just ready to go!

Returning to our baseball batting example we can see how important this is. If the batter has a large degree of muscle slack, when they contract the muscles in their leg during the stepping phase, they are going to have to remove the slack before they can begin generating force. It has been estimated that this takes about 100 msec. In other words, a full 1/3 of the time available to generate force during this part of the movement. This has led Frans Bosch to make the strong conclusion that: "The speed at which muscles can build up their tension and overcome muscle slack is usually more important to performance than the amount of force they can eventually produce" [2]

This idea of muscle preparedness is something Nikolai Bernstein also captured with his concept of *Muscle Tonus*[3]. Muscle tonus or tone is the continuous and partial contraction of the muscles while they are relaxed. For Bernstein, this was a critical part of movement control. Figure 7.3 illustrates his levels of movement construction. Without going into all the details now, we can see that the first level is muscle tone.

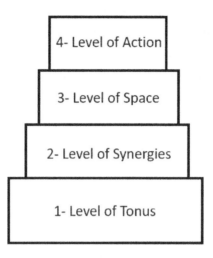

Figure 7.3 - Bernstein's Levels of Movement Construction

Bernstein proposed that the purpose of this first level was to prepare the movement apparatus to respond to commands sent from the upper levels. If we did not have this, then: "the movement apparatus would be unprepared to respond adequately to upper-level commands and the intended movement form would never be made manifest".

So, our muscles need to be ready to go for movement to be effective! We will see exactly how this can be achieved shortly but first I want to bring in another important concept. Muscle slack, or lack of muscle tonus, is a great example of a *rate limiter*. A rate limiter is an individual constraint that limits the rate at which a performer acquires and develops a movement skill. Identifying and tackling these are key to reaching higher levels of skill.

Think about baseball batting again. I very often get asked to work with hitters that need to increase their bat speed. Their swing is late on a lot of pitches, and they struggle with high-velocity pitches. In this situation, we often look in a lot of different places for the cause. Maybe they have a vision problem. Maybe they are not picking up the flight of the ball. Maybe there is a problem with their "swing mechanics". Maybe they are not strong enough and need to do some strength exercises. While any of these could be the root cause, it might also be the case that they have a large amount of muscle slack. It takes them too long to generate force. If this were the case, then coaching interventions designed to address these other factors would likely have very limited success. The benefits of getting you to pick up the ball flight earlier or increase your muscle mass are going to be restricted by the presence of muscle slack, this wasted period of movement. As we saw in Chapter 6, action capacities create opportunities for us to be more skillful. Rate limiters are the opposite – they restrict opportunities.

So how can we reduce or remove muscle slack? There are three different ways this can be done. First, an athlete can use a countermovement. If, before we begin a movement, we start moving slightly in the opposite direction this will cause the muscles to be stretched and the slack to be removed. Examples include a basketball player dipping down with their knees and hips before they jump up or our baseball batter shifting slightly forward before moving to load on the back foot. While this may work, it is problematic because it is going to take time to do the counter-movement, up to 300-500 ms which the athlete may not have. Also, in skills that require precise timing like baseball batting the countermovement now needs to be precisely timed. So, although it is a movement solution that is frequently taught, it is not the best way to remove muscle slack.

The second way to remove muscle slack is by adding load. For example, if you are just standing it is likely you have a lot of muscle slack. But if I add a load (a weighted barbell, for example) before I do a squat, the force created by the weight will cause the muscle to tense. But again this is impractical in most sporting situations because we can't just go around adding weights to people!

By far, the most effective way to remove muscle slack is by using a *co-contraction*. A co-contraction is the simultaneous contraction of two muscles around a joint: the agonist (the one that causes the movement) and the antagonist (the one that inhibits the movement). Think about doing a biceps curl. To produce this movement, the agonist biceps muscle needs to contract, and the antagonist triceps muscle needs to relax. But again, if we were doing speed curls this would be influenced by muscle slack – the delay between contraction of the biceps and elastic force production. This can be reduced if the athlete learns to contract both the biceps and triceps right before moving. Co-contractions are move effective than the other ways of removing slack because they take very little time and do not require any external force or load.

In addition to the potential to improve performance through more effective force generation, co-contractions may also serve an important role in injury prevention. When muscle slack is removed due to co-contraction it allows for faster corrections after an unexpected perturbation. For example, if when a basketball player prepares for a lateral cutting movement with a co-contraction there is an unexpected inversion of the ankle because they step on another player's foot this can be corrected by the muscles that are already pre-tensed.

This ability to co-contract to remove muscle slack is essentially another one of the action capacities we have been talking about. Once it is developed, it creates the potential for the athlete to be more skillful. To develop this capacity, we need to follow the same principles that were discussed in Chapter 6. For example, an effective way to develop co-contraction ability in the legs is by using consecutive hurdle hops under time pressure. As an athlete is forced to make quick ground contacts between hurdles, they are training their ability to pre-tense their muscles (through co-contractions) before producing force into the ground.

So, we can see, the skillful body is not just waiting around passively to receive commands from the all-powerful brain to act. It is controlling the level of readiness through adjustments in muscle tension. But this involves much more than just removing slack and having a good muscle tone. In an elite mover, the body uses tension in a much more complex and intelligent manner. It doesn't just tense one or two muscles – it creates an architectural structure through tension! It harnesses the power of biotensegrity

Biotensegrity

To illustrate the concept of tensegrity I want to start talking about architecture and structures. Think about Stonehenge for a second. How are its structure and shape maintained? It is through an external force, consistently acting on its components – gravity. What would happen if we took a very large backhoe, scooped Stonehenge out of the ground, and launched it into space? Its structure would be lost as all the components (the large rocks) would move in different directions because there is no longer gravity present. Most human-made structures are like this – they are stabilized through the external force or compression of gravity.

Figure 7.4 - Structures Stabilized Through Gravity (Stonehenge) vs Tensegrity (Pop Tent)

Next, as I did back in Chapter 1, I want to talk about tents. Think about the modern one that most people use when camping now – the pop-up tent shown in Figure 7.4. What we have here is an example of *tensegrity*. The structure of the tent is created by a balance of internal forces – the tension created by the poles sown into the material – not some external force. Once we pull the tent out of the bag, we can pick it up and move it to another location, or we could launch it into space, and it wouldn't lose its shape. As the name implies, tensegrity means integrity through tension. The structure of the tent is maintained by the internal balance of tension between the poles. Not through external compression.

Tensegrity is an architecture principle first put forth by Fuller in the 1960s[4]. Its technical definition is: "A tensegrity state is a stable self-equilibrated state of a system containing a discontinuous set of compressed components inside a continuum of tensioned components". Many examples of it can now be found in buildings. For example, as shown in Figure 7.5, the Needle Tower in Washington DC and Montreal's Biosphere.

Figure 7.5 – Examples of "Tensegrity Buildings"

Why would we want our bodies to have this? Because it has some important properties. First, because a tensegrity system is pre-stressed, that is it starts in a state of intrinsic tension, it allows for fast responses to stresses applied anywhere in the system. If you push on the side of the tent such that one of the poles move, the tension between them will cause others to move in kind leading to the structure being maintained. The system does not need to establish its structure first and then respond to the perturbation. It only needs to maintain its structure. In other words, a tensegrity system has no muscle slack. As we just saw, this idea of pre-stressing or pre-tension is very important for the control of movement. Second, tensegrity systems have energetic efficiency. Such systems maintain their structure in a highly efficient manner because the components work together, and the system is essentially storing energy itself. Third, tensegrity systems become stronger when subjected to higher forces. Finally, tensegrity systems can maintain their structure and functional properties independent of gravity. This gives them what is called omnidirectional stability –

stability in all directions not just when the system is oriented in the direction of gravity.

Why am I talking about architecture and tents in a book focused on skill acquisition? Because it has been proposed that the human body is a tensegrity system – thus, the name, BIO tensegrity. The basic idea is that the bones, muscles, tendons, etc in the human body work like the poles in a pop tent to maintain structure and posture through internal tension without the need for any external forces. Rather than maintaining stability due to compressional forces from gravity, we achieve stability through internal tension. Each body posture we put ourselves in corresponds to a different state of pre-stress or intrinsic tension across the parts of our body. This gives us all the advantages of the architectural tensegrity systems we just saw.

The concept of biotensegrity connects nicely with some of the core concepts in the ecological approach to skill acquisition. As first noted by Turvey and Fonseca[5], tensegrity is a good biological model for Bernstein's level of synergies" – the second level in the model of movement construction shown in Figure 7.3. At the highest level of skill, Bernstein proposed that skillful movement involves the use of motor synergies. That is, instead of having our muscles and joints work independently, they work together, in synergy to compensate for each other. We saw this back in Chapter 1 in Matsuo et al's study of baseball pitchers. When the shoulder rotation is too slow to get the hand to the release point, this is compensated for by speeding up the extension of the elbow a little.

Well, if you think about it, this is exactly what occurs in a biotensegrity system. Once my tent is set up, pushing on one of the poles will lead to a compensatory bending of the others. Contrast that again with what would happen in Stonehenge. If we pushed one of the stones with an external force, the other stones would not move at all. Stated another way, the pre-stress or tonus sets a biotensegrity system up nicely for implementing motor synergies. When tension is established, the system is highly sensitive to any external perturbation and can adjust globally (with the components working together) in response to it. It does this quickly because it also removes the problem of muscle slack discussed earlier in this chapter.

A final critical aspect of a biotensegrity system is that it works through a process of self-organization. Again, think about our pop-up tent. When we push on it, there is no executive command or motor plan about how to react. The poles organize themselves to maintain the structure. Like other self-organizing systems, this leads to complex, often unpredictable outcomes. For example, tensegrity systems often exhibit *non-linear stiffening*, in which the application of higher forces leads to the system becoming stronger and more stable than if there was no force present.

Implications for Coaching

What does this all mean for coaching? To develop optimal movement, we need to train our athletes to remove muscle slack and establish a biotensegrity structure within their bodies. This allows for faster, more powerful, more stable (in the face of perturbation), movement with less injury risk. Think about your bones as the metal rods in the Needle Tower shown in Figure 7.5. These provide structure and stability but cannot produce movement on their own. Movement is produced via the cables that connect them – which in the human body are called *fascia*. In doing sports training we are essentially training the fascia to organize itself.

In thinking about this there are three basic principles that I like to follow in training:

1)Moving in multiple planes.

In most strength and conditioning training, we focus on the rods in our structures – or more specifically, the muscles that hang off them. We do very little to strengthen the cables. For example, we move very carefully in one plane with very heavy loads when doing squats or bench presses. We are not creating an opportunity to train the fascial connective system to self-organize. This is discussed nicely by Bill Parisi in his book on fascial training[4]:

"It's about co-contracting muscles along the fascial lines outside of the center of mass. You're trying to create a different stress on the body that it is not accustomed to, but it will see in sport."

So, we need to have omnidirectional movements with submaximal loads not just one's in a single plane like a squat or a bench press where the load is always centered and stabilized. One of my favorite ways to do this is by using aqua bags and aqua balls. This not only creates different stresses at different angles but also creates the instability and variability we discussed in Chapter 6 when looking at action capacity.

2)Think in both agonist (creating) and antagonist (inhibiting) terms.

In a tensegrity system, there is a healthy yin and yang. The co-contraction in the system creates a state where one part of the body is pulling, and another is resisting being pulled. One is extended while the other is trying to resist this extension. As we have discussed, this serves to create a state of optimal readiness for action. But sometimes these opposing forces can become unbalanced. The most common example I see is between accelerations and decelerations in movement. We spend so much time worrying about the acceleration part (e.g., in a baseball swing we focus on generating bat speed) often without caring too much about the critical opposing deceleration (e.g., the follow-through in the swing). Having a balance between the two is critical for both performance and reducing the chance of injury. A couple of recent examples of the dangers of having an imbalance in a baseball swing can be seen here: the injuries to Miguel Cabrera and Fernando Tatis during their swing follow-through[7,8]. We must train both the force generators (the gas pedal) and the force inhibitors (the brakes) in the system!

To train this in a baseball swing we like to use activities like the one shown in Figure 7.6. For this, a pool noodle is placed near the end of the swing. Instead of trying to avoid this object, the batter is instructed to deliberately contact it.

Figure 7.6 – Pool Noodle Deceleration Activity. Photo Credit: Randy Sullivan, Florida Baseball ARMory.

3) Provide a stimulus for co-contractions.

There are a few different ways we can encourage an athlete to use these co-contractions that are essential for removing slack and establishing a biotensegrity structure. One, as I already mentioned, is time pressure. If we create activities where an athlete must quickly move between positions, it will encourage them to establish pre-tension. Another is by using the ground. For example, Figure 7.7 shows a training activity we like to use for training baseball pitchers called Glove-Side Drop-Ins. The athlete stands on an 8" box in the starting pitching position holding a baseball in his hand and glove. He steps off the box toward his back side and rotates to throw the ball into a net. Stepping off the box offers a large force that elicits a co-contraction in the back hip.

Figure 7.7– Co-contraction Activity for Pitching. Photo Credit: Randy Sullivan, Florida Baseball ARMory.

8

———

MOVING WITH EFFICIENCY & ECONOMY

M ovement comes at a cost. We must pay a bill in the form of energy expenditure. In the skill acquisition domain, we spend a lot of time considering how our movement solutions emerge to satisfy the demands of our performance goals. We talk about how these solutions are shaped by individual, task, and environmental constraints. However, something we don't consider nearly as often is the role of effort and economy in influencing how a performer solves a movement problem. I think this is an important omission for several reasons.

First, if we are looking at highly skilled performers, we typically see that not only can they consistently achieve their goals and successfully adapt their movement solution to changing conditions, but they also tend to use more economical movements. I will get into specific definitions in a little but simply put, their movement solutions require less effort. Is movement economy just a by-product of developing skills? Or is economy one of the primary criteria our perceptual-motor system is trying to achieve when learning a new skill?

Second, I think considering movement economy changes the way we look at practice design. For example, it can be related to a concept in motor learning called *overlearning*. Overlearning occurs when there is a plateau in measures of performance outcomes in training but there is still skill development occurring. So, with more and more practice the athlete is not getting any faster or more accurate. They are not hitting the ball any harder or further. But they are still making gains. A good example of this would be a situation in which the performer is continuing to use the same movement solution but with more and more practice they can do it with less energy (smaller muscle contractions, less oxygen consumption) – so it is becoming more economical. It will also make the solution more effective when they become fatigued (e.g., in the four quarter or set).

Finally, the role of movement economy emphasizes the importance of the link between skill training and strength and conditioning we looked at back in Chapter 6. Developing a system that is more efficient at using energy is going to expand the movement solutions available to a performer.

The role of movement economy, how it is developed, and the influence it has on the movement solutions we choose, is not something that is often considered in motor learning research, unfortunately. Think about the two most common laboratory tasks used in motor learning studies: reaching and key pressing. Even when we use sport-specific tasks, we study things like golf putting, darts, or throwing a ball a short distance at a target. So, essentially, even though energy expenditure seems to be an important factor in skill, we effectively remove it in most of the tasks we study. Despite this, when we read definitions of what "skill" is, we will often see reference to things like moving efficiently and smoothly.

Definitions & Measurement

So, what exactly do we mean when we use the terms movement efficiency and economy? *Movement efficiency* has been defined as the amount of work done divided by the energy used to achieve it.

Work is typically measured in terms of variables from physics like distance traveled while energy refers to calorie expenditure. So, if I burn 120 calories when running a ½ a mile and you burn 120 calories in ¾ of a mile you have greater movement efficiency.

While this is straightforward, it is somewhat limited in understanding most of the skills we are looking at in sports. In particular, those that involve the coordination of multiple limbs and degrees of freedom. In sports like baseball or cricket batting, the distance traveled by the batter in the act of hitting is essentially zero! Or think about baseball pitching. In throwing a baseball, a pitcher "travels" about 5-6 feet from their initial position on the rubber to their landing position at ball release. But this simple measure does not capture all the movements going on with all the other body parts (each of which expends some energy) in traveling that distance.

A way that efficiency can be used more effectively is by relating one aspect of the movement (i.e., an underlying process) to some aspect of performance. For example, we could compare the EMG activity in a pitcher's biceps muscle required to throw a pitch at 85mph in the 1st inning versus the 9th inning. Or we could measure the amount of elbow torque required to throw a football 50 yards for two different quarterbacks. Producing the same outcome with less muscle activity or torque force would be more efficient. We are not capturing the efficiency of the whole pattern of movement here but rather a small aspect of it. I will revisit these ideas when we consider applying this to the practice field at the end of the chapter.

Movement economy simplifies this all a bit by taking out the requirement to measure the amount of work that has been done. It is defined as the energy expenditure required to complete a task with fixed work or power demands. So, how many calories are burned by making a penalty kick in soccer, shooting a free throw in basketball, etc? In these situations, we can essentially determine the economy just by measuring energy expenditure. For example, if you burn fewer calories the next time you shoot 10 free throws you have increased your economy of movement.

Note, to keep things simple, from here on out in this chapter I am just going to use the term "efficiency" to represent both these concepts. What I mean is the general idea of the amount of energy expenditure required to move.

Fundamental Constraint or By-Product?

In traditional views of motor learning, movement efficiency has mostly been thought of as a by-product or side effect of coordination. It arises because of satisfying other more important factors when learning a skill. Specifically, efficiency has long been thought to be one of the benefits of developing low variability in movement through repetition in practice. Moving the same way every time, without a lot of variation, has been presumed to be a way to use less energy to achieve our goals.

An alternative view was proposed in 1998 by Sparrow and Newell[1]. They argue that energy expenditure is more primary in the development of skills. It is a fundamental constraint that shapes the emergence of coordination and determines why one movement solution is used over another. Think about learning to serve a tennis ball, for example. They are proposing that the coordination pattern we develop does not only depend on satisfying the task constraints. It also depends on efficiency-related ones as well. So, if we have two different ways to serve (e.g., one with an extended arm and one with a bent arm) we are not only going to self-organize into the one that results in the greatest ball velocity, but we are also going to "choose" a solution that requires less energy to produce.

This is a critical point that we are going to revisit in Chapter 15 when looking at pain and injury. While subjectively all an athlete cares about is performance outcomes and achieving their goals when exploring different ways to coordinate the movement of their body, it has another major concern in mind. Our survival! It's going to resist going into the areas of movement solution space that cause pain, and potential injury, and waste a lot of its valuable energy reserves.

If we accept that movement efficiency is a fundamental constraint that shapes the emergence of our movement solution, then it's role in skill development can be conceptualized using the model illustrated in Figure 8.1. Here we have our familiar three types of constraints (task, environment, and individual) but now with energy inputs and outputs. Energy inputs to the individual (in the form of food and oxygen) are used to create two types of energy outputs: one's to meet the demands of the task (e.g., getting a basketball to travel 15 feet on a free throw) and one's to meet the demands of the environment the athlete is playing in. One example of the latter is thermoregulation – using energy to maintain body temperature within safe limits when it is very cold or hot. So, critically, we are meeting both performance and energy demands. To quote the authors: "An organism's movements are characterized as emerging from the interaction of environment and task constraints with constraints of the individual. It is proposed, furthermore, that the process of adaptation is guided by minimum metabolic energy criteria so that task and environment constraints are accommodated with minimum metabolic cost."

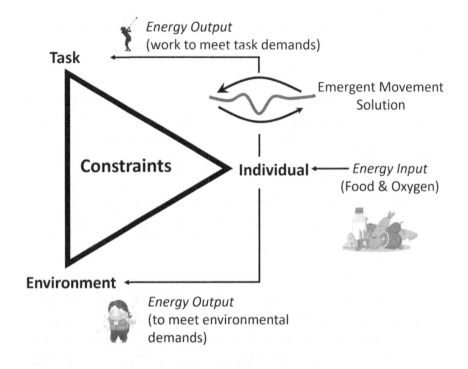

Figure 8.1 – A Constraints-Based Model of Movement Efficiency

Do We Use Efficient Movement Solutions?

Is there any evidence to support this idea that movement efficiency is a constraint on skill acquisition? With all else being equal, do we seem to use movement solutions that require less energy expenditure? Yes! In several studies, it has been shown that when asked to perform a task, individuals will adopt a movement pattern that minimizes energy expenditure – an effect called *self-optimization*. For example, Figure 8.2 depicts the results from a study by Salvendy[2] in which the energy costs (in terms of oxygen consumption) of different movement patterns (rates of pedaling or walking) were measured. The arrows show the rate at which the participants cycled or walked when they were free to choose. Critically, the chosen solutions occur at minimum points on the oxygen consumption curves even though participants were given no external feedback about energy expenditure.

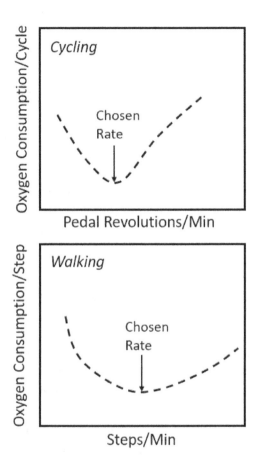

Figure 8.2 – Self Selected Rates of Pedaling or Walking Serve to Maximize Efficiency

Interestingly, movement efficiency also seems to be strongly related to gait transitions. In both humans (walk to run) and horses (walk, trot, gallop), the transitions between these different patterns of coordination closely follow oxygen consumption curves. For example, a horse will switch from a walk to a trot when the speed is such that oxygen consumption required for a trot begins to become less than required for a walk[3]. The net result is the energy cost of coordinating limb movements staying constant per unit distance traveled. This provides evidence that coordination is being organized directly based on movement efficiency rather than being a side effect produced by stability considerations.

Another well-studied effect that supports the idea that movement efficiency is a constraint on skill is the phenomenon of entrainment[4]. Entrainment occurs when there is a synchronization between the timing of a physiological process and the events within a movement pattern. The most common example is the relationship between breathing and leg movements while walking or running. There is typically a fixed ratio between the number of steps and the number of breaths. Humans typically adopt a ratio between 1:1 and 1:4. This effect can also be seen in cycling and rowing. The ability to flexibly adapt this ratio may again be a mechanism for achieving movement efficiency.

In terms of skill development, if we are doing things right, we should expect to see the pattern illustrated in Figure 8.3. That is, we are coordinating our movements to both improve performance outcomes and reduce energy expenditure. In other words, we are becoming both more skilled at a task and more efficient. Several research studies support this idea.

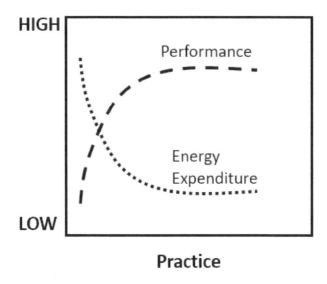

Figure 8.3 – Hypothesized Change in Performance & Energy Expenditure with Practice

In 1976, Asami and colleagues[5] examined the relationship between skill level, energy expenditure, and accuracy in a soccer ball-kicking task. Energy expenditure for kicks of different velocities was calculated based on the movement kinematics. Movement efficiency was calculated by dividing this value by the kinetic energy delivered to the ball. One highly-skilled player was compared to a lesser-skilled one. What was found? The energy expenditure required to kick the ball at a given velocity was significantly lower for the more skilled player. For example, at a velocity of 20 m/s, it was half. There was also a large difference in the maximal velocity that could be achieved – about 25 m/s for the skilled player and 20 for the lesser skilled. Interestingly, when shot accuracy was assessed it was found that maximal accuracy occurred for both players when the ball was kicked at a velocity for which movement efficiency was maximized – this was at about 80% of the maximal velocity for both players.

In 1981, Brancazio[6] examined movement efficiency in basketball shooting. He first estimated the optimum ball release angle. That is the one that required the smallest amount of force to get the ball to the basket while still having a relatively high margin for error in the shot. It was found that the actual shots performed by skilled players were close to this predicted trajectory.

Finally, in 1994, Durand and colleagues[7] examined changes in energy expenditure (using oxygen consumption), performance, and movement efficiency as a function of practice on a ski simulator task. It was found that, for complete novices at the task, with more hours of practice the energy expenditure increased over time. This makes total sense if we relate it to the concepts of freezing and freeing degrees of freedom proposed by Bernstein[8].

In their classic ski simulator study, Vereijken and colleagues[9] found that performers initially simplified the problem of movement control by *freezing* degrees of freedom –the knee and ankle joints were kept rigid so that the performer did not need to figure out what to do with them. Thus, because they are using less movement, it would be expected that they would use less energy. So, along with helping solve the degrees of freedom problem, freezing might be a solution that also serves to satisfy the requirement of minimizing energy expenditure for a new learner.

But as they begin to *free* degrees of freedom (add ankle and knee motion to allow for more skillful movement) more energy would be required. However, if you look at the amount of work achieved by the "freed" movements (in terms of the estimated speed the skier would travel at), movement efficiency (work done divided by energy used) increases with practice.

These studies all seem to provide support for a relationship between motor learning, movement efficiency, and related changes in the coordination and control of movement. To quote Sparrow and Newell: "The major principle that emerges from this literature is that, with practice, organisms learn to adapt movements to achieve the task goal with the least metabolic energy expenditure and, therefore, greater economy".

Information for Regulation of Movement Efficiency

The final component of this process I want to look at is what information might be available to a performer to allow for regulation of movement efficiency. Information coming to our central nervous system is typically classified into three types. *Proprioceptors* monitor the state of the muscles, tendons, and joints; *exteroceptors,* give information about the external environment, such as that obtained from vision; and *interoceptors* signal the condition of the internal state of the organism with respect to temperature, blood pressure, digestive functions, our cardiovascular system, etc. The first two of these have been well studied in motor control and motor learning, but interoception has been typically assumed to have little relevance to control of action. In their paper, Sparrow and Newell propose that this is an oversight and that "sensory information from internal organs, *interoceptive* information, should be considered a major component of the sensory input by which movements are coordinated and controlled".

There is some initial evidence to support this idea. For example, studies using augmented biofeedback show that we can learn to couple exteroceptive and interoceptive information. For example, while exercising on a treadmill or bicycle ergometer, healthy subjects given cardiovascular augmented feedback can better coordinate pedaling to reduce heart rate and systolic blood pressure as compared to no-feedback controls.

Movement Efficiency & Practice Design

How does practice design influence movement efficiency? There have been a couple of studies that have looked at this. In 2005, Zachry and colleagues[10] examined how focus of attention instructions influence movement efficiency. To achieve this end, a basketball free throw task was used during which energy expenditure could be assessed by measuring EMG activity from different parts of the shooter's body. Fourteen university students performed 10 shots under two different focus of attention instruction conditions. For the internal focus condition, participants were instructed to concentrate on the "snapping" motion of their wrists during the follow-through of the free throw. For the external focus condition, they were instructed to concentrate on "the center of the rear of the basketball hoop". Shot accuracy was scored on a 0-5 scale with a 0 for an airball, 5 for a swish, and points in between for hitting the rim, etc. EMG was recorded from the wrist (the body part they were told to focus on in the internal condition) and other body parts including the biceps, triceps, and shoulder.

What was found? First, consistent with the ideas discussed in Chapter 4, shooting accuracy was significantly higher in the external focus condition, by about ½ a point on average. For EMG, it was found that activity was significantly lower in the external focus condition for the biceps and triceps. So clearly this study shows higher movement efficiency with an external focus of attention – players are achieving a higher level of performance with less effort. Given the pattern of EMG activity, it suggests that this is a rather diffuse effect and not specific to the body part being focused on.

The other study was one published by Stoate and colleagues in 2012[11]. In this study, the authors wanted to examine the effect of enhanced expectancies on movement economy. To achieve this end, 20 participants from local running clubs were split into two groups of 10. After an initial assessment session, runners in both groups were asked to run for 10 minutes at 75% of their VO_2 max. Participants assigned to the enhanced expectancy group were given a feedback statement regarding their efficiency while running ("You're doing great. Your oxygen consumption is in the top 10th percentile for your age and gender"), and a similar statement was provided every two minutes. No feedback was given to the control group.

What was found? While there were no differences in heart rate or ratings of perceived exertion, oxygen consumption significantly decreased for the expectancy group, while remaining constant for the control group. The authors propose that this was due to the enhanced expectancy for performance success in the former group. However, I think it's equally plausible that the feedback statement served as augmented feedback about movement efficiency which served to alter the coordination solution that emerged.

How Can We Make Our Athletes Move More Efficiently?

If we accept the premise that movement efficiency is a fundamental constraint on the self-organization of movement then there are a couple of important implications for coaching.

1. We need to create practice environments where movements require efficiency.

Like the limitations of motor learning research discussed earlier in this chapter, we typically do not place a lot of demands on the efficiency of movements in training. There is no real cost to expending a lot of energy in the commonly-used isolated practice drill. This can easily be remedied in a couple of ways.

First, we can pre-fatigue an athlete by making them run laps, lift weights or do some other S&C exercise before they work on their skill. Alternatively, we can reduce the rest intervals between skill activities. All being done while keeping the athlete's safety in mind, of course! While we tend to think of fatigue as a negative in training if used correctly if can provide a powerful stimulus for growth and a driving force to make more efficient movements.

Second, we can take advantage of environmental constraints that influence energy expenditure. Instead of avoiding practice on hot and cold days, we could view these as opportunities to place higher demands on movement efficiency as the athlete's body will have to cope with both movement control and thermoregulation.

2. Local measures of movement efficiency can be an effective way to vary effort in practice

One of the task constraints that I see many coaches use is changes in effort. For example, when training baseball pitchers we often ask them to try to throw at 50% or 75% of their maximum. But how do we know that they are actually doing this? Subjective judgments of perceived effort and exertion have their value but can also be very inaccurate and biased. For example, in a recent pitching study, it was found that when asked to reduce their effort by 25%, on average pitchers only reduce their velocity by 11%. The title of the study says it all: "Baseball pitchers perceived effort does match actual measure effort.." [12]

An effective alternative for manipulating effort could be to evaluate it in terms of movement efficiency. For example, using wearable technology that measures things like EMG or torque we could create an efficiency metric (e.g., pitch velocity/amount of torque). This can be used to track and give feedback to an athlete about their level of effort and exertion more accurately. An example of this in baseball pitching using a wearable called the Motus Sleeve can be seen here[13].

Ok, it's now time to move beyond the basics of information-movement control to consider an equally important factor in skilled performance: how do we decide what action we intend to achieve in the first place? How do we educate our *intention*?

9

SKILLED INTENTIONALITY: KEEPING OUR OPTIONS OPEN & DECIDING SLOW

A cting is not always about achieving your goal. We saw already that sometimes we act to get more information - we act to perceive. For example, a soccer midfielder scans the area around them before they receive a pass. In this chapter, I want to look at another example of this – what I am going to call, acting to decide. I know, I know, it sounds backward – we decide to act not the other way around! But, as we will see, it is one of the most important aspects of optimal movement.

Imagine you are an ice hockey player carrying the puck up the ice and you have 2-on-1, so in other words, you have a teammate beside you and are approaching one defender. The primary opportunity that this situation (illustrated in Figure 9.1) affords (the invitation from Chapter 6) is scoring a goal. But within that there are multiple nested and related invitations – driving by the defender, passing to your teammate, trying to deceive the defender, shooting the puck yourself, etc. A *nested* affordance or invitation is one you need to take before you can accept another one – an engagement before marriage if you will. From the visual information provided by the gaps between yourself, the defender, and the goal you perceive that the affordance of shooting is the most inviting, so you wind up for a slapshot. This creates new information for the defensive player, sending them the invitation to block your shot. As they move towards you, you alter your stick movement on the fly to make a pass to your teammate who shoots and scores.

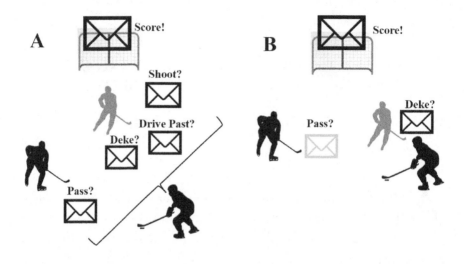

Figure 9.1 – Invitations for Action in a 2:1 Play

In a situation like this, a skilled hockey player does not just move to accept an invitation for an action (e.g., shoot or pass). They move to influence the invitations they receive! They don't just decide what action to take as quickly as possible. They <u>wait to decide</u> for as long as possible until the optimal one emerges. They demonstrate a key element of optimizing movement: *Skilled Intentionality.*

In executing a 2-on-1 like this, a skillful performer will engage with multiple invitations for action at the same. That is, they will regulate the distance between themselves and the other players to keep multiple affordances available and will alter their intention as to which invitation for action to accept based on the unfolding, online information. A lesser skilled athlete might commit to one affordance (like shooting) very early and/or get too close to their teammate, reducing the opportunity to pass without the puck being intercepted. Being skillful does not just involve picking up invitations from the

environment and acting to achieve them. That is skilled perceptual-
motor control. It also involves skilled intentionality. Moving to alter
the landscape of affordances.

How Do We Decide Which Invitation to Accept?

Before we dive more into the topic of skilled intentionality, let's go
back to invitations. As we saw in Chapter 6, an athlete with a lot of
action capacity (which we may have helped them to develop through
appropriate S&C exercises) receives a lot of invitations from their
environment to act. Shoot, pass, drive, spin, deke, etc. They perceive
a lot of affordances. But how do they decide which invitation to
accept? During the competition, they are not going to receive those
pink envelopes we sent them in practice by amplifying certain
affordances using constraints. So how do they decide what to do?

In the traditional view of skill, this is achieved through mental
representation and information processing. An athlete picks up
information from the environment (for example, the spacing of
opponents) compares it with previous experience in their mental
model, maybe makes some predictions about what will happen next,
and then makes an explicit decision (I am going to pass or shoot)
that leads to the execution of an action.

A good example of this approach is Gary Klein's Recognition
Primed Decision-Making Model (RPD)[1] illustrated in Figure 9.2.
The RPD describes how people use their experience in the form of
a repertoire of patterns. They can make decisions in two different
ways. First, they can quickly match the situation to a pattern they
have experienced before and stored it in their memory. If they find
a clear match, they can carry out the most typical course of action.
So instead of making decisions by comparing all the options, we

make decisions by matching the situation to a pattern stored in memory. In that way, people can successfully make extremely rapid decisions. So, in our 2-on-1 example, the puck carrier might detect that the defensive player is too close to the goal and recognize that this was a situation in the past where shooting lead to goals – then shoot. If the current experience matches a pattern stored in memory, they act.

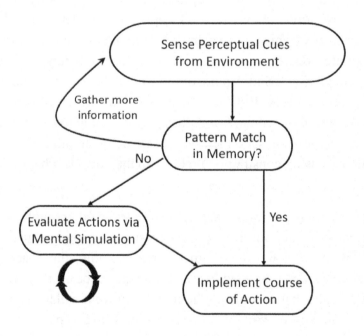

Figure 9.3 – Key ideas of the Recognition-Primed Decision-Making Model

If there is no immediate match with some previous experience, the athlete engages in the second type of decision-making process in the RPD: mental simulation. That is, in making decisions a potential course of action is evaluated by trying to imagine how it would play out within the context of the current situation. They run a simulation in their head. If the simulation indicates the option would work, then that action is initiated.

If we look at this model it captures a lot of the key beliefs people have about decision-making. First, what we want are quick decisions. If we can match the current situation to some pattern in our memory, we can act fast and decisively. As I mentioned in Chapter 5, this can also be seen in our obsession with studying reaction time in psychology research. Fast reaction times, and deciding quickly, have long been thought to be one of the hallmarks of skill and expertise. We are shocked when we bring elite athletes into a research laboratory and find that they have average or even below-average reaction times. For example, baseball great Babe Ruth[2].

Second, and relatedly, one of the main benefits of accumulating practice hours and competition experience is that it allows us to make quicker decisions. In the RPD, it gives us more patterns for matching. I have seen this defensive alignment one hundred times, I am going to do this. We are back to the Matrix – the skill comes from acquiring knowledge that allows us to interpret the confusing and ambiguous world around us. And again, the implication is that faster is better. Acquiring more patterns through experience helps us make fast decisions. We only take our time in deciding, going through this process of mental simulation, because we don't have enough patterns stored in memory.

Finally, there is no role for motor action in the decision-making process. They are completely separable, serial processes. Acting occurs after we have decided what to do. In Figure 9.3, it is regulated to one box at the very bottom of the model after all the important, complex processing occurs in our head. Again, we are back to the unintelligent body that is waiting to do the all-knowing brain's bidding.

Before I consider the alternative, ecological view I want to tell you about when my world view of decision-making changed. This involved some work I was doing on driving, not sports, but bear with me. About 15 years ago I was interested in the action of executing an across-path turn in driving. So, that is a left turn in the USA and a right turn in the UK. I am just going to use "left turns" from now on. I had a particular interest in left turn behavior because we know it is a situation where a lot of serious accidents occur and they seem to frequently be due to the driver making the wrong decision – that is, deciding to turn in front of an oncoming vehicle when the TTC was too short. So, it was an issue that seemed to fit perfectly with my research program at the time – a real-world problem related to the perception of tau!

When I started working on this, I figured it would be a fairly straightforward process to understand. Following the traditional assumptions about decision-making, I just outlined, in my mind the behavior of making left turns involved the driver reaching a critical point on the road, picking up information about the TTC of the approaching vehicle (based on the optical variable tau), combining this with prior knowledge and internal models (for example, the speed vehicles typically travel in this area), deciding whether the time gap was acceptable or not, then actually turning the steering wheel to make the turn.

A key assumption that I had adopted from traditional decision-making models but that I never really explicitly stated was that the decision to turn or not was a discrete one. That is, the person drove up to the intersection, and when they reached a certain distance from it, they made the decision, then they carried on with the turn or not. What happened before and after this critical point in time was not relevant because that was just the control of action. Because the decision occurred at a discrete point in time all I had to do was understand the perceptual information and knowledge of the driver at that point and I would be able to understand what causes us to make errors in this situation. So, I conducted a study in the driving simulator in my lab where I presented drivers with a large variety of left turn scenarios (different distances and speeds of the approaching vehicle, different sizes and types of vehicles, and different contexts like making a turn in a city where the speed limit was 40 mph vs. making it in a rural setting where it was 65 mph). I also manipulated, what I would now call the individual constraints and intrinsic dynamics of the situation, by recruiting drivers of different ages and experience levels and changing the dynamics of their simulated vehicle (in particular, how quickly it accelerated).

After collecting all that data, I started the analysis by identifying the critical decision point – or at least trying to. For this, I looked at the deceleration profile of the participants' vehicles as they approached the intersection and tried to identify the point at which it reached a particular value. But I couldn't! What I found was that how the driver's approached the intersection (both their speed and position in the lane) depended on other factors (or constraints) -- in particular, the behavior of the oncoming vehicle. How could that be the case? They hadn't decided about the left turn yet! How could their actions be related to these factors?

So, I set that issue aside, and tried to look at another question I thought would be straight forward: what is the critical time to collision gap at which drivers decide to turn? For example, was it at 3 seconds or 5 seconds? Surely, for the same set of drivers and road conditions, this must be consistent? There must be some time gap at which drivers would make the turn most of the time if the gap was larger and not very often if the gap was smaller. Like a perceptual threshold. For this, I assumed that the decision was being made at some critical distance from the intersection. Notice here, that I am again building on the assumption that decision-making is a discrete process: drivers do or do not accept the gap at some instant in time.

What did I find? This critical gap was one of the most variable things I have ever measured!! When the gap was measured relative to this assumed decision point, the critical gap for a similar set of drivers ranged between 4 and 11 seconds with a standard deviation of around 6. Sometimes drivers made turns with gaps of less than 2 seconds, other times they decided not to turn when gaps were almost 10. The values of the critical gaps were also related to a bunch of other things they were not supposed to be! For example, drivers accepted smaller gaps when the approaching vehicle was going faster. What? The whole point of doing a tau-based analysis is it takes out speed as a factor. Another interesting thing I found it that when the driver came to a complete stop (due to an interaction with another vehicle) their decision was completely different than when they were still moving as they approached the intersection. Even when all the other variables were the same. This is something that has also been found in research on pedestrian street-crossing. So, in sum, the data I had collected on left turn behavior could not fit into the traditional "perceive-decide-act" flow, no matter how hard I tried. Ok, that's enough left turns, let's look at a very different approach to understanding decision-making to the one I have been describing.

Emergent Decision Making

Let's return to our 2-on-1 example illustrated in Figure 9.1. As a skilled hockey player carries the puck down the ice, they are skating to control the space between themselves, the defender, and their teammate. They are not trying to make a quick decision. They are doing the exact opposite. They are waiting to decide for as long as possible. They are trying to let the defender decide for them. If the gap between themselves and the defender is decreasing, I pass. If this gap is increasing, I drive to the net or shoot. If the gap is not changing, I might move towards the defender to force them to make a choice. They are not trying to match what they see in the environment to some pattern stored in memory. They are waiting for the environment to send them a pink envelope as illustrated in Figure 9.1B.

Also, in this scenario, where exactly do the processes of cognition, decision-making, and "implementing course of action" start and end? The puck carrier is implementing a course of action the entire time – they are skillfully regulating the distance between themselves and the other players. They don't just stop in place, perceive the position of the defender, then move, then stop in the place, then perceive the position of the defender, then move - they are perceiving, deciding, and acting the entire time.

What we have here is *emergent* decision-making. The athlete is continuously picking up information and affordances from their environment and using it to control their movement. Their movement and the movement of the other players change the information and affordances they perceive. They are both moving to take invitations and moving to create them! A "decision" just emerges from this ongoing perception-action cycle. It is not a discrete event that happens before the player acts. They are *deciding* the whole time – again *verbs not nouns*. Deciding not decision. Decision-making is a temporally extended process, not one that occurs in one moment. They are not using their prior experience to just match the current situation to some pattern stored in memory. But rather, as we will dive into in detail in Chapter 12, they are using their past experiences to change how they relate their movement to the information they pick up from their environment. To understand this more let's get back to the concept of skilled intentionality.

The Skilled Intentionality Framework

The Skilled Intentionality Framework, first developed by Reitveld and colleagues[3], is illustrated in Figure 9.2. Starting with the left side of the figure we again have our invitations. As we saw in Chapter 6, our environment provides us with a rich landscape of affordances – lots of opportunities for action. But critically, this not only depends on the environment but also on us – the right side of the figure. The perception of affordances depends on our abilities to achieve them, and our action capacities. A hockey player that is a slow skater will not perceive the affordance of driving past a defender with the puck. Affordances do not exist independently of the capabilities (or effectivities) of the perceiver. Or as JJ Gibson so wonderfully put it:

"An affordance is neither an objective property nor a subjective property; or it is both if you like. An affordance cuts across the dichotomy of subjective-objective and helps us to understand its inadequacy. It is equally a fact of the environment and a fact of behavior. It is both physical and psychical, yet neither. An affordance points both ways, to the environment and to the observer"[4].

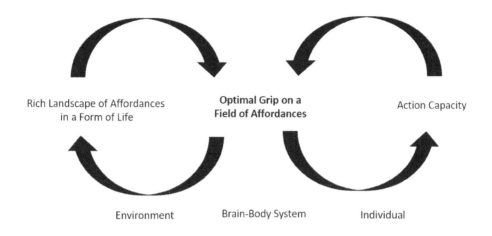

Rich Landscape of Affordances in a Form of Life

Optimal Grip on a Field of Affordances

Action Capacity

Environment

Brain-Body System

Individual

Figure 9.2 – The Skilled Intentionality Framework

Another important point they make is that affordances do not just tell us about opportunities for action, here and now, in the present – they also have a past and a future. In any situation, the opportunities are shaped by our socio-cultural conventions – as a society at large, and within the context of the environment a particular coach creates. For example, a more offensive-minded coach creates an environment where space affords a defensive player to jump in to support an attack on another team's goal, while another, a more defensive-oriented coach may not. To use the term from ecological psychology, affordances exist within a "form of life", where this is defined as a certain kind of practice or coordinated pattern of behavior between multiple individuals. For example, two years ago, if I asked to have a Zoom call instead of meeting in person, many of my colleagues would have looked at me like I am from Mars. Our form of life as a group, the opportunities different situations invite, has changed.

Two final points. First, the landscape of affordances and dynamics is changed by our actions. When I wind up to shoot, I change the affordances available to the defender, which likely will cause them to move closer to me, which changes the affordances I perceive, and so on. Second, the relevance of the different affordances is shaped by our intentions. When a hockey player is skating down the ice on a 2-on-1 there is likely a door on the side of the rink that affords leaving and going home. But that does not fit with their goal or intention at that moment.

Within this framework, skilled intentionally is defined as the selective engagement and skillful responsiveness to multiple nested affordances simultaneously. It involves what the authors call maintaining an "optimal grip" on affordances. Remember affordances are dynamic. They appear and disappear. Gaps open and close. Teammates become open and then are covered. A defender comes towards us and then backs off. As our skilled hockey player moves down the ice they are not just reacting and responding to these changing invitations for action. They are regulating their movement to keep as many of them available for as long as possible, as illustrated in Figure 9.1A. They skillfully clasp multiple envelopes in their grip so that they don't disappear. I think it is during this "optimal grip" that some athletes perceive time as slowing down. Skilled intentionality is "deciding slow", keeping multiple opportunities available. There is no rush to act so it feels like we have more time.

Training to Improve an Athlete's "Optimal Grip"

How can we improve skilled intentionality through practice design? An approach to this was discussed in a paper Passos and colleagues published in 2008[5]. The authors begin by challenging the traditional assumption that decision-making is programmable by developing simple stimulus-response relationships in training (e.g., giving the athlete more patterns to match and if X then Y rules). They emphasize that competitive team games are not stable contexts in which information is certain. Successful players need to adapt their actions to the dynamically changing environment that characterizes the typical team game.

The authors propose a four-stage model for training decision making which includes i) identifying the problem; ii) setting out a strategy to solve it; iii) creating an action model and iv) building an exercise. Let's look at these in more detail using the sport of rugby union.

An example problem that can be identified in rugby that a coach might want to improve in practice is when an offensive group of players cannot advance the ball forward effectively. This problem can be linked to two major task constraints – the timing of decisions and actions and the space left open to be used by attackers. Having identified one or more of these issues as a problem, the second step is to set a strategy. Or, in other words, a coach deciding on the constraints manipulations to be used in practice. For this, the authors recommend using video or notional analysis to identify action possibilities and strengths and weaknesses.

The third step involves creating an action model. In the author's words: "Based on the action possibilities previously identified, the coach should develop an action model which is a collective movement pattern that aims to provide stability to the team's collective actions through task constraints, such as relative positioning and outlining of roles to be performed. An action model needs to define the players' functions according to their position in the micro-unit; i.e., whether they are the ball carrier, first and second receivers, and inside and outside supporters". Finally, to build a training exercise, the authors propose focusing on task constraints including the following:

1) Changing rules without losing game logic.

An example in rugby practice is adding a rule that players can only carry the ball with two hands. This encourages young players to learn to run with two hands on the ball, which also increases passing options.

2) Changing field dimensions to leave more space available to be explored by attackers.

3) Manipulate player starting-positions; this coaching strategy varies the amount of time attackers and defenders have to act.

4) Vary the number of players involved in a practice task which again effects to space available for the attackers.

In sum, this paper proposes that the decision-making skills of players can be best enhanced under practice task constraints that provide an accurate balance between variability and stability. Stability provides structure to the players' performance; while variability allows them to deal with the uncertainty of situational-specific task demands, created by the specific opposition and performance conditions. To achieve this balance, training sessions should be based on practice tasks with constraints that are being constantly manipulated by coaches. Forcing players to satisfy specific task constraints imposed on them directs them to explore the playing environment for unique solutions to the problems created by opponents and the positioning of their teammates. We will explore these ideas more in Chapter 11 when looking at team coordination.

Implications for Coaching

If we accept the idea that decision-making is emergent, there are some important practical implications for coaching. First, it contradicts the view many coaches express that athletes must learn the "basic techniques" or "fundamentals" first before they are faced with decision-making situations in practice. Or stated another way, if an athlete can't dribble around a cone, they won't be able to dribble around an opponent. In the emergent decision-making view, this idea is flawed because it assumes that the control of the action (the so-called technique) is separable and subservient to the process of making decisions.

Second, it takes a very different view of how we become effective decision-makers. In the traditional view, this involves accumulating knowledge and enriching one's mental model so that the correct action can be selected once the situation has been identified. Again, under this assumption, it is possible to train decision-making offline (for example, by looking at schematics of plays on a whiteboard). In the emergent view, improving decision-making comes from better attunement to the information in one's environment and better calibration between one's movement and this information. Thus, decision-making can only be improved by training in context with perception and action coupled.

A third point I want to make concerns the incorrect assumption that a lot of people have about the emergent view of decision-making. That is, if actions are not preplanned based on decision processes derived from memory and internal models then they must just be purely reactive. But, as we saw in Chapter 5, the control of action in the ecological view is not simply reactive. It is prospective such that information is used in an anticipatory manner toward achieving a future state or goal.

Finally, in emergent decision-making, the most effective way to create better decision-makers in sports is by manipulating constraints in practice. Actions that emerge are highly sensitive to the initial conditions faced by an athlete (for example, the relative distances of defenders, obstacles, or goals). By giving an athlete exposure to different constraints in practice they become attuned to the relationship between the information in the environment and successfully achieving their goal.

What are the implications of the Skilled Intentional Framework for coaching? As I mentioned, it is critical to recognize that the landscape of relevant affordances for any athlete will be dependent on the socio-cultural environment of their form of life. A new learner acquires a skill within an existing form of life created by society at large and within the specific practice environment. Affordances are not solely determined by material properties in the environment. There is what is called *socio-material entanglement*. That is, the practice culture we create makes certain affordances relevant and inviting and others not. As a coach, are you inviting a broad range of affordances or creating an environment where you restrict many of them? For example, is having to play defense in practice drills like a soccer Rondo something that you make less important or even use as a form of punishment in your practice?

It is also critical that we consider the idea of having an optimal grip on multiple affordances simultaneously. We often try to separate and isolate these. For example, in team sports, we often think of and train offense and defense separately, whereas they exist together. For example, if one of the players in my 2-on-1 example is a defenseman, one of the affordances they are keeping a grip on while trying to score a goal is getting back to their position to defend if they don't. Developing athletes with this skilled intentionality requires creating rich practice activities where multiple, nested affordances are available. Think of "scoring" activities instead of "shooting" OR "passing" ones. Think nested affordances of "attacking" and "defending" not practicing offense OR defense. Think of opportunities for action (e.g., moving an opponent around on a tennis court) not just a movement (making a forehand).

10
———

LEARNING TO EXPLOIT METASTABILITY & MOTOR ABUNDANCE

There is another side to the skill coin. As we saw in the last chapter, a major part of being skillful is moving to keep multiple invitations for action available. Well, to belabor my analogy, if we train in the right way, we can also have multiple letter openers! That is, we can keep available multiple movement solutions for achieving the same action opportunity. What is called *metastability*.

The concepts of stability, metastability, and mutli-stability were discussed in the context of coordination in an article by Scott Kelso published in 2012[1]. To illustrate them, I want to use the example of catching a baseball with a glove. A common way that, especially new learners, solve the problem of coordination in this situation is by keeping their glove always pointed down to the ground and then moving their arm up or down to catch balls of different heights. Thus, if we plotted the orientation of the glove on a graph like shown in Figure 10.1, going from 0 (pointing upwards), through 180 (pointing downwards) back to 360 (upwards) there would be an attractor at 180. An attractor is a region in the solution space (in this case, the possible orientations of the hand) to which the system is drawn to. For example, if a fielder started with their hands on their hips, the glove would quickly move towards the 180 deg attractor once the ball was hit. Attractors develop via learning and practice, and there are also intrinsic attractors – ones that are due to our individual constraints. The stability of an attractor refers to how quickly the system returns to that point in state space. Which in my example, would be very quickly. For example, if you stumble while running to get the ball and your glove went a bit sideways, it will quickly get pulled back to the 180 deg angle.

Glove Angle (degrees)

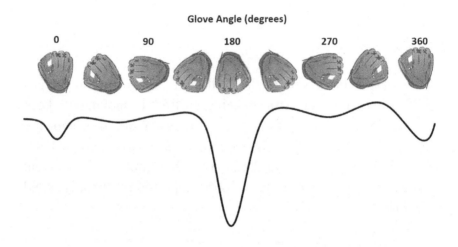

Figure 10.1 – Hand Position in Catching: Mono-stability

The situation I have just described is what is called *mono-stability*. That is having one highly stable attractor. A useful way to conceptualize attractors is as a landscape. So, in this case, if we moved through 0 to 360 deg we would have flat ground until we reached 180 where there would be a huge valley representing the single attractor. Stability is reflected in the depth of the valley – if a valley is deep, the attractor is very stable, and it takes a lot of effort to climb out of it. In most cases, mono-stability will not be an optimal coordination solution because it doesn't allow for flexibility. And this is the case in my ball-catching example. If you always try to catch a ball with your glove pointing down it is going to be very difficult to catch balls hit above your waist. Indeed, you often see this in kids learning to catch. They try to do an ineffective an awkward glove-down catch for balls hit at their chest.

A much more effective coordination solution in this situation would be of course using two different hand orientations depending on the height the ball is hit, with the glove switching to pointing upwards for higher balls. Having two stable attractors (in this case, one at 0 and 180 degrees) is the simplest form of *multi-stability*, called bi-stability. As illustrated in Figure 10.2, in the attractor landscape, we would now have two valleys with the ball height being the *control parameter* which causes a shift from one to the other. A control parameter is a constraint, like ball height or speed, that leads to the emergence of a new coordination (e.g., glove angle) when it changes. So, a system that is multi-stable is one that has two or more co-existing attractors and for which fluctuations in the system (e.g., changes in the control parameter) allow for switching between these stable states. It is good in the sense that it is adapting to the changing environment (different ball heights), but as we will see shortly it is not optimal because it does not allow for much flexibility. Changes in the environment are driving changes in the movement solution without much room for functional variability and creativity from the athlete.

Glove Angle (degrees)

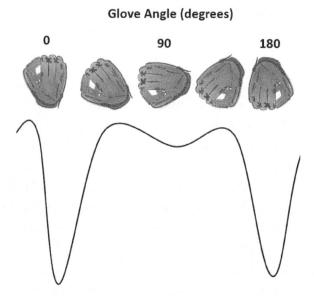

Figure 10.2 – Hand Position in Catching: Multi-stability

Why do we have multi-stability? Let's look at the good aspects of it first. It goes hand in hand with adaptability. The same movement outcome (catching the ball) can be produced by multiple different muscle configurations. Having multiple stable states allows us to harness *movement redundancy*– using different movement solutions for different constraints we are facing. To quote Kelso:

"Multistability confers a tremendous selective advantage to the brain and to nervous systems in general : it means that the brain has multiple patterns at its disposal and can switch among them to meet environmental or internal demands".

Or as Mark Latash would say it's the bliss of motor abundance[2]! The principle of *motor abundance* is that when we learn to solve a motor task, we do not seek to find one solution by eliminating some of the degrees of freedom. Instead, being multi-stable, and having a family of variable solutions to solve movement problems, allows us to be adaptable. That is, we can more easily find a solution when the task is perturbed in some way. For example, external forces are added (e.g., the wind picks up) or there are internal changes (e.g., we get fatigued). Having multiple degrees of freedom in movement control allows us to respond to the ever-changing task, environmental and individual constraints within our environment.

But it's not all sunshine and lollipops! Multi-stability does come at a cost. Due to the stability of the attractors, it can sometimes be difficult to switch from one to the other. Using my catching example again, you sometimes see this with less skilled athletes - they attempt to catch a relatively low ball with their glove pointed up, stubbornly holding on to that pattern of coordination. Another way of stating this issue is that it is difficult to be both stable and flexible at the same time – they are competing tendencies. Multi-stability can also create a very unstable region between the attractors in which fluctuations in the system will cause multiple shifts between states. Think of a new learner shifting their glove up, then down, then up for a ball hit at waist level– seemingly unable to decide what to do.

A final issue associated with both mono and multi stability is the challenge of trying to destabilize the attractors in the system if you want the learner to develop a new pattern of coordination. Say, for example, you wanted to teach a new learner to catch a ball passing to their side by rotating their glove to 90 degrees. If they were bi-stable with attractors at 0 and 180 degrees, this would be difficult because it would be hard for them to hold this new orientation. This is, of course, where methods like the CLA and differential learning (which attempt to de-stabilize existing coordination solutions) come in.

The process by which the attractor landscape changes with learning depends on the individual. If it requires a complete restructuring of the landscape (for example, as in my catching example adding a new, third attractor at 90 degrees) this is called a *bifurcation*. While if it requires just small changes in the location of the attractors in state space, we call this a *shift*. As the description suggests, a bifurcation will be more difficult and take longer than a shift. This is one of the reasons why individual performers self-organize at different rates – some seem to do it relatively easily, with others struggling to find an effective solution.

So, in sum, having multiple stable states of coordination can be advantageous in that it takes advantage of motor abundance but at the same time it is also somewhat limited in its flexibility, and it may be difficult to shift between attractors. As Kelso says in his article: bring on meta-stability!

Meta-Stability

Multi-stability and meta-stability are similar in that they both involve having more than one coordination solution. As illustrated in Figure 10.3, the difference comes in how we move between these solutions. In multi-stability there are very stable attractors (deep valleys) at the solution and a change in the constraints (in particular, the control parameter) is needed to get the system out of one of the attractor states. Meta-stability is having co-existing solutions that are weakly stable, which allows for different solutions to emerge more easily. Think of valleys in the attractor landscape that are not as deep, so they are easier to get in and out of. In Kelso's words: "in a meta-stable region, there is *attractiveness* (certain areas in the state space are more appealing to the system) but not attractors (where the system is pulled in and it can be difficult to get out)".

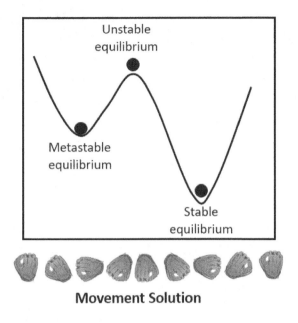

Movement Solution

Figure 10.3 – Instability, Stability & Meta-Stability

Going back to my catching example, meta-stability is being able to keep both the glove-up and glove-down solutions in a state of weak stability so that they can emerge at any time, depending on other task constraints, rather than being dependent on one control parameter to create fluctuations in the system. To understand this a bit more let's look at some studies that have investigated this concept in sports.

In a paper published in 2006, Hristovski and colleagues[3] examined the stability of different movement solutions in boxing – specifically, what parameters determine when a boxer uses a jab vs a hook vs an uppercut punch? So, we are accepting the same invitation to attack an opponent but using different letter openers to open it! Eight participants who had just completed a 12-month basic boxing course were asked to hit a heavy bag. The main task constraint manipulated was the distance of the boxer from the bag. Importantly, this distance was measured in a body-scaled manner. Instead of being expressed in meters or feet, it was measured in terms of the arm length of each boxer. So, a distance of 1.5 units, while different in terms of the actual physical distance, would by the same in body-scaled units for all boxers – one and a half arm lengths away. This is, of course, critical for the perception of affordances – whether a target affords "hit-ability" depends both on the information from the environment (the actual distance) and your action capacity (how far you can reach). The frequency of the three different types of punches was measured at different body-scaled distances.

The results are illustrated in Figure 10.4 At a relatively far distance of about 1-1.2 arm lengths boxers used almost exclusively jabs. So, in terms of what I have been discussing, there was mono stability. At a relatively short distance of 0.3 arm lengths, there was bi-stability in those boxers that used either uppercuts or hooks with roughly equal probability. Finally, for an intermediate distance range of about 0.45 to 0.65 arm lengths boxers used a varied mixture of uppercuts, hooks, and jabs. The authors argued that, in this region, boxers exhibited meta-stability because the choice of punch was not driven by a control parameter such as distance – instead boxers seemed to be able to flexibly switch between movement solutions. These findings suggest that, even after a relatively modest amount of training, regions of meta-stability can develop in which performers can exploit motor abundance in flexibly switching between movement solutions to satisfy task constraints. It also again emphasizes the critical importance of adding variability to practice conditions – it was the variation in the distance during training that led to the emergence of the different movement solutions.

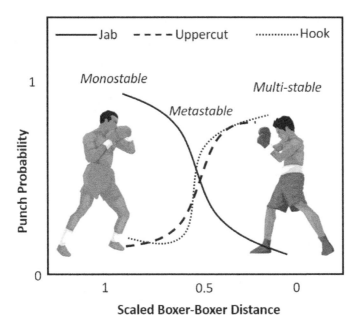

Figure 10.4 – Mono, Multi, and Meta-Stability in Boxing

A similar finding was reported by Pinder and colleagues in a 2012 study looking at cricket batting[4]. Based on the boxing findings, the authors hypothesized that there would be a meta-stable region depending on the distance of the pitch. For those that don't know, in cricket, bowlers can vary the length of the pitch (where the ball bounces) – so some are short, and the batter has to move forward while others are long, and the batter has to move backward. In this study, six skilled junior cricket players were asked to hit pitches thrown at different distances. Distances were again body scaled – in this case by the batter's height.

What was found? Again, there seem to be regions of stability and meta-stability. For short pitches, batters always moved forwards while for long ones they always moved back, but within an intermediate region, there was a flexible mix of shots played. Interestingly, within this meta-stable region, there was also higher variability in terms of swing initiation times and the durations of the back and downswing. This suggests that batters are utilizing functional variability in their swing to adapt to the task constraints.

Implications for Coaching

So, what does all this mean for coaching? Well, it seems that even moderately skilled performers can develop meta-stability for certain regions of the task parameters, like distance. And while performance wasn't assessed in these studies, it's hard to imagine that having such adaptability in being able to switch between different movement solutions flexibly and easily is not advantageous. It is also likely to make a performer co-adaptable in that they will be better able to adjust to their opponent's actions – for example, countering when an opponent tries to close the distance in boxing. I think a key for future research is understanding how these metastability regions develop – how does a performer go from very stable solutions that are hard to switch between and may be used in inappropriate conditions, to this state of flexible meta-stability?

But it seems obvious to me that there would be clear benefits of identifying these regions for each sporting skill and focusing a part of training within the meta-stable range. So, for example, given that we know that experienced boxers have a meta-stable range at a distance of about 0.45-0.65 arm lengths, I think it could be beneficial to focus training sessions for novices at this specific range. Training in an identified meta-stable range is another way that we can push a performer's system into a state of instability which we know helps exploration of new solutions. And if when we put them in this range, they are still showing mono or multi-stability such that they are overly stable in their solution this is where a constraint or differential learning type perturbation could be added to try to support the development of meta-stability.

Ok, so we have increased our action capacity to receive more invitations to act from our environment, we are moving with skilled intentionality so that we keep multiple invitations available, and we are training in metastable regions so that we have multiple, efficient movement solutions we can use to take these opportunities. Now we have one more problem to solve. Our teammates. How do we coordinate our movements so that we are all on the same page? Are we all opening the same invitation at the same time?

11

LEARNING TO COORDINATE WITH TEAMMATES: DEVELOPING SHARED AFFORDANCES

There are two opposing views of how team coordination is achieved: *shared mental models* vs *shared affordances*. The problem we are addressing here is: how do teammates get on the same page? That is, how do they coordinate their actions to produce effective outcomes like running an offensive play in football or playing zone defense in basketball? The shared knowledge or shared mental model approach argues that team coordination is based on shared information players have stored in memory. For example, all the players on a basketball team have stored a set of rules about what to do when the other team turns the ball over.

The alternative view is that team coordination is not based on knowledge stored in memory but rather hinges on teammates picking up the same affordances at the same time. So, for example, when a gap opens between two defenders in rugby (creating an affordance for making a run) both the passer and the receiver pick up this and coordinate their movements to achieve it. As we will see, corresponding to these two theoretical approaches, there have been very different methodologies used to develop team coordination. So, let's dive in a bit deeper.

Let's first look at the approach that has been around the longest: shared knowledge and shared mental models. Knowledge here refers to pieces of often unrelated information. My phone number, my birth date, and my middle name are all pieces of knowledge.

They are also pieces of knowledge that are shared with members of my family as we all can use them to call, by gifts, etc. A mental model is an internal representation of a system. So, it contains several pieces of knowledge, but the important difference is that it also includes information about how they are related and interact. The classical example of a mental model is a cognitive map. It is proposed the each of us has stored in our memory an internal representation of the area we live in, where landmarks and buildings are relative to each other, roughly how far apart they are, etc. So, we have an internal representation of a city. A mental map in our brain. Note, of course, this mental model could have errors in it and some people will have more detailed and elaborate mental models than others. And, of course, these mental models can also be shared. In this approach, it is what allows you to easily tell your neighbor how to get to the new brew pub that just opened – you both share a cognitive map of your area. OK, so let's get back to how this relates to team coordination.

At face value, *shared knowledge* is self-explanatory. It is collective knowledge shared by a team of individuals. The shared information is often stable. For example, most hockey players know what icing the puck is during a hockey game. Shared knowledge can often achieve a greater complexity than just the rules. For example, a basketball team could know before a game that a player on the opposition is poor at dribbling with their left hand, which could affect the team's defensive preparation in dealing with that player and team. Under the umbrella of shared knowledge is the idea of a mental model. When individual mental models are shared amongst team members, a *shared mental model* (SMM) may develop. SMMs provide teammates with the ability to coordinate thoughts and actions without necessarily explicitly communicating in dynamic situations. Over the years, SMMs have become a common way to articulate how teammates coordinate with each other, making them a popular method for studying team cognition. It has been suggested that team members must share mental models that describe when and how they must interact with one another to accomplish the task. In research, SMMs are typically observed at the individual level and then aggregated at the team level. Let's look at a couple of examples of research studies to make this a bit clearer.

As an example, consider the 2012 study by Bourbousson and colleagues on basketball[1]. Five players from the under-18 French national team were filmed during play and then were individually interviewed afterward. The interviews involved the experimenter and the player watching the film of the game together, with the player being asked to comment on the activity going on in the game (what they were doing, feeling, thinking, and perceiving). The main question of interest was to what degree the concerns of each teammate corresponded to each other in each instant. An example of a concern would be player A was concerned with finding the best position on the court to receive the ball. What was found? Using these concerns, the authors categorized sharedness into three forms: (1) moments of nonsharedness, which occurred during 1% of all activities (2) partial sharedness, which accounted for 87% of instances (3) and complete sharedness, which represented 12% of the total amount of shared events.

Another example is a study by Giske and colleagues published in 2015[2]. The goal of this study was to determine to what extent shared mental models exist in expert ice hockey and handball players. In particular, they were concerned with whether or not teams had established collective priorities, such as their general attack pattern. A secondary goal was to determine to what extent players engaged in practice activities to develop this shared knowledge. A total of 231 male senior players from the Norwegian elite leagues in ice hockey and handball took part in the study. Players were asked to make ratings in response to questions like: "In my team, there is an established attack movement, which is based on a common attack pattern.", "I know what the other players do when such common attack patterns are implemented" and "In pre-match meetings, the coach talks about the opponent's strengths and weaknesses" What was found? For most of the questions, high positive ratings were suggesting that athletes perceived that there were SMMs on their team and their pregame preparations were dedicated to the SMM.

So, from these examples, you can see the basic approach to studying team coordination from the shared knowledge perspective. It involves using knowledge elicitation methods (for example, ratings or interviews) for individual players and combining this at the team level to assess the level of sharedness. Another point to emphasize is that teamwork is studied retrospectively and out of context. Remember this is not an issue for the shared acknowledge approach because team coordination lies in the memory stores in the brain and thus can be accessed offline.

For me, there are a couple of clear limitations to this approach. First, it doesn't explain how players achieve coordinated actions online. Do they have a stored play or rule for every possible outcome on the field? Would accessing these be fast enough to see the kind of rapid actions we see in sports? How does this support creative plays? Is it going to be adaptable to the ever-changing conditions we have in sports?

A second issue that I have is that the fact that you can show players have knowledge about things like attack formations (and that some of this might be shared amongst them) does not necessarily mean that this is what is being used to control actions during play. We develop metacognitive-type knowledge about almost everything we do. Just ask any athlete what they think they are doing while the run, swing, kick, etc. This does not mean that this knowledge is being used to control movement in the moment. It could just be an artifact. Let's now turn to the alternative theoretical approach to team coordination which attempts to address some of the issues I just raised.

Shared Affordances

Instead of team cognition being based on shared knowledge in the form of stored mental models, coordination amongst teammates is achieved through shared attunement to perceptual information. The distinction between shared knowledge and shared attunement can be understood by considering an example from soccer. Imagine a midfielder lobs a pass over the defenders at the exact moment a striker teammate breaks for goal. How did both players come to execute such coordinated actions without any explicit communication beforehand? In the shared knowledge account, this type of coordination occurs because both players have a stored memory for the "lob pass play" and both decided to execute this action after processing the available perceptual cues (i.e., the relative positions of the players). This may also involve an intermediate step of identifying the defensive strategy that is being played by the opponent (e.g., a 3-4-3 flat formation in soccer or a zone defense in basketball).

In this account, the perceptual cues are non-informative in and of themselves – instead, they have come to be associated with this particular action or play through extensive practice and/or a coach's instruction (e.g., being told that when the defenders do X you should do Y). Thus, the keys to team coordination in this account are that:

(1) both players have similar mental models (i.e., they learned the same set of plays), and (2) these models are associated with the same perceptual cues for each player. Think The Matrix – but on a team level. Both players are using knowledge to interpret the ambiguous information coming in from the environment in the same way.

The primary distinction with the shared attunement account comes at the level of the players' perception. Instead of detecting non-informative perceptual cues that must be processed and associated with stored knowledge so that a decision about which action to execute can be reached, the ecological approach argues that perception involves the pick-up of information sources that directly specify opportunities for action. For example, in the soccer example described above, the two teammates might detect a higher-order perceptual variable like what we saw in Chapter 2 by using the tau of two gaps. Specifically, the difference between the time of arrival of the defender at the pass landing point (Tau_d) and the time of arrival of the striker at the same location (Tau_s). This difference (let's call it Tau Diff) is optically specified by the ratio of the angular gap between each player and the landing location and the rate of change of this gap. This variable is informative because it directly specifies whether there is an opportunity for a lob pass (Tau Diff is greater than 0) or is not an opportunity (i.e., Tau Diff is <0). Coordination between players occurs in this case because both players are attuned to Tau Diff and thus would simultaneously detect when the environment affords the opportunity for a lob pass.

On the surface, since the perceptual information needed for the action is available to anyone with a functional visual system and does not require one to learn the "lob pass play", it might be assumed that practice is less important for the development of team coordination in the ecological approach. However, it has been

228

shown that practice is often required for actors to become attuned to such higher-order variables as novice performers often rely on simpler (and less effective) information sources (for example, the distance of players from the ball). We will look at a specific example of this in Chapter 14. Furthermore, these information sources must be scaled by the action capacities of both performers, which again occurs through practice. For example, the Tau Diff value that affords lob passing depends on the maximum running speed that can be achieved by the striker and the maximum velocity at which the midfielder can accurately pass the ball. In summary, the keys to team cognition in the ecological account are that: (1) both players are attuned to the same information sources, and (2) both players' perceptions are effectively calibrated for the action capabilities of their teammates.

As an example, let's look at a study I conducted with a group of my colleagues from ASU[4]. A good example of the importance of coordinated decision-making can be seen on a baseball field. As illustrated in Figure 11.1, when a ball is hit on the ground and there are runners on base, each of the four infielders must rapidly decide between two options: (i) attempting to move to intercept or "field" the ball, or (ii) moving towards and ("covering") one of the bases in preparation to receive a throw. For the two middle infielders (the shortstop and second baseman) there is further complexity in that they must also decide which base to cover. For example, a shortstop needs to cover second base if the second baseman fields the ball and third base if the third baseman fields it.

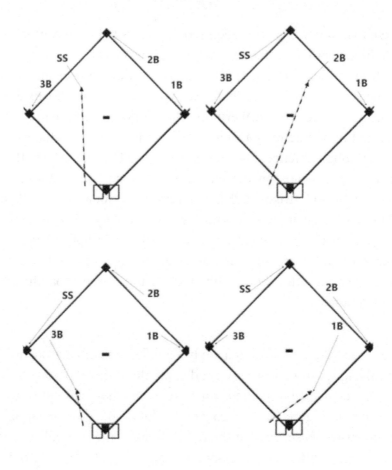

Figure 11.1 – Team Coordination in a Baseball Infield

In this situation, it is possible to assess the "correctness" of an individual player's decision -- if a player is closest to the ball and decides to field it, we could consider it to be a correct decision. However, successfully making an out on the play hinges more on the overall coordination of the teammates' decisions as opposed to their individual correctness. For example, if a player other than the closest one is going to field the ball the overall outcome would be better if the closest player decides to cover a bag.

To investigate this type of behavior we developed a joint temporal occlusion paradigm. This involves having an individual view an unfolding event (for example, an opponent serving a tennis ball) either on video or live, and then occluding (blocking their vision of it) at some point. They are then asked to decide what to do using a response that can be either passive (e.g., saying "down the line or cross court") or active (e.g., stepping in the anticipated direction of ball travel).

To scale this up to use as an assessment tool for teamwork we did the following. To create the occlusion videos, we launched balls on to an empty baseball infield at different horizontal angles. There were 8 different angles used. For example, straight ahead over 2nd base, close to the 3rd base line, etc. The balls were simultaneously filmed using 4 HD Go-Pro cameras which were each placed at the typical starting positions of one of the four infielders. So, we have the first baseman's view, the shortstop's view, etc. We then edited the videos so that only the first 250 msec of the ball flight was shown. When viewing these videos, participants were given two response choices: say "ball" if they would attempt to field the ball or say the name of the base they would cover if they decided they would let another player field it. But we didn't care so much what an individual player decided to do...we were more interested in how it coordinated with the decisions of players viewing from the other locations.

For the experiment, 120 participants were divided into 30 groups of four players. Each group including four experienced, current players: one first baseman, one second baseman, one shortstop, and one third baseman. Each of the four players watched videos from one of the four viewpoints in separate rooms and their combined performance was analyzed using the following score system:

-3 points: Best positioned player goes for the ball, and all bags are covered by other players in the group.

-2 points: A player other than the best-positioned player goes for the ball, all bags covered by other players in the group.

-1 point: Two or more players in the group indicate they would get the ball (therefore, not all bags are covered).

-0 points: No players in the group indicate they would get the ball.

There were three types of groups that participated. The first group was *teammates* --these were college baseball players from the same team who each viewed videos from the camera location corresponding to their primary playing position. The second group was *non-teammates* - these were college baseball players from different teams who viewed videos corresponding to their position. Finally, the third group was *scrambled teammates* - these were college baseball players from the same team that viewed videos from a camera position that did not correspond to their primary playing position. In particular, the first baseman viewed the video shot from the shortstop's perspective (and vice versa) and the second baseman viewed the video shot from the third baseman's perspective (and vice versa).

OK, got all that? What did we find? The results are shown in Figure 11.3, with coordination scores plotted for different ball launch directions where 0 degrees is over the 2nd base bag. First off, the Teammates group (solid line) had significantly higher coordination scores than the other two groups. That's probably not all that surprising. Through experience playing together, teammates know what each other is going to do in each situation whether that's through a shared mental model or shared perception of affordances.

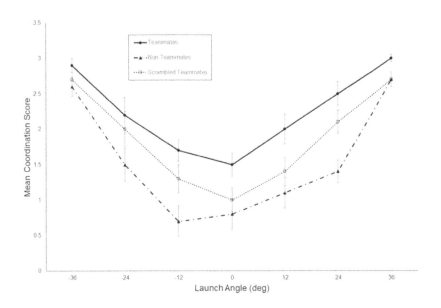

Figure 11.3 – Team Coordination Scores

What was more interesting was that the Scrambled Teammates (dotted line) had significantly higher coordination scores than the non-teammates group (dashed line). So, think about that -- players making judgments from completely different positions than they normally play but were teammates did better than non-teammates making judgments from their typical positions. We argued that this suggests, that in this task, the perception of shared affordances which includes perceiving the action capacities of one's teammates (for example, whether they have quick lateral movements or "good range") is more important for team coordination than knowledge about how to play one's position at an individual level.

Teams as Tensegrity Systems

Another interesting way to think about the use of shared affordances is the possibility that the concept of biotensegrity might not only apply to an individual body but could also be used to understand the coordination between multiple bodies – that is, team coordination in sports. This interesting idea was discussed in a 2020 article by Calderia and colleagues[5].

Of course, one of the main differences between a possible team-level biotensegrity system and the one within an individual body discussed in Chapter 7 is that there are no physical connections between the players on a team – there is no connective tissue, no fascia, that can be used to create pre-tension and allow for synergies to occur. As an alternative, the authors propose that the components of the systems are linked on an informational level rather than a physical one. In particular, via the shared affordances picked up from the environment.

The players on a team adjust their actions to information variables like the Tau Diff described above, which means that they change over time the structure they form, and thus they change the team's "informational tension". Just like our pop-up tent, the team shifts and moves together, maintaining stability and structure – but in this case, based on changes in the information picked up from the environment. By maintaining a structure that is held together internally by information, rather than externally by a coach's explicit instructions about where to be and go on the field, the team can be more adaptable and flexible. That is, they can respond in a coordinated manner to events they have never practiced.

This can also be used to understand when teamwork breaks down. To quote the authors: "A loss of efficiency in the structure can be linked to more uncoordinated actions such as unnecessary redundancies (e.g., players invading other players' areas of responsibility) or detrimental delays (e.g., players not positioning favorably to perform his or her share or to compensate teammates' less successful actions). "

An example of the tension and structure that can exist between teammates can be seen in my baseball study we just looked at. Even though they were seated in different rooms and had no way to communicate with each other, the Scrambled Teammates were still coordinated because they were held together at an informational level. They were picking up the same information from the environment and using it in the same way.

Implications for Coaching

If we accept the idea that team coordination occurs via shared affordances – teammates accepting the same invitations at the same time – then there are some important implications for coaching.

1. We need to practice in a "game context" where there are consequences for different actions.

As we saw in Chapter 9, the pickup of affordances depends on our intentions: score, kill time, defend, etc. We need to be manipulating these in team practices. For example, the goal of a passing drill should not be just "passing the ball" ☺

2. We need to create and amplify affordances during *team* practice too.

Just as we saw in Chapter 6 when developing individual action capacities, an effective way to improve team coordination is to use constraints that amplify certain information sources and information. For example, small-sided games that change the spacing and openings between players. Amplifying information sources at the same time for the same players increases the likelihood that they link the team in a biotensegrity-like structure.

3. We need to give athletes opportunities to learn the action capacities of their teammates by experiencing a variation of practice activities together.

4. We need to challenge team coordination by creating meta-stable regions on a team level.

As we saw in the last chapter, a metastable region is one where multiple movement solutions have attractiveness – they are kept active and ready to be used rather than a performer falling into a deep attractor well of one particular solution. In team sports, an equivalent are plays for which the roles of each teammate are flexible. We saw this a bit in my baseball fielder study. A practice activity we like to use that

involves working in a metastable region is the Bermuda
Triangle Fielding activity shown in Figure 11.4. For this, a
coach hits fly balls of varying heights and shapes into
metastable areas between fielders where it is not obvious who
will catch the ball. These challenge players to not only pick
up information about the flight for prospective control but
also to perceive the affordances created by the movements of
their teammates (e.g., let someone else catch it, call someone
off, potential collisions, etc).

*Figure 11.4 – Bermuda Triangle Fielding Activity. Photo Credit:
Randy Sullivan, Florida Baseball ARMory.*

ROB GRAY, PH.D.

12

REMEMBERING & USING "OFFLINE"
INFORMATION

T he next piece of the puzzle I want to consider in terms of optimizing and adapting skills is how we use, so-called, "offline" information in the control of action. As I discussed in Chapter 5, the term "offline" refers to information that is available before an event begins. Typically, in sports we define the start of an event as when the object the athlete is interacting with starts moving – a baseball pitcher releases the ball, a tennis player strikes a serve, or a soccer player contacts the ball on a penalty kick. While, as we have seen, there are abundant and rich sources of information we can use during the unfolding event (e.g., tau, optic flow, bearing angle, etc), it seems undeniable that athletes also use other information including an opponent's body language before they contact or throw the ball (commonly called "advance cues"), player tendencies, and situational probabilities. How do these fit in with the view of skill as a coupled information-movement relationship?

To understand this, I want to look at how we learn from experience. Again, we are going to focus on verbs, not nouns – emphasizing *remembering* not memory. How can our perceptual-motor system, the information-movement control laws we use, be influenced by what happened in the past? How can our system be sensitive to these "offline" sources of information without introducing complex mental models and predictions? Let's start at the beginning.

We Can Be Influenced by Past Events Without Storing Memories

Of course, one of the main types of "offline" information that an athlete uses is event history. Think about what happens in a baseball game when a pitcher throws three consecutive fastballs, a football team runs the ball on three plays in a row, or a tennis player hits the ball to your backhand three times in a row. We expect your movement on the next play to show an effect of this event history – you might gear up for another fastball, creep up to the line to stop the run, or lean to your backhand side. In sports performance, we see evidence of being influenced by the events that have happened in the recent past. It would be silly not to do this in some way. To explain this, it is commonly assumed that we must appeal to memory and inference processing going in our brains. Somewhere we have a mental model that stores the event history that is used to make some prediction about what is going to happen next. I published one of these myself for baseball batting back in 2001[1].

But what if I told you we could explain the effects of event history in sports performance without the need to appeal to these unobservable memory and prediction processes? *Hysteresis* is a phenomenon that occurs in many systems. It is when the current state of the system depends on its history. One of the most used examples to illustrate it is an elastic (rubber) band. Imagine that an elastic band is stretched out to a length of six inches. How much force is there stored in the band? We might assume that there should be a simple relationship between length and force. More length equals more force.

But it is not that simple because an elastic band exhibits hysteresis. Specifically, for a given length, say six inches, the amount of force depends on whether you got there by stretching the band from its relaxed position (loading force) or you got there by releasing it from a fully stretched-out position (unloading force). As illustrated in Figure 12. 1, you will get two completely different values for force in these two cases. It is like the elastic band "remembers" what just happened – its current state depends on the past. Hysteresis like this can be seen in numerous systems including magnetics, electrical systems, immunology, and economics - just to name a few. The existence of hysteresis makes a system decidedly nonlinear – you can't predict the outcome based on the inputs because it also depends on the history of inputs that came before. Let's look at a couple of examples of this for sports skills.

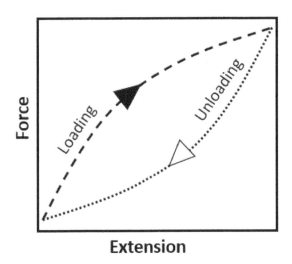

Figure 12.1 – Hysteresis in an Elastic Band

In 2001, Sorenson et al examined hysteresis in table tennis[2]. For the study, four recreational table tennis players were asked to play a series of shots from a ball machine into the target zone under two different conditions. In one condition, balls were systematically projected from the far left (location #1) to the far right (location #7) while in the other condition this occurred in reverse order. Note that all players were right-handed so "right" (position 8) is the forehand side and "left" (position 1) is the backhand side. The primary dependent variable of interest was the location at which there was a state transition – that is, the player switched from playing the ball with a forehand to a backhand or vice versa. This is, of course, like what we saw in Chapter 10 with multi-stability – there will be a switch between two attractors (forehand vs backhand) depending on the control parameter (ball direction).

What was found? As can be seen in Figure 12.2, there was clear evidence of hysteresis. When the spatial location was changed from wide right to wide left (Figure 12.2A), the transition point occurred between locations 5 and 6, 5.2 on average. When the location varied from wide left to wide right (Figure 12.2B), the transition point occurred between 3 and 4, 3.7 on average. Looking at it another way – for shot location #4, which had an identical speed and direction every time it occurred – players always made a backhand stroke for one event history and a forehand stroke for the other. The state of the system (forehand vs backhand) depends not only on the task constraints for the current shot but also on the history of task constraints in the previous few shots. AKA hysteresis. Interestingly, there was also some evidence that when the location was within these hysteresis zones (direction 3-5), the contact point from the end of the table was more variable. This reduction in stability is what is commonly observed before a state transition (or bifurcation) occurs.

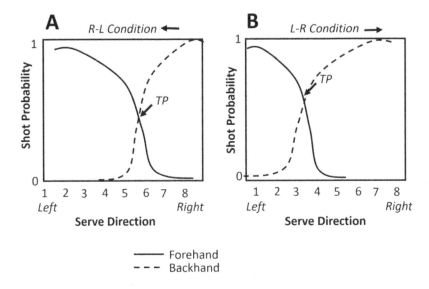

Figure 12.1 – Hysteresis in Playing Table Tennis Shots. TP = transition point between using a forehand and backhand stroke.

So, the bottom line, is we see a clear effect of event history and sequence solely due to the nature of the coordination dynamics. As discussed in Chapter 10, our attractors are not set in stone. They can shift locations and get deeper or shallower depending on experience and training. Here the attractors are developing in different locations depending on event history – just like with our elastic band.

The second study I want to look at is one published by Murase and colleagues in 2016[3]. Here, instead of looking at two different variants of the same skill, the authors looked at the transition between two completely different skills: catching and throwing. Four experienced baseball players were asked to perform two tasks: catch a launched ball (catching task) and catch a launched ball and throw it to a target (catching and throwing task). The ball was launched by a machine in one of five different directions ranging from 0 (at the player's midline) to 1.2m right of the midline. In the catching and throwing task, the participants were instructed to catch the launched ball with their left hand using a baseball glove and then immediately throw the ball as accurately as possible to another player standing 20 m (65 feet) behind them. Similar to the table tennis study, in separate blocks, the ball's direction changed systematically either from left to right or right to left. Of particular interest was at what point the players would shift attractors: from using a clockwise rotation of their body to make the throw to using a counterclockwise one.

What was found? Again, clear evidence of hysteresis. The position at which participants switched from a clockwise to a counterclockwise turn again depended on the history of the constraints – that is, whether the ball's direction was going from right to left or left to right. Importantly, the authors also found clear differences in the catching phase of the motion depending on whether the player was asked to just catch the ball or catch and throw. Specifically, when the ball was launched close to the body in the catching and throwing task, the shoulder and hip segment angles rotated in the direction of the throw, in which case, the terminal phase of catching transitioned into the preparatory phase of throwing. In contrast, the shoulder and the hip segment angles did not rotate when the ball was launched during the catching-only task because it was not necessary to transition to the next movement pattern.

This has important implications for coaching. To quote the authors:

"When mastering these skills, it is not sufficient to learn only the catching or touching movement. Our findings suggest that the movement patterns involved in catching a ball differ from those produced when a ball is caught then thrown. Moreover, when a temporal constraint is severe, it is necessary to transition from the current to the next movement quickly. Thus, learning the combination phase, which involves the terminal phase of the current movement and preparatory phase of the next movement, is important for the development of sporting skills".

This connects nicely with a concept we looked at back in Chapter 8: nested affordances. If our goal is to throw a player out at home base in baseball, we need to nest the invitation to make a throw within the invitation to catch the ball.

So critically the self-organization of movement does not solely depend on the current constraints facing the performer. It also depends both on what happened before (hysteresis) and what will happen next (whether the current action is nested with another affordance like catching a ball to make a throw). We can see that a dynamical system is also influenced by "offline" information – things that happen outside the window of the event itself. And, given that an elastic band can do it, these things can influence movement solutions without the need to bring in some unnecessary memory or inference processes.

How exactly does this occur? Well, as discussed in the last chapter, our experience with particular events can cause changes in the locations and depths of the attractors for different movement solutions. This is particularly likely to occur for a performer that has metastability because the attractors are less stable and easier to move around. Thus, I would argue that another advantage of developing metastability is an increased ability to adapt to context and event history.

It is also possible that these effects of event history are due to the process of *calibration*. Calibration refers to the scaling of the relation between information and movement in our control law. So, we are not changing the information variables we use or the aspect of our movement we control, just the relationship between them. For example, a batter learns how hard they must push off on their back foot or rotate their upper body to produce the required rate of closure between the bat and the contact point. When the dynamics of the actor change (e.g., the hitter is fatigued) a re-calibration will be required - a larger amplitude and perhaps earlier onset of muscle activity will be needed to close the same gap. Re-calibration also occurs in response to the change in the dynamics of the environment such as an increase in the pitch speeds the batter is facing (e.g., when a batter is called up from the minor to major leagues). Therefore, it is possible that effects of event history (e.g., pitch sequence in baseball as I have found in my research[1]) are due to recalibration produced when a series of the same pitch type (e.g., fastballs) occur in a row.

Next, let's consider the use of "advance cues", the body language of an opponent.

"Advance Cues" are Used for Prospective NOT Predictive Control

As we say back in Chapter 4, the term *advance cue* is used to refer to any aspect of the behavior (in particular, the movement kinematics) of an opponent that can be used to anticipate the

246

upcoming event. For example, advance cues in baseball batting include variations in the pitcher's body posture at the point of ball release (e.g., a pitcher's grip on the ball, as illustrated in Figure 12.2) the size of their leg kick, and the speed of their delivery which is sometimes slower for changeups compared to fastballs.

Figure 12.2 – Typical Grips for a Fastball, Curveball, and Changeup

The traditional view is that we use advance cues to make a discrete prediction about the event that's coming up. In baseball, we predict it will be a fastball, change-up, or curveball. In tennis, we predict that the server is going to hit the ball cross-court or down the line. We then use this cue to pre-program our movement in some way. For example, we start shifting our weight to our back foot a bit earlier if we predict it's a fastball – commonly called "sitting on a fastball".

What evidence is there to support this view? Well, it is largely based on the excellent body of research, started by Bruce Abernethy[4], using the temporal occlusion paradigm we saw in my baseball fielding study discussed in the last chapter. When we show an athlete an unfolding event like a baseball pitch, block their vision, then ask them to anticipate what will happen next (e.g., "it is a fastball right down the middle of the plate") we find a similar pattern of results across a wide range of sports. Using baseball as an example, relative to lesser-skilled batters, expert batters have superior anticipation accuracy and can perform at an above-chance level for shorter views[5] e.g., displays in which the scene is occluded at the instant the pitcher's front foot contacts the ground. Furthermore, pitch recognition accuracy has been shown to be significantly correlated with in-season batting statistics for Minor League baseball players[6]– in particular, on-base percentage (a measure of how often a batter gets on base via any means including a hit or walk). This seems to provide irrefutable evidence that skilled athletes are predicting what is going to happen next.

But, in my opinion, we have been looking at this all wrong. I think the superior ability of experienced athletes to anticipate in these experiments is just an artifact of their attunement to different information sources as compared to less experienced athletes. When we ask them to make a discrete prediction, they are better at it because they are picking up different information, but this is not actually what they are doing when they perform their skill. Instead of making a categorical prediction based on advance "cues", I believe skilled athletes are using information from the movements of their opponents to continuously control their own movement. In other words, they are using it for prospective not predictive control.

Evidence for this view can be seen in a recent study by Takamido and colleagues[7]. Fifteen male softball players were asked to perform a simulated hitting task in which they timed their swing movement based on a large video projection of the pitcher. Video recordings of the pitcher were presented at different playback speeds to create quicker and slower deliveries. Swings were analyzed using a high-speed camera and force plates positioned in the batter's box. It was found that the kinematics and kinetics of the swing were significantly influenced by the playback speed. Along with altering the timing of the different phases of the swing shown in Figure 7.2, playback speed was found to influence the distribution of forces in the back foot (i.e., the relative amounts on the big and little toe) during the weighting phase.

Evidence for the use of online, prospective control was found in the result that movements were initiated earlier (relative to the time of ball release) for slower playback speeds. Think about that. Why would I start moving earlier for a pitch that was going to be slower? If I were predicting the event, shouldn't I do the exact opposite? But this is exactly what we expect with prospective control. We start moving as soon as information becomes available (the pitcher starts their delivery) because we are using it to continuously control our movements. To quote the author's main conclusion from the study: "in particular, the preparatory movement pattern is adjusted by coupling the hitting movement with the advanced kinematic information of the opponent pitcher".

These findings are also consistent with some research I have done on baseball batting[8] showing that changing the time at which the pitcher is occluded from the batter's view has a systematic effect on their swing kinematics. They don't just switch from a "fastball swing" to a "curveball swing" as would be expected based on pitch recognition studies.

So, yes "advance cues" are important for the control of movement in sports, but they can be used in a much better way if we think of them as information used to prospectively control the early parts of our movement rather than as just cues used to make a discrete prediction. As we saw in the softball study, this information seems to be used to regulate things as subtle as how much weight you put on your big toe versus your little toe! If we accept this, it has the very important consequence that using this information needs to be trained in a coupled manner rather than watching videos and making a passive verbal response about what will happen next.

Player Tendencies and Situational Probabilities

What about player tendencies (this pitcher throws mostly fastballs) and situational probabilities (they are more likely to throw a curveball when there are 0 balls and 2 strikes)? How can these things influence prospective movement control without appealing to some form of prediction? Again, I think we are looking at these in the wrong way. Instead of using them to predict and control action, I propose their primary role is as information sources to change intentions.

For example, it is possible that the observed effects of situational probabilities (e.g., the ball-strike count) on batting performance in baseball may reflect an education of intention process rather than predictive control. Intention here refers to the actor's goal or what they intend to actualize with their action. Beyond just getting a hit, there are other intentions a batter can have depending on the game situation. These include taking (not swinging at) a pitch, trying to pull the ball, or trying to hit the ball to the opposite field. It is common for batters to change their intentions based on the pitch count.[9] For example, when ahead in a 3-0 count they might intend to pull the ball because such hits are more likely to result in homerun. Conversely, when behind in a 0-2 count they might try to hit the ball up the middle or to the opposite field to avoid striking out. Given that pull and opposite field hitting involve distinctly different patterns of coordination,[10] it is likely they would also involve different information-movement control laws. Different intentions organize the perceptual-motor system differently.

Another example can be seen from studies showing that batters use a different pattern of eye movements when they intend to take a pitch as opposed to when they intend to swing.[11] If a batter's intentions do depend on the count it could explain why this is an important factor in hitting and why there is a difference in performance when the pitch affords the intention (i.e., an inside fastball a batter can pull on a 3-0 count or not). It might also explain why, on some occasions, batters decide not to swing for seemingly hittable pitches, namely, the pitch didn't afford their intended goal.

Implications for Coaching

Using "offline" information sources effectively is important for optimizing movement. We need to take advantage of patterns that arise from interactions with our environment rather than being purely reactive to what is happening at the moment – just not in the ways people have traditionally thought! Our perceptual-motor system remembers (changes with experience) without memory (passive storage of programs and plans). From this there is one strong implication – we need to have patterns present in practice so athletes can learn to pick them up and use them.

One easy way this can be achieved is by using *serial practice*. When manipulating the structure of practice, we tend to focus on two extremes in motor learning: blocked vs. random practice. Blocked is having everything stay the same while random obviously involves changing things randomly. An interesting middle ground is the use of serial practice. In serial practice, we are switching the skill or the task constraints but not doing so in a completely random order. So, for example, serial practice in golf might be: putt, chip, drive, putt, chip, drive, etc. Or, if we stay within one skill: long putt, medium putt, short putt, long putt, etc. Previous research has shown that serial practice can provide a good middle ground between blocked and random practice. It gets the adaptability benefits of random practice without the high variability in conditions that can be too difficult for novice learners[12]. But for our purposes here, serial practice has the benefit that there is an order and structure to the conditions that can encourage the development of processes like hysteresis in the control of movement.

OK, so we have looked at perceiving, acting, and how we can build an adaptable relationship between the two. Now it's time to turn to the dark side – how can we keep this relationship together (and perhaps make it even stronger) in the face of things that are trying to break it apart?

13

AFFECTIVE PRACTICE: LEARNING TO HANDLE PRESSURE & EMOTION

I f you think about it most of the practice we do is at a different temperature than the game. I am not talking about degrees Fahrenheit or Celsius, but rather the level of emotion involved. Competition is "hot" – there is pressure, anxiety, anger, sadness, etc. Practice is mostly "cold", not involving a lot of emotion, pressure to perform, etc. In terms of thinking about skill acquisition and the design of practice, emotions have typically been viewed as something uncontrollable and negative. Unwanted "noise" in the learning process that is better to remove, at least until the skill is very well established. But if you think about it this is a flaw in our efforts to have representative design and sports-specific training. We put a lot of effort into ensuring that the information and movements are similar in training to the real sport – but we don't often try to match the emotional context. In this chapter, I want to show you the benefits of incorporating "hot" practices into your training. Having not just effective practice but *affective* (relating to moods and feelings) practice too!

The Benefits of Adding Pressure to Practice

As I briefly mentioned in Chapter 4, 'choking under pressure' is thought to occur because our attention is pulled around in some way – either towards our body leading to us over-controlling our movement or away from our body to some form of distraction. However, there is also some evidence that we can learn to fight this tendency though the use of self-regulatory processes and increasing effort. So, a simple prediction is that training under high anxiety might improve these processes and make an athlete better able to handle the stresses of competition. We also know that stress can be adaptive in that it increases readiness to perform and makes us more prepared to act so it may also have additional benefits in making an athlete more focused during practice.

One of the first studies to investigate these ideas was by Oudejans and Pipers in 2010[1]. This experiment involved having participants throw darts using the unique setup they have a Vrije University in Amsterdam. Imagine climbing halfway up a mountain, leaning off the side a bit, and playing darts! Within their lab they have a dartboard sticking out from a rock-climbing wall that can be raised to different heights. During training, 24 participants were split into two groups. The control group threw darts while only .14m (6 inches) off the ground – so low anxiety. The experimental group did the same except they also faced competitive and evaluative pressure during training (prize money for performance and being videotaped). Following this training, both groups then threw from three different heights: .14m, 4 m (13 feet), and 5.6 m (18 feet). Obviously, as the height increases, anxiety is going to go up. Believe me, I tried it!

What was found? For the group that trained under competitive and evaluative anxiety, scores did not change at all as the height above the ground was increased. For the control group, which trained under low pressure, there was a drop in score of nine points on average when going from the ground to 18 feet above it. So, training with anxiety improves performance under anxiety. An important point to note here: the pressure in training was completely different from the pressure in testing. While the former was centered around the actual task of dart throwing, the latter was essentially fear of falling. I will return to this issue of how similar the pressure in practice must be to that in competition shortly.

The second study I want to look at is one by Gav Lawrence and colleagues from the University of Bangor[2]. In this experiment, 32 novice climbers trained on an indoor climbing wall and were split into two different groups. Group 1 was a control group that performed all training under low anxiety conditions. Group 2 was a group that always trained under high anxiety conditions. In this case, anxiety was created by videotaping and telling participants that their video would be evaluated by a professional climber and that the evaluation would be posted in a public area. After training, the speed and accuracy of climbing were measured under two conditions (a low anxiety test, and a high anxiety test in which participants were offered a prize for performance).

What was found? For the low anxiety control group, when they were tested under low anxiety conditions, performance was about the same as it was at the end of training. However, when they were tested under high anxiety conditions, there was a large increase in the time required to traverse the course (by about 7 seconds). Consistent with the findings of the dart-throwing study we just looked at, the group that was trained under conditions of high anxiety showed no adverse performance effects when tested under high anxiety.

Here is where it gets interesting. When the high anxiety group was tested under low anxiety conditions, they had a significant decline in performance (an increase in time of about 5 seconds). Therefore, there is an important practical message here: just as always practicing in low anxiety conditions is bad, so is always practicing in intense, high anxiety conditions. Not only would it completely mentally exhaust an athlete, but it would also likely make them unable to "psych themselves up" to perform in lower-stress moments in competition.

Before diving into the next study, I want to re-emphasize an important point we will consider in detail next chapter: the distinction between performance and learning. The goal of adding emotional context, like anxiety, to practice is learning. In other words, making the athlete better in the future. The athlete will likely perform poorly in practice when you add these things. And if they don't look bad in practice you probably aren't doing it right! So, the question here is not whether the pressure can cause performance to get worse. We know it does. The question is will experience with it in practice prevent you from getting worse in the future, in competition?

The next study I want to look at was by Hordacre et al in 2016[3]. In this, the authors' main goal was to look at the effects of pressure training in a situation where the pressure was completely separated from the task being performed. In the studies I have talked about so far, the pressure was applied while the action was being executed (e.g., while throwing darts or rock climbing). In the Hordacre study, the anxiety was induced before the motor task training began, not at the same time. Specifically, 36 participants were split into two groups. A control group first completed a set of speeded math problems involving one-digit numbers, so 3 minus 2. An experimental group did the same except with 3-digit numbers, so 817 minus 342. Not surprisingly, previous research has shown that the 3-digit task creates significantly higher levels of anxiety. Following this manipulation, both groups were trained in precision pinch tasks. That is, they had to learn to squeeze their thumb and forefinger together to exactly produce forces of three different magnitudes. They then went away and came back to perform a retention test 24 hours later.

What was found? As expected, the group that did the 3-digit problems beforehand had significantly higher perceived anxiety at the start of the training for the pinch task. However, this group's anxiety went away very quickly, within about 1-2 blocks of training. Looking at performance during training, the 3-digit group performed the task significantly faster and had shorter movement times immediately from the first block of training and maintained this advantage throughout the entire training session. These effects were likely due to the adaptive effects of stress. That is, getting the 3-digit group all riled up before training likely increased their motor readiness resulting in better performance in training.

But what about the more crucial test of learning? How did the two groups do in the retention test? In terms of performance on the pinch task, the 3-digit group was significantly more accurate and again had shorter movement times. So, in sum, putting an athlete through a high anxiety experience may be beneficial even if this occurs before the practice of the sport and it involves a completely unrelated task.

One last study I want to mention is by Stoker and colleagues in 2017[4]. The goal of this study was to try and identify which type of stressors have the biggest effects on performance. In most of the research I have reviewed so far, the researchers have used what I call the kitchen sink approach – throwing a whole bunch of different types of pressure (competitive, social, fear) at the participants. But if you don't have the time or resources to do all of that what are the most important elements you need?

In their study, Stoker and colleagues compared two things that they had found are mostly commonly used by elite coaches in an earlier survey study. These are manipulating the demands of training and manipulating the consequences of training. In terms of demands, their survey revealed that coaches manipulated tasks (for example, the rules of play) and environmental stressors (for example, using noise from a loudspeaker) to create high-pressure training exercises. For consequences, coaches used rewards, forfeit, judgment, and evaluation to expose athletes to meaningful performance-contingent outcomes.

The goal of their study was to determine which had a bigger effect on perceived anxiety in athletes, demands, or consequences. To achieve this end, 15 netball players from England's international squad trained under three conditions: a demands condition, a consequences condition, and a control condition. Across the three conditions, participants performed the same Netball-specific drill. For the conditions in which the demands were manipulated shot sequences were randomized, they were required to play while wearing occlusion glasses, and a noise distractor (a loud repeating beep) was added. For the conditions in which consequences were manipulated players were judged by having to perform the drills in front of the head coach and while being videotaped. There was a $50 reward for the best performance and the player with the lowest score in training had to do a one-minute presentation in front of the team on one of four topics. What was found? Both when measured through questionnaires and assessed via heart rate, anxiety was higher (and performance level lower) in the consequences condition.

Before getting into some recommendations for practice design, I wanted to mention two other practical methods people have used for pressure training. The first are vignettes. So instead of letting a golfer just repeat swing after swing on the driving range or a baseball batter taking repeated swings at balls thrown by a pitching machine, a coach can paint a picture of an emotionally laden situation for them. "Imagine it's the 18th hole at The Masters and you are winning by one stroke". "It's the bottom of the 9th. Two outs.." That kind of thing.

The second method is using the Game Intensity Index (GII) concept developed by Renshaw and Chow[5]. For the GII, it is proposed that in team sports the intensity of practice is equal to the size of the playing area divided by the number of players. So, if you want to turn up the heat a bit, make the playing area smaller in a soccer or football practice. An analogous method in ball sports like baseball or cricket is to have a coach pitch the ball from a closer distance than is used in the real game. This helps to better approximate the extreme timing demands and associated emotions that occur in high-level competition.

Implications for Adding Pressure to Practice

From this research, I think we can pull some key principles for designing pressure training in practice:

1. There does not seem to be a high level of specificity required in pressure training.

   The pressure in training does not need to exactly match the competition pressure – which is typically impossible to recreate anyways. So, for example, if an athlete is worried about performing in front of a large crowd, you don't need a large crowd to prepare them for it. Other things like being videotaped may be just as useful.

2. You might not even have to add anxiety to the actual sports task.

    Having an athlete do something stressful before practice, like playing a difficult mental game, is likely to also have motor learning benefits.

3. Mix up pressure levels in practice. It's not good to always train using either low or high pressure.

4. Don't leave it at failure.

    If you are doing things right, it is likely that an athlete's performance will get significantly worse when first introduced to pressure training. As a coach, it is critical that you don't leave them there. It is important to adjust practice conditions, so they see some success and discuss the goal of the training with them. Most importantly, let them know poor performance is expected. In all of this, you want to avoid creating an expectation of failure in an athlete.

5. Consequences including rewards, forfeits and judgment seem to be more powerful than demand manipulations in creating pressure.

One of the most powerful pressure manipulations in my experience is telling the athletes you are coaching that the person that scores the lowest will need to make a speech in front of the team. What we are trying to do here is make them worry about the consequences of their actions just like they might in competition. We are training them to become resistant to the urge to turn their attention inwards to control movement (i.e., the creeping hand of pressure) as we saw in Chapter 4.

For those interested in more information on this topic, Hendrick and colleagues also give some good general guidelines for other types of emotional experiences[6]. Emotion can be thought of as an individual constraint that is going to shape the emergence of different movement solutions. Thus, it can be manipulated in practice just like other constraints.

The Power of Expectations

The final point I want to consider in this chapter is the role the coach plays in setting an athlete's expectations. Are you making them feel like they are doomed to fail or full of hope to succeed? This is more important than you might think. In their OPTIMAL theory of motor learning[7], Wulf and Lewthwaite argue that increasing an athlete's expectancy of success is one of the key factors in learning a new skill. In support of this, they cite some interesting studies looking at the use of optical illusions in sports.

In a study published in 2015[8], Chauvel and colleagues trained golfers to putt under two different conditions: a regular golf hole and a hole that's perceived size was changed as the result of an optical illusion. As shown in Figure 13.1, the Ebbinghaus illusion is created by putting circles of different sizes around a central circle. Most people see the central circle as being larger when it is surrounded by small circles (right side) as compared to when it is surrounded by large circles (left side) even though the two are in reality the same physical size.

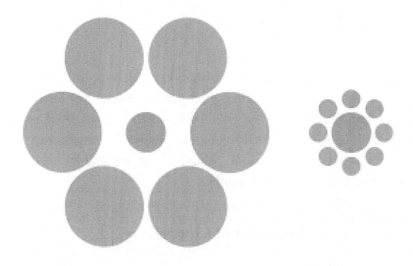

Figure 13.1 – The Ebbinghaus Illusion

What happens when you recreate this on a putting green? That is, you surround regulation-size golf holes with either large or small circles. Even though the task constraints (in terms of the size of the ball and the hole) haven't changed, there seem to be changes in how effectively novice golfers learn to putt. Specifically, after training with either a normal hole or the Ebbinghaus illusion, participants were tested with just a normal hole. The golfers that trained with the illusion perceived a normal golf hole to be bigger, had higher ratings of confidence, and, most importantly, putt the ball closer to the hole (by about 5cm on average) than those that did not. The authors argued that this effect is due to enhanced expectancies. When you perceive the hole as being bigger you expect to make it and it helps you perform and learn better.

All this talk about expectancies leads nicely into the next topic I want to consider: how difficult should a task be in practice? How should we be manipulating the level of challenge to enhance skill acquisition?

14

HOW DIFFICULT SHOULD PRACTICE BE? THE "70% RULE" & GETTING THE LEVEL OF CHALLENGE RIGHT

How difficult should practice be? This is a question that I get asked all the time by coaches. And, indeed, it is a very important one. On the one hand, practice needs to be difficult enough that the athlete is not performing every movement and skill perfectly. They need to be challenged. In motor learning, we often make the distinction between performing and learning. Performing is doing things well right now, in practice. Learning is doing something that will make you perform well in the future, in competition. We will get into this more in a moment, but very often effective learning requires poor performance. But, on the other hand, we don't want practice to be too difficult such that our athletes are having very little success at all. This can be de-motivating, cause them to have reduced feelings of competence and lead them to put less effort into practice or even stop showing up for practice altogether. So, we need to get the balance of success and failure right!

The most prominent theory related to task difficulty and motor learning is the Challenge Point Hypothesis proposed by Guadagnoi and Lee in 2004[1]. The first important element of this framework is that there are two types of task difficulty: nominal and functional. The nominal difficulty of a task is determined by its perceptual-motor requirements, independent of who is performing it and under what conditions it is being performed. So, for example, a 20-foot jump shot is nominally more difficult than a 10-foot shot due to the greater distance. Functional task difficulty, on the other hand, refers to how challenging a task is relative to both the skill level of the individual performing the task and the task constraints under which it is being performed. So, a 20-foot jump shot is more functionally difficult for a novice basketball player than an NBA player. A 20-foot shot over a defender is more functionally difficult than an open shot, even though in all these cases the nominal difficulty is the same. So, the first important implication for coaching is that we need to think in terms of varying the functional, not just nominal, difficulty of our practice. As most coaches already do, we need to have lower nominal task difficulty (slower speeds, closer shots, less variability in conditions, etc.) for performers at lower skill levels.

Next, as illustrated in Figure 14.1, the authors emphasis the distinction between performance and learning I made at the start of this chapter. At low levels of functional task difficulty (so adjusted for skill level), an athlete is going to perform well but not have many opportunities to learn and improve. While at very high levels of functional task difficulty they are going to do neither. In the middle somewhere is the optimal challenge point for the athlete that is going to have the highest potential learning benefits.

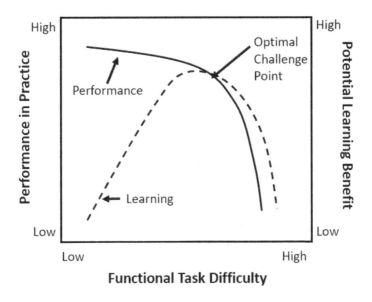

Figure 14.1 – Performance vs Learning

To understand this relationship between performance and learning, let's compare blocked vs random practice. Blocked practice involves executing the same skill repeatedly, typically under the same set of task constraints, for several trials before moving on to working on another skill. For example, a golfer might hit 50 balls on a driving range, then 50 putts on a practice green, and then head over and make 50 chip shots out of the sand. In random practice, the skills are randomly intermixed. So, the golfer might practice one drive, then two putts, then one chip, then two drives, etc.

The typical pattern of results you get when comparing these two types of practice structures is illustrated in Figure 14.2. Most notably, during the practice sessions, athletes that engage in blocked practice typically have better performance (in our golfing example they make straighter drives, sink more putts, and get the ball out of the sand more often) as compared to the athletes engaging in random practice. But then two interesting things happen when we give them a competition-like test after training is over. First, the athletes that did blocked practice struggle mightily when you place them under random test conditions while the random practice group typically performs well – often at an even higher level then they achieved in practice. Second, what happens if we test the athletes on a shot that they didn't attempt in practice, what motor learning researchers call a transfer test (e.g., a long iron shot in golf)? Again, the learners that engaged in random practice excel while the blocked practice group struggles. I will look at the reasons why this might occur in a little bit but think about these effects for a moment. Random practice makes you better at switching between skills or performing something a little bit different from what you learned. Isn't this exactly what the athlete will be doing in competition?! Struggling a bit in practice, and having lesser performance, makes you better in the long run. You learn more effectively.

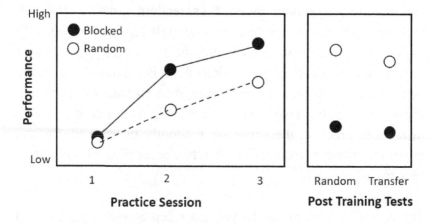

Figure 14.2 – Typical Blocked vs Random Practice Results

While we are on this topic, I want to address another important issue – a performer's ability to assess the degree to which they are learning and improving in different practice conditions. I often hear coaches say that isolated, decomposed practice drills (like dribbling around cones in soccer or hitting off a tee in baseball) should be used because some athletes like and prefer them over more variable, coupled activities. Well, just like with a lot of other things in life, what we like is not always what is good for us! This point was made very nicely in a recent paper by Hodges and Lohse[2]:

"What is particularly interesting about these practice order effects is the sense of fluidity and apparent feeling of learning, which accompanies people who practice under repetitive, drill-like, blocked practice conditions. Fast gains in practice give the impression that learning is taking place, even though faster acquisition is not necessarily good for long-term learning. When participants who study under blocked conditions are asked how well they will do at a future time, they show optimism in their retention capability, compared to people who study under random conditions. This sense of learning which accompanies rapid gains in practice is despite data gathered from retention tests, which show the opposite pattern".

Even though an athlete may like and feel more confident when a coach implements things like repetitive, isolated practice drills and prescriptive instruction telling them exactly what they should be doing – the research clearly shows these are not the best conditions for actual learning and transfer to competition.

Ok, Rob, we buy what you are selling here. We need to find the optimal challenge point of functional difficulty in our practice where the athlete is learning not just performing. But how do we know how to do this? The answer that works well for me and a lot of the coaches I work with is the "70 % rule". That is, we want to change the task difficulty in practice such that the athlete is successful on roughly 70% of their attempts. If they are doing a lot better than this we increase speeds, use a smaller ball, shorten distances, add more variability, etc. If they are doing much worse than 70% we do the opposite. There is a large body of research that shows 70% to be the optimal mix of enough success to keep athletes motivated and enough failure for them to improve and learn[3].

Information for Learning

The second key part of the Challenge Point Hypothesis is that not all difficulties are equally beneficial for learning. It is not difficulty per se that we want, but rather information for learning and improving. That is, we want an athlete's failures to be informative in some way, showing them a path to a better movement solution. What this information is exactly can be conceptualized in different ways depending on the theory of skill acquisition[2], but of course, I want to look at it from an ecological perspective where we consider the relationship between the athlete and their environment – not just the processing that is going on in their head.

From an ecological perspective, we can understand this by considering the concept of "information for learning" in the theory of Direct Learning proposed by Jacobs and Michaels[4]. In Direct Learning, a critical part of skill acquisition is movement through information space. What the authors call "Education of Attention". For example, Figure 14.3 illustrates a common pattern I have seen in my studies on baseball batting over the years (see also the excellent study by Smith et al[5] that shows similar effects).

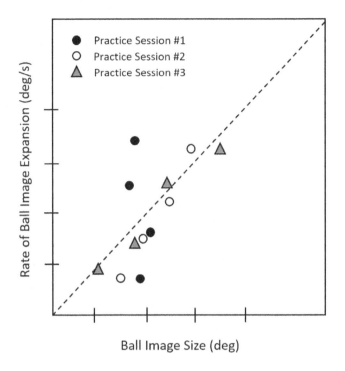

Figure 14.3 – Moving Through Information Space

Here we have a bunch of swings plotted in an information space created by looking at the image size of the ball (θ) and the rate of change of the ball's image size ($d\theta/dt$). Another way to think of this is the ball's distance plotted against its speed. Because the ball always remains the same physical size, the size of its image will be directly related to its distance from the batter's eye (bigger equals closer) and its velocity will be directly related to the rate of change in the image size (faster expansion rate equals higher velocity).

Early in training, I often see the pattern illustrated by the solid circles in Figure 14.3 which shows the initiation point for different swings. Here the batter is using the ball's angular size (or distance) as the information source to control their movement – they are starting their swing when the angular size reaches a critical value no matter how fast it is going. This, of course, does not work very well when we start varying things as it makes them too early for slow pitches and too late for fast ones.

Later in training, this changes. As shown by the open circles and triangles, batters seem to switch the information they are using as they accumulate more practice time. They move through the information space from using just θ to control their swing to, eventually, using the ratio θ divided by $d\theta/dt$ (dashed line). Which, of course, is our good friend tau. This is a more effective hitting control law because they are using specifying information about the time to arrival of the ball to time their swing. And, indeed, their batting performance dramatically improves.

What guides this movement through information space? The process starts with some error or non-optimality in performance. If we are performing the task successfully there is no reason to change anything. Let's look back at the information-movement control law for baseball batting I discussed back in Chapter 2. Recall, as shown in Figure 14.4, to time the swing successfully the batter is coupling the tau of two gaps: the gap between the ball and the front of the plate (ϕ_{Ball}) and the gap between the current length of their arm muscle and the length when it is fully extended (ϕ_{Bat}). If they are unsuccessful in achieving this control law then, as shown in Figure 14.4, there is going to be some difference between the size of these two gaps when the ball reaches the plate. This difference is information for learning, in that it informs the batter about what they need to do to reduce the performance error.

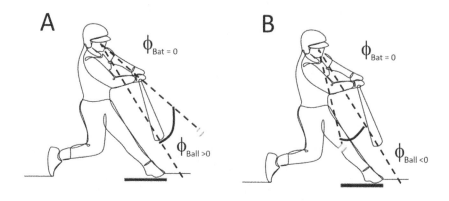

Figure 14.4 – Information for Learning in Baseball Batting

Let's look at a couple of scenarios to illustrate this further. First, imagine that instead of using the control law illustrated in Figure 14.4, the batter was using the one seen in the early stage of learning in Figure 14.3 – using the angular size of the ball to control their swing. This would result in the difference between the gaps between positive for some (slow) pitches (as shown in Figure 14.4 A, the arm reaches full extension before the ball arrives) and negative for other (fast) pitches (as shown in Figure 14.4 B, the arm reaches full extension after the ball has already crossed the front of the plate). This difference between the visual and proprioceptive tau gaps is information for learning. That is, it provides the batter a guide to how they can change their movement solution to perform better. If they have the pattern of results I just described, there is no simple change in their movement pattern that can correct the problem, so they will be encouraged to search for a new information source.

Imagine instead, that every time the batter swings, the tau of the gap in the arm muscle is positive (Fig 14.4A). This is information that a *re-calibration* is needed. For a given ϕ_{Bat} gap, they need to put more force into their muscles to close it faster. There is not only information in our environment that we can use to control our actions but there is also information that indicates the required change in our movement solution. In this case, the direction and magnitude of the difference between the tau gaps when the ball crosses the plate.

And this brings us back to challenge and task difficulty. If the task difficulty for an athlete is too high in practice, there will be very poor information for learning. That is, it will be difficult for their perceptual-motor system to identify what needs to be done to improve performance. For example, if we use pitch speeds that are way too high, or we vary pitch speed too much for a novice baseball batter the differences between the tau gaps for the swings shown in Figure 14.4 will not be good information for learning. because they are likely to have no consistent pattern from swing to swing.

Creating Information for Learning via Practice Design

There are two important implications of this for coaching. First, we can't have information for learning if the conditions are constant and unchanging. For example, if we have a batter practice hitting off a pitching machine throwing the ball at the same speed every time they are not going to get the information they need to find an effective movement solution. This leads me to a conclusion that many will find sacrilegious: blocked practice is not the devil – constant practice is! There is nothing wrong with working on the same skill (be it driving a golf ball, hitting a baseball, or serving a tennis ball) over and over. The problem comes when we practice them, in the same way, every time. That is, we don't vary things like the size of the fairway, the position of the ball in the stance, the position of opponents, speed, etc. from execution to execution. Information for learning requires variability. As evidenced in recent studies of differential learning[6], when we vary the task constraints while performing the same skill, we get the same long-term benefits we see with random practice (switching between skills).

Second, we need to think about how and why we are varying task difficultly in practice. Again, we don't want to just think about making things difficult for difficulty's sake. We want to make things harder to provide more information for learning. For me, this is where we really need to consider the skill level of the performer. Are they a novice trying to develop the basic pattern of coordination for the skill or are they a highly skilled athlete that is trying to optimize the control of an already effective movement solution?

For less-experienced performers, I like to think about varying the constraints at or even outside the borders of the movement solution space. For example, one of my favorite activities to use when working with a new golfer is to have them deliberately try to hit the ball as far right as possible and then as far left as possible. Then try hitting the ball on the toe of the club and then on the heel. In other words, I am trying to get them to do it wrong! For me, this is a very effective way to give information for learning. Experiencing what I need to do with my body to get a ball to go way right or way left, provides me with information about what I need to do to get it to go straight. So, when we are working to establish the basic pattern of coordination, I try to vary things to create these extremes in performance outcomes. Because the athlete is less experienced, they need very coarse information to first get the movement solution in the right ballpark.

While there would likely still be some benefits for doing this type of practice with experienced golfers, it is not likely to help them optimize their already effective movement pattern. The sensory feedback you get from hitting the ball way to the right and way to the left is likely going to be too coarse to provide information for learning to hit the ball with a slight draw (a shot that curves slightly in one direction), for example. For athletes at higher levels of skill working at the borders of the solution space is not likely going to help much. Instead, I like to think in terms of using focused variability. Instead of creating large variations in task constraints, I focus them on the specific aspect of the skill we want to improve.

An example of this can be seen in my work looking at training opposite field hitting in baseball batting[7]. The players in my study were already good hitters so I did not use the type of broad task variations I might use with a novice trying to get them to learn the basic pattern of coordination used to swing a bat (e.g., trying hitting the ball way left, all the way right, pop it up in the air, hit it into the ground, move way back in that batter's box, now way forward, etc.). Instead, I focused the variability on the task of opposite-field hitting. Specifically, I asked them to hit through different gaps on that specific side of the field and used physical constraints (a connection ball and objects placed on the ground) to encourage, smaller, more specific changes in the movement solution. The constraints were used to de-stabilize certain movement solutions: the connection ball for swings in which there was an early separation between the batter's arms and their body and the object on the ground for ones in which the batter stepped away from the plate. Because the batters in my study were already proficient at hitting, they needed more focused and specific constraint manipulations to provide information for learning.

Of course, in this process, the coach also plays a vital role in shaping information for learning and helping to guide the athlete's movement through information space. We are not just standing back and letting them figure it out all on their own. To quote from the paper by Hodges and Lohse:

"To help make this new information useable, the coach often provides a valuable role in helping direct attention and determine key information. This help may be through adapting of task-specific constraints, changing rules or augmenting practice through verbal instruction or video".

Practice should be iterative and adaptive based on how the athletes are performing and taking (or sometimes not taking) the opportunities for learning you are providing as a coach. For this I am again going to say something that many will find sacrilegious: it is OK to give explicit instructions every once and a while as long as they are used to help guide the athlete not give them the solution. For example, if an athlete is struggling in some practice activity, I have no problem with saying "why don't you try bending your knees more" or "maybe keeping your elbow in would help you stay more balanced". For me, this is just getting them to explore another part of the movement space which is a good thing. But critically, if the instruction does not seem to help I don't keep repeating it. I am not "correcting" the movement pattern. I am helping them get more information for learning not giving them the solution. For more on this please check out my video presentation "Roots Not Branches"[8].

Another point to consider here is how we provide feedback to an athlete. Frequently pointing out when they do things wrong can be de-motivating and lead to reduced expectations. An effective strategy to address this is to let the player choose when they receive performance feedback. Research has shown that we learn better under conditions of self-controlled feedback as opposed to when someone else (like a coach) decides when it is given[9]. This also serves to reduce the amount of external feedback the player is given which encourages them to focus on their own intrinsic, sensory feedback.

Finally, it is important to note that the optimal practice difficulty for an individual performer is always dynamic and changing. As an athlete gets better at a task, the amount of new information they get from practice activities is going to decrease so we need to keep pushing them to create new opportunities to learn. In other words, we need to periodize skill acquisition just like we do with strength and conditioning.

Periodizing Skill Acquisition

An interesting approach to changing task difficulty within and across training sessions is the Periodization of Skill Training (POST) framework proposed by Otte and colleagues[10]. The framework is built on the CLA and identifies three challenges facing coaches in planning practice. Challenge #1 is appropriately introducing representativeness and task specificity in training. Because, as we saw in earlier chapters, more advanced performers typically are attuned to different and more specifying information sources as compared to their lesser skilled counterparts, it is critical that training represent different levels of the dynamic

278

information present in competition so that a learner's attention can be educated to this specifying information.

Challenge #2 is finding a balance between stability and instability. When we look at motor learning as a search through a perceptual-motor landscape, a key to effective skill development seems to be balancing *exploitation* (developing a movement solution that is stable in the face of perturbations in the environment) and *exploration* (going through periods of instability to find new and more effective solutions).

Challenge #3 is managing the level of information complexity in training. This is like the concepts we just saw for information for learning. If a task has too high a level of functional difficulty there likely will not be effective information from the pattern of performance outcomes.

The authors propose that skill should be broadly structured into the three stages shown in Figure 14.5. The first stage, "Coordination Training", is focused on searching for and exploring different coordination patterns within the training environment. In my experience, this is best achieved by starting with the "variability at the borders" manipulations I described above (e.g., hit way right then way left) and then using a relatively small amount of variability in constraints (e.g., hitting to the same target) to help stabilize the solution.

Figure 14.5 – The Periodization of Skill Training (POST) Framework[9].

A key element of this stage is reducing the functional task difficulty in some way while still keeping the information-movement coupling intact. A great example of this is reducing the size of equipment (scaling) for new learners. For example, using lower compression balls in tennis, smaller diameter balls for baseball pitching, and reducing the size of the playing area in cricket. In a 2016 paper, Buszard and colleagues[11] reviewed a total of 25 studies investigating equipment scaling for sports tasks including tennis, basketball, volleyball, cricket, throwing, and catching. They found that for 18 of them there were significant performance benefits as compared to training with standard, adult equipment.

In the second stage, "Skill Adaptability Training", the idea is to move the athlete away from using solutions that permit just some basic level of proficiency (e.g., freezing degrees of freedom, using non-specifying information) towards more optimal solutions (e.g., motor synergies, using specifying information). To facilitate this process, the framework proposes three sub-stages: (1) "Movement Variability Training" (2) "Complex Training" and (3) "Team-based Training"

Movement variability training focuses on enhancing the ability of the athlete to adapt movement parameters in response to changing constraints in the environment. To quote the authors:

This sub-stage is driven by the aim of challenging performers to more actively search for relevant information sources and adapt micro-component features of movement solutions (i.e., "within skill variability"). Predominantly, this would be within a stable affordance landscape and under varying levels of task complexity. Methodical approaches within this stage of "Movement Variability Training" could include, for example, the differential learning approach or the addition of changing parameters and modified equipment to the movement task at hand.

For example, if we were training a soccer goalkeeper, this could involve adjusting the ball speed or size, or the shooting distance. Peripheral vision could be limited with special glasses, etc. So, in general, this stage still focuses on single movement tasks in training environments including one or two athletes.

Conversely, in the complex training stage, the goal is to confront performers with multiple movements via a further increase of information complexity (e.g., small training groups consisting of a larger number of players). This is where variability in practice schedules can also be emphasized focusing on "between skill variability" of unrelated movement skills.

Finally, team-based training reintroduces game-like structures to practice through, for example, the use of small-sided or conditioned games.

The third and final developmental stage in the POST framework is Performance Training. This is meant to occur close to competition at a point in training where the goals are increasing efficiency and confidence as opposed to skill development, necessarily. This training should be at the highest level of representativeness (e.g., using 11 vs 11 in soccer) and focus more on aspects like pre-game routines and strategy in facing a specific opponent.

Overall, I think this framework is a good way to conceptualize the key principles of periodizing skill acquisition. In the early stages of training, we are focusing on basic coordination while later we are working on optimizing and stabilizing movement solutions. It is also important that we have some sessions, in particular ones close to competition, for which the goal is not learning or large changes in movement. Rather, we should be focusing on confidence and pressure-proofing the skill. This will typically involve less variation and lower task difficulty in practice. Finally, it is important to note that the arrows in Figure 14.5 are bi-directional indicating that skill acquisition is not a one-way street! Sometimes we will need to go back to coordination training even for highly skilled athletes.

15

ADAPTING TO PAIN & INJURY & BECOMING ANTI-FRAGILE

In "How We Learn to Move" I presented two somewhat radical ideas about dealing with an injury that I feel even more strongly about today. The first is the idea that we need to shift our focus from injury *re*habilitation to injury adaptation. Since writing my first book, I have been witnessing a young family member go through rehabilitation for serious injuries that occurred in a driving accident. In observing this process, I can't help but think the focus on trying to get him back to where he was is counterproductive. You need to have the same range of motion you had before. You need to be able to do this lunge movement like you used to. All this is showing him is what he can't do leading to a lot of frustration and demotivation. The exercises he is doing are all also very decomposed and isolated – the movements he is making in therapy have no real purpose (other than to satisfy the therapist). He has no real intent or goal.

I think injury *re*covery (there is another word we use that implies going back) could be improved if we make two primary changes to how we work with injured athletes. First, rather than having so much emphasis on getting back, I think the focus should be on exploring and learning about your new body. Injury fundamentally and often permanently changes the individual constraints of a performer. They need to learn about their new solution space by living in it for a while.

A good example of how this can be achieved is the *Feldenkrais Method*[1]. In this method, developed by Israeli engineer Moshe Feldenkrais, participants are asked to perform a series of very slow movements (typically while lying on the floor) with a strong emphasis on awareness of how the movement feels. Each class focuses on a particular functional theme, such as flexing the spine, mobilizing the hips, or coordinating the feet and ankles. Critically, movements are often non-typical (e.g., trying to roll from your back to sitting while holding a knee or foot), and variable (participants are encouraged to try different ways of achieving the same thing). There are no "keep your knees over your toes" instructions. As Feldenkrais himself once said: "it is incorrect to correct."

There is a large body of research showing the benefits of this method. In 2015, Hillier and Worley[2] conducted a systematic review that included 20 randomized control trials comparing the Feldenkrais Method to control or placebo groups. Across the individual studies, there was evidence for reduced perceived effort in movement, increased comfort, improved body image perception, and more movement dexterity. Consistent with the ideas of exploring and learning about your "new" body the authors concluded that research "supported the proposal that the Feldenkrais Method works on a learning paradigm rather than disease-based mechanisms". For more information on this method, I would encourage you to check out the podcast interview I did with Todd Hargove[3].

The second change I think we need to make is putting more focus on affordances in rehabilitation sessions. We need to create environments in which patients have an intention – they are trying to achieve something other than just the movement itself. And they receive invitations (plural) to act from the environment. We need to start rebuilding the information-movement relationship not just focus on the movement part of things.

The other radical idea I put forth in my first book was that movement variability is an injury prevention mechanism. Counterintuitively, being inconsistent and not having "perfect form" every time is a good thing! Not only does it give us more options for solving movement problems it also seems to reduce the stresses we put on our body, decreasing the likelihood we are going to hurt it.

As further evidence for this idea let's look at a recent paper published by Ghanti and colleagues[4]. In this study, the authors compared three different approaches to strength and conditioning training. All groups performed a series of exercises including different types of squats, lunges, and jumps. The training lasted for eight weeks. Before and after training, participants performed a single-leg landing test in which they dropped to the ground from a box. Knee valgus (how much the knee turns outward from the body midline) and ground reaction force was measured and used as markers of a potential ACL knee injury.

The first training group was a traditional, prescriptive instruction group that received internal focus of attention instructions. Each exercise was shown to athletes, and they were asked to copy and repeat it. If the athletes requested it, the trainer instructed them on the proper technique using verbal feedback. Feedback was focused on the correct body positions and movements.

The second training group was a prescriptive group that received external focus of attention instructions. Participants were again instructed in the "correct" way to perform the different exercises with the difference being that they were now focused more on external objects in the environment instead of just their body movements. For example, "point your knees towards the cone" or "jump and touch the hanging ball".

The final training group was a *differential learning* group. In this approach, the goal is not to get the athlete to have the correct technique. Instead, we are trying to get them to explore the movement solutions space by deliberately not ever having them perform the same exercise in the same way. In other words, lots of movement variability! For example, Table 15.1 shows some of the different options that were used for a double-leg jump. On each attempt, the instructor randomly chooses one of these, so the athlete is doing something different every time.

Task Constraints	Environmental Constraints
Jump as high as you can	Exercise in the sand with and without shoes
Before jumping do three bunny hops in different directions	Exercise in a dark room
Make a jump with a full turn to the left and then to the right	Exercise with music in the background
While jumping keep your arms behind your back, across your chest, above your head…	
When you land have one arm in front of you and one behind	
Land with a very narrow or very wide stance	
Land on your toes	

Table 15.1 – Example Variants of a Double Leg Jump in Differential Learning

What was found? For knee valgus, both the external focus and differential learning group showed a reduction after training with the effect being larger for the latter group. For differential learning, the angle was reduced by about 7 degrees while for the external focus group it was reduced by about 3. There was no significant change in valgus angle for either the internal group or a no-training control group. The same pattern was observed for the ground reaction forces. For the differential learning group, there was about a 6 N/kg reduction in force while there was only about a 1 N/kg reduction for the external focus group.

Overall, I think this study adds to the growing body of work demonstrating the potential benefits for injury prevention of training methods that encourage self-organization and movement variability[5]. It also demonstrates a powerful possibility. In training, the tendency has been to try and not break athletes by focusing on things like correct technique and perfect form. Studies like this one show that deliberately trying to mess with technique, trying to "break" it by making an athlete perform in a set of highly variable conditions, might make them less likely to get injured in the end. It might even make them anti-fragile.

Anti-fragility

Anti-fragility is a concept from evolutionary biology that refers to a system getting stronger from exposure to stressors[6]. Exposure to adverse conditions does not always lead to disruption in our performance. Sometimes it can bring about a change in our behavior that leads to growth and strengthening. Paula Silva and colleagues have proposed that this can also occur in sports training[7]. Specifically, they draw a connection with the topic we looked at back in Chapter 10, metastability:

"Growth from stress, termed antifragility is nicely illustrated when athletes implement novel and creative task solutions "on the fly" in response to challenges created by opponents in the field of play"

The authors propose that it is *metastability* (keeping multiple movement solutions available) that grants athletes the ability to implement these creative task solutions. Critically, the focus here is not just resilience (recovering from a stressful event like missing a free throw to win a game). It is adapting and growing from the stressor.

A good discussion of how we can design practice to promote this anti-fragility can be seen in a paper looking at rock climbing by Hill and colleagues[7]. The authors begin by bringing in another concept from biology: *hormesis*. As illustrated in Figure 15.1, the concept of hormesis captures the idea that there is a biphasic relationship between the dosage (loading) of a stressor and the organism's response to it. Specifically, if the dosage is too small there will be no adaptation while if it is too large it will lead to system breakdown (toxicity). Thus, much like we saw with challenge in the last chapter, we need to find an optimal level of stress loading to encourage anti-fragility.

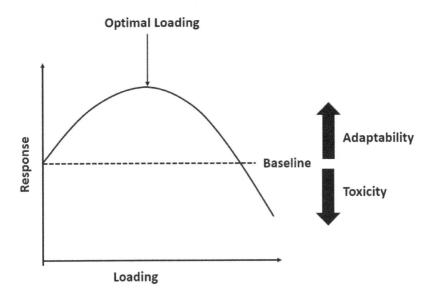

Figure 15.1 – Hormesis. The relationship between stress loading and the system response.

To help identify this optimal loading, 37 climbers were asked to complete different routes of varying difficulty. To quantify the stress loading each climber's response (defined as the % of the route that was completed divided by the # of attempts) was plotted as a function of the loading (determined by the route difficulty). The results for four climbers are shown in Figure 15.2. Like what we saw with the challenge point hypothesis, from these curves it is possible to identify the optimal loading to produce anti-fragility. For example, for the climber shown in the top left figure, we might target a difficulty level of 6 while for the bottom right we might use a route difficulty level of 3.

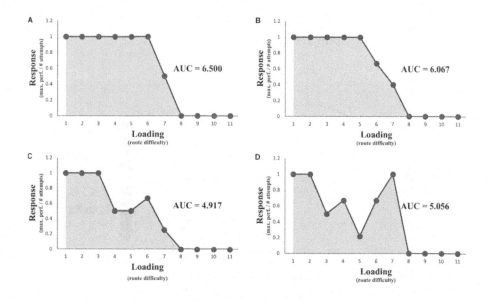

Figure 15.2 – Loading-Response Curves in Climbing[7].

Pain as a Constraint

The last topic I want to look at in this chapter is pain – in particular, how it influences motor learning and rehabilitation of injury. This is a topic that I have been interested in for a long time but, to be honest, I found it hard to fit into my worldview of skill. So, here I want to look at a couple of ways of conceptualizing pain using an ecological, performer-environment relationship approach.

The most straightforward way to think about pain from an ecological perspective is that it acts as a constraint on movement coordination. Remember, a constraint is something that takes away a movement solution. So having pain, for example when I extend my elbow, is likely to push me away from a coordination solution that involves that movement, toward something else.

There are a few studies that have attempted to investigate pain from this perspective. Arieh and colleagues[9] asked participants to learn dart throwing. They compared a control group with one that had lotion made of red pepper sauce applied to either their knee or elbow to induce topical pain. While there were no effects on performance, there was some evidence that the different groups coordinated their movements differently – in particular, in terms of variability. Specifically, as we might expect, the pain group exhibited less movement variability. However, it is difficult to take too much from studies like these because (unlike with a real sports injury) the pain is not linked to a specific movement solution.

Another way of looking at pain from an ecological view is to consider how it changes the field of affordances (invitations) available to a performer. This is something that was examined in an interesting paper by Coninx and Stillwell[10]. Expanding on what I discussed in Chapter 6, the authors define the field of affordances in terms of four dimensions: salience, valence, mineness, and temporal horizon.

Salience refers to the strength of the invitation of a given affordance. Using my analogy, is it in a bright pink or plain white envelope? Valence refers to whether the affordance is positive or negative. This is a point that we often don't talk a lot about in the ecological approach - things in our environment can have negative affordances – that is, they can create opportunities for bad, unwanted outcomes. As Gibson put it. affordances are conceptualized to account for the relation between the subject and environment "either for good or ill". For example, in football, passing a ball into a double-team can afford (offer the opportunity for) an interception for a quarterback. Or streetlamps offer opportunities for collisions while we are walking. As positive affordances create attractors, negative affordances can be thought of as repellors that push us away from that area of solution space.

The third dimension of mineness refers to the degree to which a person feels that an affordance is part of their identity or character. For example, the fact that a course affords running a marathon to some people is part of who they consider themselves to be – I am a "distance runner" or "marathoner". The fact that opportunity for action is available to them is part of their identity.

The fourth and final dimension is the temporal horizon which refers to the time over which the opportunity for action is perceived. The field of affordances can be narrowed to the here and now or integrate a wider temporal perspective providing more flexibility. For example, "I can't make that pass because there is a defender in the way" is an affordance with a short temporal horizon while "I can't make that pass because my arm is not strong enough" is one with a longer horizon.

How does pain influence the field of affordances? The authors consider this separately in terms of acute (temporary) and chronic pain. Acute pain mainly influences the salience of some attractors with a negative valence. That is, we temporally avoid specific movement solutions that hurt. They don't influence mineness (the subject's identity derived from affordance) and they typically have a short temporal horizon. The effect is very different for chronic pain:

"In chronic pain, positively valenced possibilities to act seem to overall lose their salience or change their valence becoming negative affordances. Some possibilities for action disappear or they appear less attractive. Various actions are experienced as to be avoided as otherwise benign daily tasks become threatening. For example, stairs no longer afford what they used to. Instead, they signal potential for injury, increased pain, or embarrassment. Chronic pain alters the field of affordances with respect to a variety of activities beyond simple motoric tasks"

So, in chronic pain, we again have increased salience of negative affordances but with a much longer temporal horizon and increasing effects on mineness – the person begins to adopt the idea that they are incapable of doing certain things.

Finally, the authors make some really good points about the role of treatment and rehab in dealing with pain that is highly consistent with the ideas I presented at the start of this chapter:

"The central goal of treatment is not to find and treat an underlying 'cause'; instead, the goal is to help patients to better attune to their environments. In other words, the central goal of treatment is to guide patients so that they can perceive possibilities for (meaningful) interactions with the world where the body is no longer the intruding object of attention and the source of alienation or isolation".

The authors also note that this is consistent with the recent trend towards the so-called positive health approach for dealing with pain which focuses on the patient's strengths rather than their weaknesses – affordances with positive valence rather than just all negative.

Injury adaptation (NOT rehabilitation) should focus on getting an athlete to learn to connect with the new field of affordances available to them, not focus on getting back to ones that were previously available. And we need to spend more time in treatment on actions with goals and intentions (so that the affordances can be perceived) rather than trying to get the form of isolated movements correct.

16

SOME TOOLS TO SUPPORT PRACTICE DESIGN

One of the real challenges in following an ecological approach to skill, in which we allow the athlete to develop their own relationship with their environment,t is there are no simple templates or practice routines that can be used. This approach to skill is not an alternative set of drills or practice activities. Rather, it is a set of principles that can be used to apply almost any coaching method (e.g., instruction, demonstration, using video, etc.) to practice. With this in mind, in this chapter, I want to present some tools that I have found to be highly useful in the application of an ecological approach to coaching. Note, although they are illustrated for baseball they can be used for any sports skill. Along with providing specific metrics and guides, I have found that going through the exercise of developing these tools yourself is a great way to get coaches to think more deliberately and purposefully about practice design.

The Constraints Matrix

Developing a constraints matrix is essentially akin to putting all the tools in a coaching toolbox down on paper into a structured framework. It is comprised of a list of potential constraints that can be manipulated in practice (categorized into individual, environment, and task), the levels of the constraint that can be used, and the potential affordance or movement solution they might invite. The beginnings of a constraint matrix for baseball batting practice is shown in Table 16.1.

Constraint Class	Constraint	Levels	Potential Affordances
Task	Viewing condition	-Occlude 1st half of delivery	-Bat-ball skills, online control of bat path
		-Occlude 2nd half of delivery	-Gaze control, picking up early information from pitcher's delivery
	Pitch spin rate	2400 rpm 2200 rpm 2000 rpm 1800 rpm 1600 rpm	-Recalibrate information-movement control law, pick up higher order information about ball flight
Environment	"Crowd"	None Scouts in stands Cameras recording swing Hecklers	-inhibiting attentional shifts to distracting stimuli and/or an internal focus
Individual	Intention (via advance information)	No info Pitcher attacks the outside corner Pitcher likes to mix speeds ...	-Developing approach, attentional focus, decision making

Table 16.1 – Constraints Matrix for Batting Practice

Working on developing a constraints matrix on your own or with a group of coaches in your organization will have several benefits:

1. It helps to clarify the "why" of different practice activities.

2. It is a good way to keep track of any new technology or resources that become available and to see how they might

fit in with the current practice. For example, a new pitching machine that allows you to vary spin in different directions, a new set of weighted bats, etc.

3. It provides a quick reference for options to address specific problems/challenges an individual player might be struggling with e.g., what are some practice activities I can use for a batter that is chasing pitches out of the zone?

4. It can help achieve more consistency and compatibility in coaching across the different levels of an organization.

    While I am not saying that all coaches must use the exact same set of activities, it is helpful if different coaches working with the same player use ones that are designed with a similar purpose in mind (e.g., promote self-organization, not prescription, mostly external not internal focus of attention, etc.).

Representative Practice Assessment Tool

While a constraints matrix shows what we could be doing in practice, it is critical that as coaches we take a hard look at what we ARE doing. In many cases, there will be large gaps between the two! If our goal is positive transfer of training (better performance in competition) we need to look at our practice activities through the lens of the concept of representative design. Building on the excellent work of Krause and colleagues[1] in tennis, Table 16.2 shows an example Representative Practice Assessment Tool (RPAT). Having a knowledgeable, independent observer assess practice using this tool can be an effective way to identify areas that could be improved.

PRACTICE ASSESSMENT TOOL								

Player: _____ Coach: _____ Date: _____ Name of task: _____
Goal of task: _____
Type of activity: ☐ Machine ☐ Live ☐ Weighted Bat ☐ Tee ☐ Soft Toss

	Not at all		Could be better		Definitely	NA	Suggestions for improvement
Does the goal detail a specific purpose?	1	2	3	4	5	NA	
Is the information used for control like what is used in a game?	1	2	3	4	5	NA	
Does the task require the player to make decisions?	1	2	3	4	5	NA	
Does the task require the player to adapt their intentions?	1	2	3	4	5	NA	
Does the task require the player to adapt their movement solution?	1	2	3	4	5	NA	
Does the task provide an appropriate level of challenge for the player?	1	2	3	4	5	NA	
Are the task dynamics (e.g., timing, force) like what is required in the game?	1	2	3	4	5	NA	
Does the task induce pressure/emotional reaction in the player?	1	2	3	4	5	NA	
					TOTAL SCORE _____		

Table 16.2 – Representative Practice Assessment Tool (RPAT)

Planning & Quantifying Variability in Practice Drills

I strongly encourage coaches to utilize some methodology for planning and tracking the amount of variability in their different practice activities. In my experience, adding variability to practice is the lowest-hanging fruit in creating better conditions for skill development. It has well-documented benefits and is becoming increasingly easier to implement. This can be done by laying out the details of planned activities ahead of time or having someone record what is being done in a practice session. For example, Table 16.3 shows the different conditions that a batter may have faced in one batting practice session. You can then take data like this and calculate a simple variability metric using the R code provided by Buszard and colleagues[2] or create a simple scoring system of your own.

Swing #	Swing Type* (Between Skill Variability)	Pitch Speed (Within Skill Variability)	Pitch Type (Within Skill Variability)
1	Machine	FB	90
2	Machine	FB	90
3	Machine	FB	90
4	Machine	FB	90
5	Machine	FB	90
6	Machine	CB	80
7	Machine	CB	80
8	Machine	CB	80
9	Machine	CB	80
10	Machine	CB	80
11	Live	FB	75
12	Live	FB	75
13	Live	FB	75
14	Live	FB	75
15	Live	FB	75
16	Live	CB	65
17	Live	CB	65
18	Live	CB	65
19	Live	CB	65
20	Live	CB	65
...			

Table 16.3 – Example Conditions for a Batting Practice Session. FB=fastball, CB=curveball.

Tracking variability of practice across sessions like this can have many benefits:

1. Frequently, it brings to light the fact that a lot of our practice sessions have very little variability thus we are

missing opportunities to create dexterous, adaptable athletes.

2. It can be used to help set the appropriate level of challenge for players at different skill levels.

   For example, for lower levels and younger players, the amount of variability in a practice session should be lower. If a player is struggling, we should dial back a bit on the variability, etc.

3. As discussed in Chapter 15, there is a growing body of evidence that encouraging variability in movement patterns reduces injury risk.

   More variability in practice conditions promotes more variability in movement. Thus, the level of variability is a factor that should be considered in calculating and monitoring workload.

4. It can be used to help periodize practice activities across a season and in the off-season.

   As discussed in Chapter 14, we want to have more variability the further we are from game competition and have at least a few sessions we lower variability mixed in to help promote confidence and keep the athlete motivated.

Developing Instructional Constraints & Cues

As discussed in Chapter 4, there is a large body of research showing the benefits of external focus of attention cues over internal cues. Does this mean that a coach should never refer to a player's body during instruction? In my opinion: no. There is a time and place for internal cues – in particular, during activities focusing on improving proprioceptive awareness and feel. However, I do agree that there can be benefits from expanding the coaching toolbox by developing external versions of commonly used internal cues. It is also useful to create a taxonomy of the cues being used based on other dimensions that have been shown to influence performance and learning of skills. In particular, the direction (are we getting the athlete to move towards or away from something?) and distance (are we getting them to focus on something close to their body like the bat or far away like an infielder?). In Table 16.4, I show an example of this type of cue classification for baseball batting. Again, I would recommend going through this exercise with your group of coaches. For more information on developing and modifying cues I highly recommend the excellent book The Language of Coaching by Nick Winkelman[3].

Focus	Internal				External				Analogy/Holistic			
Distance	Near		Far		Near		Far		Near		Far	
	T	A	T	A	T	A	T	A	T	A	T	A
"Throw your hands at the ball"			X									
"Squash the bug"										X		
"Push off your back foot"	X											
"Keep your shoulder in"									X	X		
"Move like a jackhammer"												
"Get on the plane of the pitch"								X				
"Let the ball get deep"							X					
"Turn your belt buckle to the pitcher"						X						
"Crack the whip"												X
"Pull the knob to your hip"	X											

Table 16.4 – Taxonomy of Hitting Cues. T=Towards, A=Away

EPILOGUE

If you have made it this far, thank you so much for sharing my journey with me. Understanding, developing, and applying the principles of skill acquisition has been pretty much a lifelong pursuit of mine. From trying to keep my hockey career going for much longer than my individual constraints should have allowed to researching skills in the lab to, more recently, dealing with the messiness and challenge of trying to apply my ideas in the field.

In writing this book and "How We Learn to Move" I have tried to capture a moment in my journey. As Tim Ingold might say, I am trying to be "enskilled": writing in a place and time rather than somehow trying to create a timeless, context-free document – if that is even possible. Consistent with the main message I have been preaching here, my books are a product of the current relationship I have with my environment. The information I am most attuned to. The articles and books I have read recently. The podcasts I have listened to. The athletes and coaches I consult. The amazing colleagues I share and explore ideas with.

I find viewing knowledge and understanding in this way, as a current relationship, very freeing. It frees me from any attempt to find every relevant article or piece of content before writing. It frees me from trying to make every chapter perfect, addressing every issue. Just today I had an amazing discussion with my Patreon supporters which made me want to go back and write another chapter focused on the individual constraints of motivation, autonomy, and confidence and how they interact with other types of constraints during skill acquisition. But I resisted – that will be for another part of my journey!

I would highly recommend that anyone interested in pursuing a career in this area share their own journey in this way. Don't worry if you have read every book or paper, understand every term, or have coached every type of athlete – sharing where you are here and now in your skill acquisition journey is incredibly valuable to people. In my career, I have published nearly 100 journal articles, been invited as a keynote speaker at several prestigious conferences, and won some big research awards. But looking back now, the single biggest turning point, the act that got me to where I am today, living out my dream of getting to work with some of the greatest athletes in the world, was starting the Perception & Action Podcast. I have received lots of feedback from people saying how much they appreciate me sharing what I am reading, my experiences at conferences, my current thinking about topics, etc.

So, thanks for reading, cheers for now, and keep on keeping em' coupled.

NOTES

Preface: Beyond How We *Learn* to Move

1. Glazier, P. S., & Davids, K. (2009). Constraints on the complete optimization of human motion. *Sports Medicine, 39*(1), 15-28.
2. Ingold, T (2000). *The perception of the environment: essays on livelihood, dwelling and skill.* London and New York: Taylor & Francis Group.
3. This quote has bounced around on Twitter for many years. Not sure who exactly said it first! Ric Shuttleworth?
4. Gray, R. (2021). *How We Learn to Move: A Revolution in the Way We Coach & Practice Sports Skills.* PACE Publishing.

1. Harnessing the Power of the Athlete-Environment Relationship

2. Mace, W. (1977). James J. Gibson's strategy for perceiving: Ask not what's inside your head, but what your head's inside of. In R. Shaw and J. Bransford (Eds.), *Perceiving, acting, and knowing: Toward an ecological psychology* (pp. 43–65). Hillsdale, NJ: Erlbaum.
3. The Black Cloud. http://www.amazon.com/Black-Cloud-Valancourt-Century-Classics/dp/1941147429
4. Rushton, S. K., & Gray, R. (2006). Hoyle's observations were right on the ball. *Nature, 443*(7111), 506-506.
5. Derivation of tau
6. Lee, D. N. (1976). A theory of visual control of braking based on information about time-to-collision. *Perception, 5*(4), 437-459.
7. Lee, D. N., Lishman, J. R., & Thomson, J. A. (1982). Regulation of gait in long jumping. *Journal of Experimental Psychology: Human perception and performance, 8*(3), 448.
8. Lee, D. N., & Reddish, P. E. (1981). Plummeting gannets: A paradigm of ecological optics. *Nature, 293*(5830), 293-294.

9. Brian Bushway – Seeing without Sight
   https://www.youtube.com/watch?v=EFvH7NF4MSw
10. Interview with Brian Bushway. https://perceptionaction.com/380/
11. Turvey, M. T., Fitch, H. L., & Tuller, B. (1982). The Bernstein perspective: 1. The problems of degrees of freedom and context conditioned variability. Human motor behavior: An introduction.
12. Matsuo, T., Jinji, T., Hirayama, D., Nasu, D., Katsumata, Y., & Morishita, Y. (2020). Consistent Hand Dynamics Are Achieved by Controlling Variabilities Among Joint Movements During Fastball Pitching. *Frontiers in sports and active living*, *2*, 159.

2. "Seeing Through the Matrix" – Picking up Information from the Environment

1. Gibson JJ. The Perception of the Visual World. Boston: Houghton Mifflin; 1950.
2. The Dress Illusion. https://en.wikipedia.org/wiki/The_dress
3. Lee, D. N. (1998). Guiding movement by coupling taus. *Ecological psychology*, *10*(3-4), 221-250.
4. Chapman S. Catching a Baseball. Am J Phys 1968;36:868-70.
5. Lee, D. N. (1976). A theory of visual control of braking based on information about time-to-collision. *Perception*, *5*(4), 437-459.
6. Lee, D. N. (1976). A theory of visual control of braking based on information about time-to-collision. *Perception*, *5*(4), 437-459.
7. Cutting, J. E. (1986). *Perception with an eye for motion* (Vol. 1). Cambridge, MA: MIT Press.
8. Koenderink, J. J., & van Doorn, A. J. (1987). Representation of local geometry in the visual system. *Biological cybernetics*, *55*(6), 367-375.

3. Optimizing the Control of Gaze

1. Allsop, J., & Gray, R. (2014). Flying under pressure: Effects of anxiety on attention and gaze behavior in aviation. *Journal of Applied Research in Memory and Cognition*, *3*(2), 63-71.
2. Regan, D. (1985). Visual Flow and Direction of Locomotion. *Science*, *227*(4690), 1064-1065.

3. Vine, S. J., Moore, L., & Wilson, M. R. (2011). Quiet eye training facilitates competitive putting performance in elite golfers. *Frontiers in psychology*, 8.

4. Button, C., Dicks, M., Haines, R., Barker, R., & Davids, K. (2011). Statistical modelling of gaze behaviour as categorical time series: What you should watch to save soccer penalties. *Cognitive Processing*, *12*(3), 235-244.

5. Vickers, J. N. (2007). *Perception, cognition, and decision training: The quiet eye in action.* Human Kinetics.

6. Ryu, D., Abernethy, B., Mann, D. L., Poolton, J. M., & Gorman, A. D. (2013). The role of central and peripheral vision in expert decision making. *Perception*, *42*(6), 591-607.

7. Hausegger, T., Vater, C., & Hossner, E. J. (2019). Peripheral vision in martial arts experts: The cost-dependent anchoring of gaze. *Journal of Sport and Exercise Psychology*, *41*(3), 137-145.

8. Regan, D., & Vincent, A. (1995). Visual processing of looming and time to contact throughout the visual field. *Vision research*, *35*(13), 1845-1857.

9. Mann, D. L., Abernethy, B., & Farrow, D. (2010). Visual information underpinning skilled anticipation: The effect of blur on a coupled and uncoupled in situ anticipatory response. *Attention, Perception, & Psychophysics*, *72*(5), 1317-1326.

10. FTC vs Ultimeyes. https://www.ftc.gov/news-events/news/press-releases/2016/02/ftc-approves-final-order-prohibiting-ultimeyes-manufacturer-making-deceptive-claims-app-can-improve

11. Hubbard, A. W., & Seng, C. N. (1954). Visual movements of batters. *Research Quarterly. American Association for Health, Physical Education and Recreation*, *25*(1), 42-57.

12. Bahill, A. T., & Laritz, T. (1984). Why can't batters keep their eyes on the ball. *American scientist*, *72*(3), 249-253.

13. Mann, D. L., Spratford, W., & Abernethy, B. (2013). The head tracks and gaze predicts: how the world's best batters hit a ball. *PloS one*, *8*(3), e58289.

14. Justin Langer. https://en.wikipedia.org/wiki/Justin_Langer

15. Head Stabilization in Birds. https://www.audubon.org/news/for-birds-steady-head-key-incredible-focus

16. Frost, B. J. (1978). The optokinetic basis of head-bobbing in the pigeon. *Journal of Experimental Biology*, *74*(1), 187-195.

17. Jordet, G., Aksum, K. M., Pedersen, D. N., Walvekar, A., Trivedi, A., McCall, A., ... & Priestley, D. (2020). Scanning, contextual factors, and association with performance in english premier league footballers: an investigation across a season. *Frontiers in psychology*, *11*, 553813.
18. McGuckian, T. B., Chalkley, D., Shepherd, J., & Pepping, G. J. (2018). Giving inertial sensor data context for communication in applied settings: An example of visual exploration in football. *Multidisciplinary Digital Publishing Institute Proceedings*, *2*(6), 234.
19. Wood, G., & Wilson, M. R. (2011). Quiet-eye training for soccer penalty kicks. *Cognitive processing*, *12*(3), 257-266.
20. Harle, S. K., & Vickers, J. N. (2001). Training quiet eye improves accuracy in the basketball free throw. *The Sport Psychologist*, *15*(3), 289-305.
21. Khalaji, M., Aghdaei, M., Farsi, A., & Piras, A. (2022). The effect of eye movement sonification on visual search patterns and anticipation in novices. *Journal on Multimodal User Interfaces*, *16*(2), 173-182.
22. Constraining Vision to Education Attention. https://perceptionaction.com/164-2/
23. Oppici, L., Panchuk, D., Serpiello, F. R., & Farrow, D. (2018). The influence of a modified ball on transfer of passing skill in soccer. *Psychology of Sport and Exercise*, *39*, 63-71.
24. Practice Activity Analysis. https://perceptionaction.com/417/

4. Focusing Attention in the Right Place

1. Castaneda, B., & Gray, R. (2007). Effects of focus of attention on baseball batting performance in players of differing skill levels. *Journal of Sport and Exercise Psychology*, *29*(1), 60-77.
2. Gray, R. (2013). Being selective at the plate: processing dependence between perceptual variables relates to hitting goals and performance. *Journal of Experimental Psychology: Human Perception and Performance*, *39*(4), 1124.
3. Gray, R. (2015, September). The Moneyball problem: what is the best way to present situational statistics to an athlete?. In *Proceedings of the Human Factors and Ergonomics Society*

Annual Meeting (Vol. 59, No. 1, pp. 1377-1381). Sage CA: Los Angeles, CA: SAGE Publications.

4. Gray, R. (2020). Changes in movement coordination associated with skill acquisition in baseball batting: freezing/freeing degrees of freedom and functional variability. *Frontiers in Psychology, 11*, 1295.

5. van der Graaff, E., Hoozemans, M., Pasteuning, M., Veeger, D., & Beek, P. J. (2018). Focus of attention instructions during baseball pitching training. *International Journal of Sports Science & Coaching, 13*(3), 391-397.

6. Wulf, G., Höß, M., & Prinz, W. (1998). Instructions for motor learning: Differential effects of internal versus external focus of attention. *Journal of motor behavior, 30*(2), 169-179.

7. Chua, L. K., Jimenez-Diaz, J., Lewthwaite, R., Kim, T., & Wulf, G. (2021). Superiority of external attentional focus for motor performance and learning: Systematic reviews and meta-analyses. *Psychological Bulletin, 147*(6), 618.

8. Fitts & Posner Model. https://perceptionaction.com/129-2/

9. Zachry, T., Wulf, G., Mercer, J., & Bezodis, N. (2005). Increased movement accuracy and reduced EMG activity as the result of adopting an external focus of attention. *Brain research bulletin, 67*(4), 304-309.

10. Herrebrøden, H. (2022). Motor Performers Need Task-relevant Information: Proposing an Alternative Mechanism for the Attentional Focus Effect. *Journal of Motor Behavior*, 1-10.

11. Gray, R. (2018). Comparing cueing and constraints interventions for increasing launch angle in baseball batting. *Sport, Exercise, and Performance Psychology, 7*(3), 318.

12. Differential Learning. https://perceptionaction.com/dl/

13. Studies Comparing Prescriptive & Self-Organization Approaches. https://perceptionaction.com/comparative/

14. Oftadeh, S., Bahram, A., Yaali, R., Ghadiri, F., & Schöllhorn, W. I. (2021). External Focus or Differential Learning: Is There an Additive Effect on Learning a Futsal Goal Kick?. *International Journal of Environmental Research and Public Health, 19*(1), 317.

15. Toner, J., & Moran, A. (2015). Enhancing performance proficiency at the expert level: Considering the role of 'somaesthetic awareness'. *Psychology of Sport and Exercise, 16*, 110-117.

16. McNevin, N. H., Shea, C. H., & Wulf, G. (2003). Increasing the distance of an external focus of attention enhances learning. *Psychological research*, *67*(1), 22-29.
17. Mullen, R., Jones, E. S., Oliver, S., & Hardy, L. (2016). Anxiety and motor performance: More evidence for the effectiveness of holistic process goals as a solution to the process goal paradox. *Psychology of Sport and Exercise*, *27*, 142-149.
18. Becker, K. A., Georges, A. F., & Aiken, C. A. (2019). Considering a holistic focus of attention as an alternative to an external focus. *Journal of Motor Learning and Development*, *7*(2), 194-203.
19. Gray, R. (2020). Attentional theories of choking under pressure revisited. *Handbook of Sport Psychology*, 595-610.
20. Gray, R., & Cañal-Bruland, R. (2015). Attentional focus, perceived target size, and movement kinematics under performance pressure. *Psychonomic bulletin & review*, *22*(6), 1692-1700.
21. Gray, R., & Allsop, J. (2013). Interactions between performance pressure, performance streaks, and attentional focus. *Journal of sport and exercise psychology*, *35*(4), 368-386.
22. The Hot Hand: The Mystery & Science of Streaks
23. Gray, R. (2015). Differences in attentional focus associated with recovery from sports injury: Does injury induce an internal focus?. *Journal of sport and exercise psychology*, *37*(6), 607-616.

5. Moving to Control the "Current Future"

1. Schiff, W., & Detwiler, M. L. (1979). Information used in judging impending collision. *Perception*, *8*(6), 647-658.
2. Gray, R., & Regan, D. (1998). Accuracy of estimating time to collision using binocular and monocular information. *Vision research*, *38*(4), 499-512.
3. Gray, R., & Regan, D. (2000). Estimating the time to collision with a rotating nonspherical object. *Vision Research*, *40*(1), 49-63.
4. Brenner, E., & Smeets, J. B. (1997). Fast responses of the human hand to changes in target position. *Journal of motor behavior*, *29*(4), 297-310.
5. Craik, K. J. (1948). Theory of the human operator in control systems. II. Man as an element in a control system. *British journal of psychology*, *38*(3), 142.

6. Heald, J. B., Lengyel, M., & Wolpert, D. M. (2022). Contextual inference in learning and memory. *Trends in Cognitive Sciences*.

7. Gibson JJ. The Perception of the Visual World. Boston: Houghton Mifflin; 1950.

8. McBeath, M. K., Shaffer, D. M., & Kaiser, M. K. (1995). How baseball outfielders determine where to run to catch fly balls. *Science*, *268*(5210), 569-573.

9. Shaffer, D. M., Krauchunas, S. M., Eddy, M., & McBeath, M. K. (2004). How dogs navigate to catch Frisbees. *Psychological science*, *15*(7), 437-441.

10. Suluh, A., Sugar, T., & McBeath, M. (2001, May). Spatial navigation principles: Applications to mobile robotics. In *Proceedings 2001 ICRA. IEEE International Conference on Robotics and Automation (Cat. No. 01CH37164)* (Vol. 2, pp. 1689-1694). IEEE.

11. Asai, T., Sugimori, E., & Tanno, Y. (2010). Two agents in the brain: motor control of unimanual and bimanual reaching movements. *PloS one*, *5*(4), e10086.

12. Higuchi T, Nagami T, Nakata H, Watanabe M, et al. Contribution of Visual Information About Ball Trajectory to Baseball Hitting Accuracy. PLoS ONE 2016;11:e0148498.

13. Stepp N, Turvey MT. On Strong Anticipation. Cogn Syst Res. 2010 Jun 1;11(2):148-164. doi: 10.1016/j.cogsys.2009.03.003.

14. Stepp, N., & Turvey, M. T. (2008). Anticipating synchronization as an alternative to the internal model. *Behavioral and Brain Sciences, 31*(2), 216–217

6. Pink Envelopes NOT Push Signs: Affordance-Based Coaching

1. Gibson, J. J., & Carmichael, L. (1966). *The senses considered as perceptual systems* (Vol. 2, No. 1, pp. 44-73). Boston: Houghton Mifflin.

2. Zhu, Q. (2013). Perceiving the affordance of string tension for power strokes in badminton: Expertise allows effective use of all string tensions. *Journal of Sports Sciences*, *31*(11), 1187-1196.

3. Gray, R. (2020). Comparing the constraints led approach, differential learning and prescriptive instruction for training opposite-field hitting in baseball. *Psychology of sport and exercise*, *51*, 101797.

4. Fajen, B. R. (2007). Affordance-based control of visually guided action. *Ecological Psychology, 19*(4), 383-410.

5. Oudejans, R. R., Michaels, C. F., & Bakker, F. C. (1997). The effects of baseball experience on movement initiation in catching fly balls. *Journal of Sports Sciences, 15*(6), 587-595.

6. Scott, S., & Gray, R. (2010). Switching tools: Perceptual-motor recalibration to weight changes. *Experimental brain research, 201*(2), 177-189.

7. Dicks, M., Button, C., & Davids, K. (2010). Examination of gaze behaviors under in situ and video simulation task constraints reveals differences in information pickup for perception and action. *Attention, Perception, & Psychophysics, 72*(3), 706-720.

8. Caldwell, J. M. E., Alexander, F. J., & Ahmad, C. S. (2019). Weighted-ball velocity enhancement programs for baseball pitchers: a systematic review. *Orthopaedic Journal of Sports Medicine, 7*(2), 2325967118825469.

9. Reinold, M. M., Macrina, L. C., Fleisig, G. S., Aune, K., & Andrews, J. R. (2018). Effect of a 6-week weighted baseball throwing program on pitch velocity, pitching arm biomechanics, passive range of motion, and injury rates. *Sports Health, 10*(4), 327-333.

7. Stronger Tent Poles: Harnessing Muscle Tension & Biotensegrity

1. Bosch, F. The Anatomy of Agility. HHMR Media.

2. Van Hooren, B., & Bosch, F. (2016). Influence of muscle slack on high-intensity sport performance: A review. *Strength and Conditioning Journal, 38*(5), 75-87.

3. Bernstein, N. A., Latash, M. L., & Turvey, M. T. (2014). *Dexterity and its development*. Psychology Press.

4. Sadao, S. (1996). Fuller on tensegrity. *International Journal of Space Structures, 11*(1-2), 37-42.

5. Turvey, M. T., & Fonseca, S. T. (2014). The medium of haptic perception: a tensegrity hypothesis. *Journal of motor behavior, 46*(3), 143-187.

6. Fascial Training – A Whole System Approach.
https://www.amazon.com/Fascia-Training-Whole-System-Bill-Parisi/dp/1797818864
7. Miguel Cabrera Injury
https://www.cbssports.com/mlb/news/tigers-miguel-cabrera-done-for-2018-season-with-ruptured-biceps-tendon/
8. Fernando Tatis Injury. https://www.mlb.com/news/fernando-tatis-jr-injured-on-strikeout

8. Moving with Efficiency & Economy

1. Sparrow, W. A., & Newell, K. M. (1998). Metabolic energy expenditure and the regulation of movement economy. *Psychonomic Bulletin & Review, 5*(2), 173-196.
2. Salvendy, G. (1972). Physiological and psychological aspects of paced and unpaced performance. *Acta Physiologica Academiae Scientiarum Hungaricae, 42*(3), 267-274.
3. Hoyt, D. F., & Taylor, C. R. (1981). Gait and the energetics of locomotion in horses. *Nature, 292*(5820), 239-240.
4. Bechbache, R. R., & Duffin, J. (1977). The entrainment of breathing frequency by exercise rhythm. *The Journal of physiology, 272*(3), 553-561.
5. Asami, T. (1976). Energy efficiency of ball kicking. *In Biomecanics VB, 135.*
6. Brancazio, P. J. (1981). Physics of basketball. *American Journal of Physics, 49*(4), 356-365.
7. Durand, M., Geoffroi, V., Varray, A., & Préfaut, C. (1994). Study of the energy correlates in the learning of a complex self-paced cyclical skill. *Human Movement Science, 13*(6), 785-799.
8. Freezing DF an Early Movement Solution
https://perceptionaction.com/185/
9. Vereijken, B., Emmerik, R. E. V., Whiting, H. T. A., & Newell, K. M. (1992). Free (z) ing degrees of freedom in skill acquisition. *Journal of motor behavior, 24*(1), 133-142.
10. Zachry, T., Wulf, G., Mercer, J., & Bezodis, N. (2005). Increased movement accuracy and reduced EMG activity as the result of adopting an external focus of attention. *Brain research bulletin, 67*(4), 304-309.

11. Stoate, I., Wulf, G., & Lewthwaite, R. (2012). Enhanced expectancies improve movement efficiency in runners. *Journal of Sports Sciences*, *30*(8), 815-823.
12. Melugin, H. P., Larson, D. R., Fleisig, G. S., Conte, S., Fealy, S. A., Dines, J. S., ... & Camp, C. L. (2019). Baseball pitchers' perceived effort does not match actual measured effort during a structured long-toss throwing program. *The American Journal of Sports Medicine*, *47*(8), 1949-1954.
13. New Study Suggests Motus Sensors Can Take the Guesswork Out of Pitching and Save Arms https://www.sporttechie.com/mlb-baseball-motus-sensors-pitcher-exertion-load-management/

9. Skilled Intentionality: Keeping Our Options Open & Deciding Slow

1. Klein, G. A. (1993). A recognition-primed decision (RPD) model of rapid decision making. *Decision making in action: Models and methods*, *5*(4), 138-147.
2. Testing Babe Ruth. http://psychclassics.yorku.ca/Fullerton/
3. Rietveld, E., Denys, D., & Van Westen, M. (2018). Ecological-Enactive Cognition as engaging with a field of relevant affordances. *The Oxford handbook of 4E cognition*, *41*.
4. Gibson JJ. The Perception of the Visual World. Boston: Houghton Mifflin; 1950.
5. Passos, P., Araújo, D., Davids, K., & Shuttleworth, R. (2008). Manipulating constraints to train decision making in rugby union. *International Journal of Sports Science & Coaching*, *3*(1), 125-140.

10. Learning to Exploit Metastability & Motor Abundance

1. Kelso, J. S. (2012). Multistability and metastability: understanding dynamic coordination in the brain. *Philosophical Transactions of the Royal Society B: Biological Sciences*, *367*(1591), 906-918.
2. Latash, M. L. (2012). The bliss (not the problem) of motor abundance (not redundancy). *Experimental brain research*, *217*(1), 1-5.
3. Hristovski, R., Davids, K., Araújo, D., & Button, C. (2006). How boxers decide to punch a target: emergent behaviour in nonlinear

dynamical movement systems. *Journal of sports science & medicine, 5*(CSSI), 60.

4. Pinder, R. A., Davids, K., & Renshaw, I. (2012). Metastability and emergent performance of dynamic interceptive actions. *Journal of Science and Medicine in Sport, 15*(5), 437-443.

11. Learning to Coordinate with Teammates: Developing Shared Affordances

1. Bourbousson, J., Poizat, G., Saury, J., & Sève, C. (2012). Temporal aspects of team cognition: a case study on concerns sharing within basketball. *Journal of Applied Sport Psychology, 24*(2), 224-241.

2. Giske, R., Rodahl, S. E., & Høigaard, R. (2015). Shared mental task models in elite ice hockey and handball teams: Does it exist and how does the coach intervene to make an impact?. *Journal of Applied Sport Psychology, 27*(1), 20-34.

3. Passos, P., Milho, J., Fonseca, S., Borges, J., Araújo, D., & Davids, K. (2011). Interpersonal distance regulates functional grouping tendencies of agents in team sports. *Journal of motor behavior, 43*(2), 155-163.

4. Gray, R., Cooke, N. J., McNeese, N. J., & McNabb, J. (2017). Investigating team coordination in baseball using a novel joint decision making paradigm. *Frontiers in Psychology, 8*, 907.

5. Caldeira, P., Fonseca, S. T., Paulo, A., Infante, J., & Araújo, D. (2020). Linking Tensegrity to Sports Team Collective Behaviors: Towards the Group-Tensegrity Hypothesis. *Sports Medicine-Open, 6*(1), 1-9.

6. **Gray, R.** & Sullivan, R. (In press). *A Constraints-Led Approach to Baseball Coaching*. Routledge.

12. Remembering & Using "Offline" Information

1. Gray, R. (2002). "Markov at the bat": A model of cognitive processing in baseball batters. *Psychological Science, 13*(6), 542-547.

2. Sørensen, V., Ingvaldsen, R. P., & Whiting, H. T. A. (2001). The application of co-ordination dynamics to the analysis of discrete

movements using table-tennis as a paradigm skill. *Biological cybernetics*, *85*(1), 27-38.

3. Murase, D., Yokoyama, K., Fujii, K., Hasegawa, Y., & Yamamoto, Y. (2016). Baseball catching patterns differ according to task constraints. *Advances in Physical Education*, *6*(3), 151-157.
4. Abernethy, B., & Russell, D. G. (1987). Expert-novice differences in an applied selective attention task. *Journal of Sport and Exercise Psychology*, *9*(4), 326-345.
5. Moore CG, Muller S. Transfer of Expert Visual Anticipation to a Similar Domain. Q J Exp Psychol 2014;67:186–96.
6. Müller S, Fadde P.J. The Relationship Between Visual Anticipation and Baseball Batting Game Statistics. J Appl Sport Psychol 2016;28:49-61.
7. Takamido, R., Yokoyama, K., & Yamamoto, Y. (2019). Task constraints and stepping movement of fast-pitch softball hitting. *PloS one*, *14*(2), e0212997.
8. Gray, R., & Cañal-Bruland, R. (2018). Integrating visual trajectory and probabilistic information in baseball batting. *Psychology of Sport and Exercise*, *36*, 123-131.
9. Williams T, Underwood J. The Science of Hitting. New York: Simon and Schuster; 1970.
10. Mcintyre DR, Pfautsch EW. A Kinematic Analysis of the Baseball Batting Swings Involved in Opposite-Field and Same-Field Hitting. Res Q Exerc Sport 1982;53:206-213.
11. Fogt N, Persson TW. A Pilot Study of Horizontal Head and Eye Rotations in Baseball Batting. Optom Vis Sci 2017;94:789-96.
12. Porter, J. M., & Beckerman, T. (2016). Practicing with gradual increases in contextual interference enhances visuomotor learning. *Kinesiology*, *48*(2.), 244-250.

13. Affective Practice: Learning to Handle Pressure & Emotion

1. Oudejans, R. R., & Pijpers, J. R. (2010). Training with mild anxiety may prevent choking under higher levels of anxiety. *Psychology of Sport and Exercise*, *11*(1), 44-50.
2. Lawrence, G. P., Cassell, V. E., Beattie, S., Woodman, T., Khan, M. A., Hardy, L., & Gottwald, V. M. (2014). Practice with anxiety improves performance, but only when anxious: evidence for the

specificity of practice hypothesis. *Psychological research*, *78*(5), 634-650.

3. Hordacre, B., Immink, M. A., Ridding, M. C., & Hillier, S. (2016). Perceptual-motor learning benefits from increased stress and anxiety. *Human Movement Science*, *49*, 36-46.

4. Stoker, M., Maynard, I., Butt, J., Hays, K., Lindsay, P., & Norenberg, D. A. (2017). The effect of manipulating training demands and consequences on experiences of pressure in elite netball. *Journal of Applied Sport Psychology*, *29*(4), 434-448.

5. Renshaw, I., & Chow, J. Y. (2019). A constraint-led approach to sport and physical education pedagogy. *Physical Education and Sport Pedagogy*, *24*(2), 103-116.

6. Headrick, J., Renshaw, I., Davids, K., Pinder, R. A., & Araújo, D. (2015). The dynamics of expertise acquisition in sport: The role of affective learning design. *Psychology of Sport and Exercise*, *16*, 83-90.

7. Wulf, G., & Lewthwaite, R. (2016). Optimizing performance through intrinsic motivation and attention for learning: The OPTIMAL theory of motor learning. *Psychonomic bulletin & review*, *23*(5), 1382-1414.

8. Chauvel, G., Wulf, G., & Maquestiaux, F. (2015). Visual illusions can facilitate sport skill learning. *Psychonomic bulletin & review*, *22*(3), 717-721.

14. How Difficult Should Practice Be? The "70% Rule" & Getting the Level of Challenge Right

1. Guadagnoli, M. A., & Lee, T. D. (2004). Challenge point: a framework for conceptualizing the effects of various practice conditions in motor learning. *Journal of motor behavior*, *36*(2), 212-224.

2. Hodges, N. J., & Lohse, K. R. (2022). An extended challenge-based framework for practice design in sports coaching. *Journal of Sports Sciences*, *40*(7), 754-768.

3. McKee, S. P., Klein, S. A., & Teller, D. Y. (1985). Statistical properties of forced-choice psychometric functions: Implications of probit analysis. *Perception & psychophysics*, *37*(4), 286-298.

4. Jacobs, D. M., & Michaels, C. F. (2007). Direct learning. *Ecological Psychology*, *19*(4), 321-349.
5. Smith, M. R., Flach, J. M., Dittman, S. M., & Stanard, T. (2001). Monocular optical constraints on collision control. *Journal of Experimental Psychology: Human Perception and Performance*, *27*(2), 395.
6. Valença, M., Coutinho, D., Schöllhorn, W., Ribeiro, N., & Santos, S. (2022). Investigating the Effects of Differential Learning on Golfers' Pitching Performance as a Function of Handicap. *International journal of environmental research and public health*, *19*(19), 12550.
7. Gray, R. (2020). Comparing the constraints led approach, differential learning and prescriptive instruction for training opposite-field hitting in baseball. *Psychology of Sport & Exercise, 51,* 101797.
8. "Roots Not Branches: Why the Ecological Approach is NOT Just a Set of Alternative Training Methods https://youtu.be/s-flnv9BUnY
9. Huet, M., Camachon, C., Fernandez, L., Jacobs, D. M., & Montagne, G. (2009). Self-controlled concurrent feedback and the education of attention towards perceptual invariants. *Human Movement Science*, *28*(4), 450-467.
10. Otte, F. W., Millar, S. K., & Klatt, S. (2019). Skill training periodization in "specialist" sports coaching—an introduction of the "PoST" framework for skill development. *Frontiers in Sports and Active Living*, 61.
11. Buszard, T., Garofolini, A., Reid, M., Farrow, D., Oppici, L., & Whiteside, D. (2020). Scaling sports equipment for children promotes functional movement variability. *Scientific reports*, *10*(1), 1-8.

15. Adapting to Pain & Injury & Becoming Anti-Fragile

1. The Feldenkrais Method https://toddhargrove.substack.com/p/the-feldenkrais-method#
2. Hillier, S., & Worley, A. (2015). The effectiveness of the feldenkrais method: a systematic review of the evidence. *Evidence-Based Complementary and Alternative Medicine, 2015.*

3. 389 - Interview with Todd Hargove
   https://perceptionaction.com/389/
4. Ghanati, H. A., Letafatkar, A., Shojaedin, S., Hadadnezhad, M., & Schöllhorn, W. I. (2022). Comparing the Effects of Differential Learning, Self-Controlled Feedback, and External Focus of Attention Training on Biomechanical Risk Factors of Anterior Cruciate Ligament (ACL) in Athletes: A Randomized Controlled Trial. *International journal of environmental research and public health, 19*(16), 10052.
5. An Ecological Approach to Sports Injury
   https://perceptionaction.com/injury/
6. Taleb, N. (2012). *Antifragile: Things that Gain From Disorder (Incerto)*. New York, NY: Random House.
7. Kiefer, A. W., Silva, P. L., Harrison, H. S., & Araújo, D. (2018). Antifragility in sport: leveraging adversity to enhance performance.
8. Hill, Y., Kiefer, A. W., Silva, P. L., Van Yperen, N. W., Meijer, R. R., Fischer, N., & Den Hartigh, R. J. (2020). Antifragility in climbing: Determining optimal stress loads for athletic performance training. *Frontiers in psychology, 11*, 272.
9. Arieh, H., Abdoli, B., Farsi, A., & Haghparast, A. (2022). Assessment of motor skill accuracy and coordination variability after application of local and remote experimental pain. *Research in Sports Medicine, 30*(3), 325-341.
10. Coninx, S., & Stilwell, P. (2021). Pain and the field of affordances: an enactive approach to acute and chronic pain. *Synthese, 199*(3), 7835-7863.

16. Some Tools to Support Practice Design

1. Krause, L., Farrow, D., Reid, M., Buszard, T., & Pinder, R. (2018). Helping coaches apply the principles of representative learning design: validation of a tennis specific practice assessment tool. *Journal of sports sciences, 36*(11), 1277-1286.
2. Buszard, T., Reid, M., Krause, L., Kovalchik, S., & Farrow, D. (2017). Quantifying contextual interference and its effect on skill transfer in skilled youth tennis players. *Frontiers in psychology, 8*, 1931.

3. Winkelman, N. C. (2020). *The language of coaching: The art and science of teaching movement*. Human Kinetics Publishers.

ABOUT THE AUTHOR

Rob Gray is a professor at Arizona State University who has been conducting research on and teaching courses related to perceptual-motor skills for over 25 years. He received his MS and Ph.D. from York University in Canada with a focus on the visual control of movement. He has served as an expert consultant with Nissan Motor Corp, the US Air Force, and several sports teams and organizations. In 2007 he was awarded the Distinguished Scientific Award for Early Career Contribution to Psychology from the American Psychological Association. He is the author of the best-selling book on skill acquisition, *How We Learn to Move: A Revolution in the Way We Coach & Practice Sports Skills*. Finally, he hosts and produces the popular Perception & Action Podcast. Explore the episodes at https://perceptionaction.com/

Made in United States
Orlando, FL
21 November 2023

39218296R00183